# Building on
# Student Diversity

## ONE WEEK LOAN

# Building on Student Diversity

*Profiles and Activities*

*Joy R. Cowdery*
*Linda Ingling*
*Linda E. Morrow*
*Vicki A. Wilson*
*Muskingum College*

SAGE Publications
Thousand Oaks ▪ London ▪ New Delhi

*For information:*

Sage Publications, Inc.
2455 Teller Road
Thousand Oaks, California 91320
E-mail: order@sagepub.com

Sage Publications Ltd.
1 Oliver's Yard
55 City Road
London EC1Y 1SP
United Kingdom

Sage Publications India Pvt. Ltd.
B-42, Panchsheel Enclave
Post Box 4109
New Delhi 110 017  India

Printed in the United States of America

*Library of Congress Cataloging-in-Publication Data*

Building on student diversity: Profiles and activities/Joy R. Cowdery . . . [et al.].
    p. cm.
Includes bibliographical references and index.
ISBN 1–4129–3693–4 or 978-1-4129-3693-4 (pbk.)
    1.  Multicultural education—United States.  2.  Children with disabilities—Education.
3.  Teacher-student relationships—United States.  4.  Effective teaching—United States.
I. Cowdery, Joy R.
LC1099.3.B84 2007
372.9′046—dc22                                        2006009933

This book is printed on acid-free paper.

06   07   08   09   10   10   9   8   7   6   5   4   3   2   1

| | |
|---|---|
| *Acquiring Editor:* | Diane McDaniel |
| *Editorial Assistant:* | Erica Carroll |
| *Associate Editor:* | Elise Smith |
| *Production Editor:* | Beth A. Bernstein |
| *Copy Editor:* | Barbara Coster |
| *Typesetter:* | C&M Digitals (P) Ltd. |
| *Cover Designer:* | Candice Harman |

# CONTENTS

# PREFACE

**A**s teachers of students of all ages, abilities, and backgrounds, we firmly believe that everyone can learn. As former classroom teachers, we put this belief into action by designing classrooms and learning activities that promoted the intellectual, emotional, and social growth of each of our students. Now, as professors who prepare college students to become teachers, we struggle to develop the dispositions and teach the strategies that will help our students promote the growth of each of *their* future students.

In the past, we relied on short case studies and field experiences to teach our students about the challenges of teaching children from a wide variety of backgrounds and with a wide range of abilities. How much more beneficial it would be, we thought, to have a group of children that all our students knew who could help us show them how to create powerful learning experiences in classrooms and schools that were respectful and supportive of all. So we began to write stories—stories about children we made up from the knowledge and experiences we had had as parents, teachers, and professors. And we began to develop activities that would allow our college students to learn about these special children and their potential for growth as whole persons.

As we began to use these stories in our classes, the children became an integral part of our teacher education program. They showed our students what it was like to be "different." They showed our students how to create a caring school environment, to accommodate for special learning needs in instructional activities and assessments, and to interact with families and communities. They showed our students that all children, even those who are most challenged and challenging, have faces, names, and lives outside the classroom.

In this book, which evolved from our writing project, we introduce you to six prototypical children—Casey, Sarah, Malcolm, Raul, Leslie, and Yu-shin—who have a wide variety of backgrounds and abilities. If you are a teacher candidate, they will help prepare you for working with real children in real classrooms. If you are a professor in teacher education, you will find that the stories of these children can bring your classroom instruction to life, from initial classes in diversity, through general methods and content-specific methods courses, and even into student teaching or clinical practice seminars. Because all of your students know all of these children, there is a common basis for instruction and discussion. If you are a dean or department chair, or the accreditation director, you will find that the activities in this book contribute to meeting Standard 4 of the National Council for the Accreditation of Teacher Education (NCATE), specifically Element 1: Design, Implementation, and Evaluation of

Curriculum and Experience in relation to diversity. All of the faculty in our teacher education department have been using these stories and activities in undergraduate and graduate education classes for more than 3 years and recognize their contribution to the effectiveness of our candidates in understanding and building on the diverse backgrounds and abilities of students. This book can be used alone or can complement other textbooks in multicultural education, special education, family and community collaboration, general methods, specific-content methods, and student teaching or clinical practice seminars.

## ORGANIZATION

The book is organized with an introduction to the setting of the stories, followed by

- Part I: Profiles and cumulative folders of students
- Part II: Activities

Chapter 1 includes a profile of Midland, U.S.A., a small town in which the children live, as well as profiles of the schools they attend. These descriptions help place the children in a community context and provide insight into their own and their families' lives. The three activities included in this chapter provide experience in thinking about the children in relation to their families and communities. For courses in which family and community backgrounds are central, faculty will want to begin with this section. For other courses, setting may be less important, and faculty may wish to have their students skip this section and move right into the children's stories.

Part I includes Chapters 2 through 7, the children's stories and their cumulative folders. The children include Casey, a European American child from an impoverished background with a specific learning disability in reading; Sarah, a working-class European American child identified as intellectually gifted; Malcolm, an African American child diagnosed with ADHD (attention-deficit/hyperactivity disorder); Raul, a Mexican child who is an English Language Learner in kindergarten and the early grades who recognizes in high school that he is gay; Leslie, who is in a wheelchair because of an automobile accident; and Yu-shin, an English Language Learner in middle school and high school who is reluctant to adopt the language and culture of his new home.

The children's situations are captured at three points: early childhood (prekindergarten through Grade 3), middle childhood (Grade 4 through Grade 8), and high school (Grade 9 through Grade 12). Raul is an English Language Learner in early childhood but experiences cultural dissonance throughout his school career. Yu-shin is an English Language Learner in middle school and high school. The English Language Learners are profiled at the time they enter Midland schools.

For this book, we have attempted to produce prototypes, not stereotypes, and have used both the relevant literature and our own experiences to develop characters who are interesting individuals as well as representative of the groups we wish to illustrate. The characters themselves are purely fictional and do not represent any one of the many children we have worked with over the years. Where characteristics of known persons and places have been used in developing the stories, names and circumstances have been changed to protect their identities.

One of the unique aspects of this book is the inclusion of cumulative folders, or permanent record files, for each of the children profiled. In our experience, teacher education candidates and even entry-year teachers have little experience in working with the tool most likely to provide information about students and their specific learning challenges—the cumulative folder or permanent record file. In developing these folders, we have included examples of real-world documentation, including grades, medical records, results of standardized tests and state assessments, parent-school communications, and student work. And although these records are not complete—some of the children would have folders as thick as this book— they will give teacher education candidates insight into the kinds of information available to teachers and practice in using this valuable primary resource.

Part II includes Chapters 8 through 12, the activities designed to be used with the children's profiles and folders in Part I. The chapters highlight the following areas:

- Getting to Know Your Learners
- Designing Environments That Support Your Learners
- Developing Lessons to Meet the Needs of Your Learners
- Gathering Data to Improve Instruction
- Communicating With Families: Activities

The activities employ a variety of instruction strategies, including reflective journaling, group discussion, role playing, and preparation of letters, posters, and other products of communication. Explicit instructions are given for classroom experiences, and rubrics for assessment of learning are included for many activities.

The activities have been piloted in our institution and have been revised and improved with the insights and experiences of our colleagues and students. In our experience, these activities have helped candidates to understand the lives of children whose experiences are far different from their own, to incorporate student backgrounds into curriculum in order to maximize motivation and academic success, to adapt learning activities and assessments that better meet students' abilities and disabilities, and to include families and communities in the learning process.

The profiles in Part I are intentionally *not* "cases" or "case studies," in that they do not contain specific dilemmas for discussion and analysis. They are simply the stories of students. It is the activities in Part II that present teacher education candidates with the directions for how to interact with the profiles—and the students—through reflection, discussion, and action. And because the profiles are not bound by specific problems, faculty are encouraged to use the stories of the children in ways that are useful in their own courses, in any activity in which having a collection of children to "put a face" on diversity might be useful. It is our intention that Casey, Sarah, Malcolm, Leslie, Raul, and Yu-shin become students in your simulated professional development school, much as they have in ours. We hope that they will help your teacher candidates learn to understand and build on student diversity in ways that value every child and ensure that every child is both successful and challenged in the learning process.

Many people have contributed to this project, and we would like to acknowledge the following and thank them for their assistance: to Dr. Kaye M. Martin for her help in conceptualizing the project; to Dr. Sandy Long for her contribution to the development of Malcolm's cumulative folder and for sharing her expertise in special education; to our colleagues in teacher education at Muskingum College who used the "Raul Project" and offered corrections and suggestions that made the activities more useful and the stories more real; to our students at Muskingum College who piloted the activities, offered their insights into the profiles and activities, found the typos and inconsistencies in our stories, and encouraged us by sharing with us their revelations and their passion for teaching; to our conference colleagues who made suggestions that improved the effectiveness of the project and encouraged us to publish our work; to the editors at Sage who made excellent suggestions for improving the final project; to our peer reviewers for their helpful feedback: Patricia J. Wall, University of Portland, Elaine Foster, Grambling State University, Jean Ann Foley, Northern Arizona University, Patricia G. Maiorino, University of New Haven, Gail P. Gregg, Florida International University, Sheryl Conrad Cozart, George Mason University, Miroslava B. Vargas, Texas A&M International University, Denise Blum, California State University Fresno, Mary Curran, Rutgers State University of New Jersey, Winston Vaughan, Xavier University, Terrence O. Harewood, University of Indianapolis, and Anonymous Reviewer, Temple University; to Marilyn Spragg Jenrette, MD, for verifying Leslie's medical records; to Rachael Hrisak and Heather Frese for allowing us to borrow their early work for Sarah's folder; to Susan Larson for helping to develop documents for Sarah's folder; to Megan and Brett Butler for their childhood experiences as gifted children; to Dr. Donna Adornetto and Lori Morrow for assistance in developing Casey's individualized educational program; to Aaron, Benjamin, and Dylan Cowdery for their contributions to the prototypes of our fictional students.

# Chapter 1

# MIDLAND U.S.A. AND ITS SCHOOLS

Every good story has a setting. For the children whose stories are contained in Part I of this book, that setting is Midland U.S.A. Although not Everytown, Midland has the businesses, schools, and populations that are characteristic of many towns, and its values and customs influence and are influenced by the people who live there. As you meet Casey, Sarah, Malcolm, Raul, Leslie, and Yu-shin, you will see that their stories are intertwined with those of others—their families, their friends, their teachers, and the other children and adults who interact with them. You will also see that their stories are influenced by the places they live, work, and play in—their homes, their schools, and the other venues they frequent. This chapter introduces you to those places and provides a context in which to understand the children and to make decisions about how you, as a teacher, can best build on their diverse backgrounds and abilities to create effective and empowering classrooms and schools.

## MIDLAND

Midland, with a population of 10,000, is nestled in the southeast corner of a state in the center of the United States. As the county seat, it serves as the commercial center for the 18,000 residents of its surrounding villages and countryside. Its nearest large city, with a population of 250,000, is 60 miles away, about an hour's drive on an interstate highway.

### Commerce

Midland's businesses include Nisota Inc., an automobile manufacturing plant; several small factories that serve the automobile after-market; the Welbuilt Box Company, a midsized manufacturer of cardboard boxes; and Serv-Right Company, a distribution center for rubber kitchenware. Cowon Inc., a Korean-owned electronics company, plans to locate a major manufacturing plant in Midland.

A four-block downtown houses three banks, a drugstore, two local clothing stores, a bookstore, a variety of arts and crafts stores, a mom-and-pop breakfast and lunch counter, and all of the city and county services. On the outskirts of town are a major discount store, two supermarkets, a large home improvement store, a chain drugstore, and a handful of small specialty stores, along with a few national chain fast-food restaurants.

Sprinkled along the town's two main streets are car dealerships, tire stores, equipment rental stores, law offices, insurance agencies, branch banks, and funeral homes. Midland serves the people who live throughout the county as well as those who live within the city limits.

Although much of the county's land is agricultural, the number of people making a living from farming is less than 5% of its population.

## Features

In addition to being the county's center of commerce, Midland is also the county seat. A century-old courthouse graces the city's center. The annual county fair is held in Midland in July. A harvest festival sponsored by local civic groups is held in the fall.

Midland College, located in the center of the city, is a private liberal arts college, with 1,100 undergraduate students and 100 graduate students in education and business. A small YMCA is affiliated with the college and serves as the center of the college's indoor sports program. It is open to the public and is widely used for community events.

A large local park features tennis courts, baseball diamonds, and basketball courts. One of the old school buildings has been converted into an after-school youth center with outdoor sports facilities and a skateboard park. A 2-mile bike path follows an abandoned railway. The city has two golf courses, one private and one public. There is a private swim club, open only to members. A state park with a fishing lake is located about 5 miles outside the city.

## Schools

The Midland City School District serves 2,300 students: 800 in Midland High School, 600 in Midland Middle School, and roughly 300 in each of three elementary schools. The school board consists of five members, each elected by voters in the district. The district's motto is "Reaching Higher, Every Day in Every Way." It is currently under "Continuous Improvement," the middle of the categories assigned to districts by the state department of education, based on its scores on required achievement tests.

## Cultural Background

The earliest settlers of Midland were English farmers who migrated west in the early 1800s. The descendents of these first families are still in Midland; some are still farmers, some own businesses, and some are the town's professionals.

As the town grew, it attracted other European Americans, and throughout the early 20th century, African Americans. In the past 5 years, Mexicans have come to work in the small manufacturing plants; some have sought and achieved U.S. citizenship. There is a very new group of Laotians, sponsored by a local church. A few Japanese families are here with the Nisota plant. It is anticipated that several Korean families will come to town with the new Cowon plant.

| Ethnic demographics are as follows: | |
| --- | --- |
| European American | 78% |
| African American | 10% |
| Mexicans and Mexican Americans | 5% |
| Laotians | 1% |
| Japanese | 2% |

## Religion

Most of Midland's residents are Protestants, with about 40% claiming membership in mainline churches, including Methodist, Presbyterian, and Baptist, and about 20% in evangelical sects, including Jehovah's Witnesses. About 15% are Roman Catholic. There are very small numbers of Jews, Buddhists, and Muslims, who must drive to the nearby large city to find organized religious services. Most of the religious organizations in Midland have active youth groups.

## CLOVER VALLEY ELEMENTARY SCHOOL

Located at the eastern edge of Midland is Clover Valley Elementary School. Built in 1925, the town's former high school houses 300 students in kindergarten through fifth grade. It is a rather imposing two-story square brick structure with a large front lawn and several acres of playground space in the back. There are two sections of each grade, putting the average class size in the high 20s. In addition to 12 classroom teachers, there are "specials" teachers in art, music, and physical education. There are two "intervention specialists" to work with children with identified special needs and their regular classroom teachers. There are three teachers' aides, who work primarily with prekindergarten, kindergarten, and first-grade classes. Classes are self-contained through the third grade, but teachers of the same grade often collaborate on lesson plans and units. The fourth and fifth grades are partially compartmentalized, with one teacher specializing in science and math and the other in language arts and social studies. Although there is an increasing number of English Language Learners (ELLs), there is as yet no schoolwide plan to accommodate their needs.

### Activities

Special events include a Round-Up for kindergarteners in the summer, a Fall Festival to raise money for the parent-teacher organization, a Winter Holiday Song Fest, and a Spring Music Review. Events and parent-teacher conferences are well attended.

### Students

About a quarter of the children are from the town's wealthiest subdivision. Their parents are the town's doctors, lawyers, business owners, and senior management of the automobile plant. More than half of the children are from the working-class neighborhood around the school, which was built just after World War II. Most of their parents work in the town's service industries, and a few have jobs in the auto parts and box factories. The remaining students come from a trailer park just at the outskirts of town and a three-block section where most of the town's African Americans live. Their parents work primarily in the town's service industries: fast food, retail, and maintenance. A handful of students are children of the Japanese managers of the automobile plant. Fifty percent of the children receive free or reduced-price lunch.

The school district is rated by the state as a "Continuous Improvement" district. For the district as a whole, the scores on the mandated achievement tests continue to be below the state average. At Clover Valley, the scores vary widely from very high to very low, with the average for most tests just at the state average. In an effort to raise scores districtwide, each elementary school has an intensive summer school program, a volunteer-based tutoring program, and an extensive testing skills and review program for those students who do not pass the achievement tests at their grade level.

## Words From the Staff and Students

Mrs. Sloan, principal: "I just love working at Clover Valley! This is my third year here, and we've really made some strides at making this building a good place for boys and girls. I've been working with the teachers to institute a new schoolwide discipline plan that puts more responsibility on the children to solve behavior problems. We've had some consultants in working with us, and I think that most of the teachers are starting to think it's a good idea. I don't see as many names on the board as I used to!"

Mr. Peters, janitor: "This building is pretty old, and sometimes I feel like I'm just keeping it glued together. Still, it's always clean, and nobody's complained yet that I don't do a good job. The kids here are pretty well behaved for the most part, although you do get a wild one from time to time. Mrs. Sloan does a good job of keeping things under control."

Ms. Kearns, art teacher: "You should see some of the children's artwork at Clover Valley! There are some real talented young artists here, and I try to display as much of their work as possible. Overall, this is a pretty good place to work. Some of the teachers act like they'd rather be doing something else, but most are very good and like the students a lot."

Mr. Bush, intervention specialist: "We instituted inclusion here quite a few years ago, but we're just starting to get a handle on how to integrate the regular kids with the ones with special needs. I still have a couple of teachers who wish I'd just take "my kids" back to the resource room! I've taken some courses at the local college to help me work with kids and teachers, and I think I'm making some progress."

Mrs. Kettering, third-grade teacher: "I'm still not sure about that Mrs. Sloan. She has a lot of new ideas—and sometimes I think we'd be better off doing things the way we used to."

Leslie Carr, first grader: "This is a really good school. My teacher is Mrs. Clawson, and she's really good. We have class meetings to see how we can make things better."

Tonya Yosaka, fifth grader: "I like it here at Clover Valley. We get to read a lot, and the teachers are very nice. I really like art and music. I want to sing in the show choir when I get to high school."

# MIDLAND MIDDLE SCHOOL

Located on the outskirts of the city limits and within sight of the high school is Midland Middle School. Built in 1990, it is a one-level building with four wings. The wings surround a common area that consists of a dining facility that can be transformed into a large meeting room, a gymnasium with a small stage area, a library, two smaller meeting rooms, and administrative offices. The building is fully disability accessible and houses the county's middle school unit for students with multiple disabilities.

Like the other buildings in the district, Midland Middle School is well maintained. The building recently won a Spruce Up Midland award from the Midland Chamber of Commerce for the innovative landscaping that the eighth-grade students completed as a service learning project last year. In the evenings after ball games, the building is accessible for community meetings, and the large, well-equipped computer lab is open to district families until 9 p.m. Monday through Thursday.

Midland Middle School serves 600 students in Grades 6 through 8. It is one of the few area middle schools that went through the North Central Association of Colleges and Secondary Schools optional middle school accreditation process. It is also one of only a few regional middle schools that embrace the middle school philosophy. Three of the four wings each house all the classrooms for one grade level, as well as a teacher workroom and two small intervention classrooms. The fourth wing houses classrooms for music, visual arts, living skills, and a computer lab with 25 desktop computers. The classroom for students with multiple disabilities and a resource classroom for students identified as gifted are also housed in this wing.

## Grade-Level Organization

The approximately 200 students per grade level are divided into family groups of 50 students. Eight content teachers provide instruction for the 200 students, with four teachers assigned to two family groups—one teacher for reading/language arts, one for math, one for social studies, and one for science. The family groups are flexibly subdivided into groups of 25, so that the groupings can be more or less heterogeneous as needed. Thus each day, each content teacher provides instruction for four groups of 25 students.

Each grade level has one intervention specialist and one special education paraprofessional who provide support to general education teachers and special education instruction in the classrooms reserved for intervention services. The home-base teacher for each group of 25 students also serves as that group's intervention coordinator and monitors his or her students' progress across academic subjects, as well as their behavior. The middle school has recently applied for an adolescent literacy/reading intervention grant that will provide funds to hire a reading specialist to provide intensive reading instruction for the most challenged readers. Although there is a small and growing number of students who are ELLs, there are no special services available to them beyond what individual teachers choose to do in their own classrooms.

## Scheduling

Midland Middle School uses a "double blocking approach" to scheduling. Every day each student receives 80 minutes of mathematics instruction, 80 minutes of reading/language arts instruction, and either 80 minutes of science or social studies. One semester each family group takes science, and the next semester each family group takes social studies. In addition, all students rotate through 80-minute 9-week minicourses in computer technology, music, art, and life skills each year. Finally, all students have a 40-minute physical education period each day, as well as a 40-minute lunch and recess period.

Last year, in an effort to improve achievement scores, 40 minutes were added to the middle school day to provide one intervention period per day for each student. However, this time is also the time used for sixth- to eighth-grade band and choir, which alternate every other day every two weeks. Students who choose to be in both band and choir do not have a regular intervention period and use recess time for any intervention needs they have.

## Behavior Management

Midland Middle School has struggled with inconsistent building and classroom rules both within and across wings for several years. Disrespect for peers, teachers, and the facility seemed to be increasing. Last year the building established a buildingwide positive behavioral support team, which consisted of one teacher from each 50-member family group, a teacher from each special area, two intervention specialists, and representatives from the secretarial staff, custodians, and cafeteria workers. Led by the building principal, this group established five buildingwide rules and several routines for the common areas. In addition, each wing has established a common set of classroom rules and routines shared by all the teachers their family group shares. The buildingwide and wing-specific rules and routines are now in the process of being implemented, with every teacher taking time to discuss and model what the expected behaviors look and sound like, what the positive consequences for appropriate behavior are, and what the negative consequences for inappropriate behavior are.

## Activities

In addition to sixth- through eight-grade band and chorus, there are several informal clubs that meet periodically over the lunch recess period. One teacher leads a poetry-writing club and another hosts a foreign language club in which eighth graders have the opportunity to learn basic conversational Spanish. Several teachers oversee intramural volleyball and basketball during lunch recess times. A small group of students meets in a room weekly during recess to have a Bible study. This group is student led, but a teacher is in the room to ensure that acceptable standards of behavior are maintained.

Approximately 25 students serve as the Midland Middle School yearbook staff, and another 20 participate in a minitheatrical production that the seventh-grade language arts teacher produces each spring. Several eighth-grade students have indicated an interest in starting a peer mediation and conflict resolution program similar to one they heard about from friends who attend a nearby middle school. They presented their suggestion to the student council, whose members had little interest in promoting the development of such a program. However, one of the student council advisers seemed quite interested.

Midland Middle School also has after-school competitive seventh- and eighth-grade girls' volleyball, soccer, and basketball programs and seventh- and eighth-grade boys' soccer, basketball, and wrestling programs. The games of these teams are often almost as well attended as some of the high school athletic events. Approximately 50% of the students participate in one or more sports; however, this number is skewed toward those who either live within walking distance or can afford transportation to and from practices and games. Due to decreased funding, the district is contemplating a "pay-to-play" policy for competitive sports at the middle school.

## Students

The students at Midland Middle School reside in nearby Midland and in some small surrounding rural communities. The population is primarily made up of blue-collar manufacturing and rural employees. Eighty-one percent of the student body is European American and 96% is Christian. African American students comprise about 10% of the student population. There is a growing Mexican population (approximately 5%), and 4% of the students are from Southeast Asia. To date, the school has not had consistent ESL (English as a second language) services available to their students, an issue that is being discussed by the building's parent advisory council and district's community advisory group.

Other issues on the agenda for the building-level parent advisory council are the continued below-state-average achievement test scores and a growing concern about weekend alcohol and marijuana use among seventh and eighth graders. Last year, three students had to be rushed to the hospital with alcohol poisoning, and four were put on probation for illegal drug use. Rumors of illegal substance use by members of the eighth-grade basketball teams have begun to tarnish the school's reputation in the community and throughout the county.

The building's DARE officer does not believe that his activities in the building are having any positive impact and is soliciting parent and teacher input. Two seventh-grade girls and three eighth-grade girls gave birth last year. All but one of the girls has returned to school this year.

As a part of the schoolwide behavioral support initiative, there have been several concerted efforts to address the increasing number of cliques and escalating name-calling. From the first day of school forward, sixth graders enter from their respective elementary buildings with the stereotypes those buildings have developed over time. Students coming from the most rural of the elementary buildings are known as "hayseeds" before they get in the door, and the children coming from the elementary school that serves the area nearest the factories are known as "boxers." Carefully configured family groups that blend students from all four buildings do much to minimize geographical name-calling by the end of the sixth-grade year. However, those negative messages are replaced with ones more related to physical appearance, race, or religion. Several "cultural sensitivity" assemblies and follow-up homeroom-based activities have done little to lessen the name-calling. Graffiti has begun to be a problem.

## Words From the Staff and Students

Mr. Geiser, principal: "I retired from a high school principal's position in another district but came to Midland Middle School when Mrs. Sanders, the previous principal, died unexpectedly. I've lived in Midland all my life. Mrs. Sanders and her staff worked hard to develop a solid program for our kids, so why let it go to pot? Every year, though, it seems harder to stay on top of all the new initiatives and state requirements."

Ms. Biddle, assistant principal: "Last year I was really getting worried about the discipline and student attitudes at Midland. However, it seems like we've begun to turn the corner with this new schoolwide behavioral support plan. Now if I could just find something that might help with the name-calling. I received two calls last week from board members who had heard rumors about the graffiti. So which do I focus on—clean walls or implementing this reading intervention grant? I'm already here 10 hours a day.

Mrs. Piper, secretary: "I know I don't make much money here, but I love the kids. It breaks my heart when I see some of them come in without breakfast or watch them sleep away their day in the sick room because they've been up all night. And it makes me so mad when I hear them be mean to each other. I never let my girls talk like that. How can parents just not care what their kids say and do?"

Ms. Jasper, sixth-grade science teacher: "I'd never thought I'd like it here in Midland, but this middle school was the only one that offered me a position. Whoever thought that there would not be a teacher shortage in this day and age! But, you know, the town is growing on me, and I've become really attached to so many of the kids. Some seem to have all the advantages and don't even realize it. Others just seem to have had no breaks at all. Surprisingly, I find myself being their champion more often than not. Having the double-blocked periods for labs has really let me learn my students' strengths and difficulties. How can teachers so misunderstand their students? You just have to get to know them and see them in action."

John and Julie Jackson, parents of two boys who attend the middle school (John serves on the building's parent advisory committee, and Julie speaks on health-related careers every year on eighth-grade career day). John: "The name-calling and conflicts among groups of students seem to be escalating. It just wasn't an issue when I was in school. All these move-ins are diluting the quality of our children's education. It's silly to think that teachers should have to 'teach' kids how to behave in the lunchroom and hallways. When I got in trouble at school, I got in bigger trouble that night at home. Man, I learned not to act up a second time. What's wrong with these parents anyway?"

Julie: "What parents? Some of these kids are just about living on their own. I just don't understand why they don't put their kids first. We always do."

Raul Ramirez, eighth grader: "This school is OK. But sometimes the kids are mean. Really mean."

## MIDLAND HIGH SCHOOL

Located just outside the city limits is Midland High School. Built in 1981, it is a fairly modern two-story structure with an attached gymnasium/auditorium. The halls are wide and fully disability accessible. One elevator is available for the second floor, and a ramp as well as a staircase connects the gym to the main building. About 15% of the student population is in a special education program, including a multiple-handicapped unit. There is ample parking surrounding the school, and most students drive or ride a bus to school. The closest housing development is over 2 miles from the building. Being located outside of city limits and surrounded primarily by fields and rows of trees has protected the school from frequent vandalism. The physical buildings look almost new.

Midland High School is a 4-year comprehensive high school of about 800 students. MHS is accredited by the Mid-Central Association of Colleges and Secondary Schools and by the state department of education. It operates on a nine-period day, and classes are 42 minutes in length. Laboratory classes are often double periods. Its stated mission is to provide, along with the family and community, an excellent educational experience for all students to prepare them to achieve success in their careers, communities, and personal lives. MHS has competitive interscholastic athletics and an award-winning marching band and show choir, along with a variety of other extracurricular programs that afford opportunities for personal growth, citizenship, and leadership.

## Activities

Extracurricular activities include student government, National Honor Society, jazz band, marching band, choirs, cheerleading, Academic League Team, newspaper, yearbook, Youth-to-Youth drug program, chess club, Leadership Council, pep squad, International Club, Future Farmers of America (FFA), and Educators of Tomorrow.

Interscholastic sports for boys include football, cross-country, soccer, golf, basketball, wrestling, baseball, tennis, and track. Among the girls' interscholastic sports are cross-country, soccer, golf, volleyball, tennis, basketball, softball, and track.

## Requirements

Twenty-one credits are required for graduation: four credits of English, three of science, three of math, three of social studies, two of physical education and health, one of arts, and five of electives in foreign languages, the arts, business, or other academic areas. Fifty percent of the student population attend college or postsecondary education. More than 30% of the teachers have their master's degrees and an average of 17 years of teaching experience.

## Students

Students reside in nearby Midland and some small surrounding communities. The population is primarily made up of blue-collar manufacturing and rural employees. Most students are working-class students who also hold part-time jobs after school and in the summers. By high school, though, the number of students applying for free lunch has dropped to 28%. Eighty-three percent of the student body is European American, and 98% of the student body is Christian. African American students comprise about 10% of the student population. Most African American students live in the eastern section of town and have attended the same elementary school. A growing Mexican population has risen to 5%, and some teachers have begun to talk about starting ELL services at the high school. A small group of Southeast Asian students also lives in the community, but most of these children are in elementary or middle school. About half the student population participates in athletics and extracurricular activities. The high school's events attract a large audience from the wider community. The high school provides a center of social activity and identity for the small city's population.

Despite the relatively high graduation rate, the school district is rated as a "Continuous Improvement" status by the state. The scores on the mandated proficiency test continue to be below the state average. As a result, several initiatives have been instituted in the last 2 years. Tutoring during study halls for those failing to pass the test, mandatory summer school, and stricter enforcement of truancy rules are some of the ways that the school has tried to address the problem.

In addition, traditional problems of absenteeism, teen pregnancy, and alcohol have been complicated recently by increasing drug problems among the students. As the economy has declined and jobs in the area have disappeared due to factory closings and moves, part of the population has turned to illegal sources of income. Because a large city is only 1 hour from the town, the availability of harder drugs has become more accessible. While alcohol is still the most popular drug among the city's teenagers, more and more cases of overdoses of heroin and crack cocaine are being seen at the local hospital. The high school has had to beef up its discipline staff to stop the increasing sales of drugs and related drug activity in the schools. Consequently, more student-on-student assaults and petty theft are being seen in the high school every year.

## Words From the Staff and Students

Mr. Roberts, principal: "Midland High School is an excellent educational institution. It provides opportunities for all students. Like many high schools, we have our share of problems, but we have an excellent staff to work toward solving those problems."

Ms. Gross, assistant principal: "Most students at Midland do not take advantage of the education that is offered to them. I find it frustrating that students today expect others to do things for them rather than to work hard for their goals. Too many parents spoil their children and then blame the school when those children get into trouble. There should be parenting classes required of anyone wanting to have children."

Mr. Bond, janitor: "The school and the kids are pretty much the same as when I started 30 years ago. I've seen kids, teachers, and principals come and go, and still the school is pretty much the same. Seems like more kids are having bigger troubles these days, but you've got good kids and bad kids. Kids are kids."

Ms. Flack, ninth-grade English teacher: "I've seen a decline in the interest level of my students. It worries me. Each year it is more and more challenging to motivate my students. So many outside activities drain them of a focus on their academics. The best time, though, is when I can light a fire, when my whole class is involved and excited about a concept or a piece of literature. Just last week, one of students, who rarely participates, came up to me and told me that he had been so interested in *To Kill a Mockingbird* that he had decided to do his social studies report on the civil rights movement. Now that's rewarding."

Coach Marks, social studies teacher, track coach: "I really like teaching. I like the kids here. I thought this was what I wanted to do with the rest of my life. Ever since I was in high school track, I dreamed of coaching. But now I'm starting a family and I'm having a hard time making a living. Being gone all day and most of the night is a hardship as well. My brother has his own insurance agency, and I'm seriously thinking about switching careers."

Mrs. Huttman, special education teacher: "I feel as if I'm an **advocate** for my students. If no one will speak up for them, it is my responsibility. Sometimes I'm not a very popular person, but I think that it is my job to make sure my students are treated fairly and afforded the same opportunities as all other students. None of my kids is ever cheerleader or football star or class president, but each of them has the right to have the same chance at an education and in activities as any other kid in this high school. Our school and our community have a long way to go before every child feels that he or she can succeed."

Jessica Linn, 12th-grade student: "I have to thank my parents and my teachers for giving me a wonderful education. Midland High School has been a great place to get a solid foundation for college. I will really miss my friends and my teachers when I leave this year. There are so many things to be involved in here, and students should take advantage of those activities. I do believe I had a very well-rounded experience here."

Malcolm Singer, 10th-grade student: "This place is really boring. If it weren't for my friends and the awesome parties, I would've quit a long time ago. The teachers here all seem to have their pets, and if you're not part of a certain crowd, nobody cares about you. I can't wait to leave."

## ACTIVITY 1: EXAMINING THE SCHOOL AND COMMUNITY

### Directions

Choose one of the Midland schools and consider the following:

1. What is the cultural, ethnic, and socioeconomic makeup of the community?

2. How is this reflected in the school?

3. What makes this school unique or challenging?

4. How is this school attempting to meet the diverse needs of its students?

5. Does this school provide equal educational opportunities for all students?

## ACTIVITY 2: EXPLORING THE "HIDDEN CURRICULUM"

Every school has a hidden curriculum—the behaviors, attitudes, and expectations it unintentionally teaches its students. Ask yourself, in addition to the planned curriculum, what else do students learn in this school.

### Directions

Choose one of the Midland schools and consider the following:

1. From the organization of time, materials, and priorities, what do students learn about what is important?

2. From policies, routines, procedures, and the physical structure, what do students learn about what is expected? Does this match with all of their home experiences? If not, describe the differences.

3. From comments from the principals, teachers, staff, and students, what are students learning about their worth in this school system?

4. Consider the students in the biographies. Which ones will have the hardest time adjusting to the school's hidden curriculum? Why?

## ACTIVITY 3: SCHOOL AND COMMUNITY COLLABORATION

### Directions

Divide into small groups as directed by your instructor. Choose one of the following sets of questions to discuss. Plan to share your answers in class in the format determined by your instructor.

1. Clover Valley Elementary School would like to start a school-business partnership with one of Midland's businesses. What first steps should it take? Who should take them? How would you contact the businesses? What benefits might there be for the school, the schoolchildren, and the business partner? What type of a planning group might you establish? Who might be part of it?

2. The Midland Council of Churches has approached one of the teachers, Ms. Jasper, at Midland Middle School about sponsoring an after-school tutoring and support program for at-risk middle school students. What steps should she take? What are some of the issues that need to be discussed? What might be the potential benefits? What might be some potential challenges? What type of a planning group might you establish? Who might be a part of it?

3. The guidance counselor at Midland High School is painfully aware that it is the only high school in a three-county area that doesn't have a career development program and job shadowing. Midland had tried to start a program 5 years ago but could not generate sufficient interest in the community to keep a local program going for more than a year. Several parents have asked him to try to develop this program again and have agreed to help him. He is not sure where his principal stands on the issue, since the principal received much bad press the last time the program was established. What steps should he take? With whom should he talk? In whom should he generate interest? What are some of the potential benefits and challenges of this type of program.

4. You are Mrs. Sloan, the principal at Clover Valley Elementary School. As more and more students enter your building with limited English skills, you are increasingly bothered by the central administration's refusal to establish an ESL program. You have been approached by several business leaders whose employees' non-English-speaking children attend your school. They would like to help you start an ESL program. They have pledged both financial and people support if you can get the administration to let you pilot a program that is based on sound principles of ELS instruction. What first steps should you take? With whom should you talk? What type of a planning group should you assemble? Where should you turn for program models? What might a good ESL program include?

**Box 1.1**    Rubric for Activity 3

| Unacceptable | Acceptable | Exemplary |
|---|---|---|
| Not all group participants involved in discussion | All group participants involved in discussion | All group participants equally involved in discussion |
| Not all questions addressed | All questions addressed | All questions addressed in detail |
| Outside resources not considered | Outside resources considered | Outside resources used to answer questions |
| Several relevant stakeholders not considered | Most relevant stakeholders involved in planning process | Creative options included in planning process |
| Format guidelines not consistently followed | Format guidelines consistently followed | All relevant stakeholders involved in planning process |
| | | Creative use of format |

# Part I

## Profiles and Cumulative Folders

In Part I, you will meet children from a variety of backgrounds with a wide range of abilities and disabilities. They are African American, European American, Hispanic, and Korean. They are native speakers of English and English Language Learners (ELLs). They are from poor, working-class, and middle-class families. They are identified as intellectually gifted and as average in their abilities to learn. They have been diagnosed with a learning disability and with attention-deficit/hyperactivity disorder (ADHD). They have physical abilities and disabilities. They are gay and straight. As you read their stories and examine their cumulative folders, imagine that they are the students in a classroom—your classroom. And as in a real classroom, you will learn from the children what it is you can and must do to ensure that all are valued and that all are both challenged and successful in the classrooms and schools that you create.

# Chapter 2

## CASEY GRIFFITH

*Motivating and Modifying for Learning Disabilities*

## SECOND GRADE

### Clover Valley Elementary School

Casey Griffith is a 7-year-old European American boy who lives with both parents and a 10-year-old sister, Claudia, in a rural area 4 miles from Clover Valley Elementary School. At the beginning of the school year, Mr. Jones, Casey's second-grade teacher, learned from Casey's previous first-grade teacher, Mrs. Simpson, that his mother, Juanita Griffith, is a licensed practical nurse in an area hospital. Mrs. Griffith had told Mrs. Simpson that she is quite proud of her job, since she earned her LPN license after going back for her GED a year after Claudia was born.

Mrs. Simpson had also learned that Casey's father, Sam Griffith, quit high school when he and Juanita decided to get married. Unlike Mrs. Griffith, he did not earn his GED; school had never been easy for him, and he still cannot read. Ever since he was little, he always had enjoyed tinkering with cars, and he had quickly found a job as a mechanic at a Midland auto repair shop.

Unfortunately, toward the end of Casey's first-grade year, Mr. Griffith was fired for irregular attendance at work. Since he was known for being good with his hands, he began to pick up handyman jobs in the area, which helped a little with expenses. However, it seemed like extended family began calling on him for help with odd jobs they needed to have done, and his immediate response to their needs put him behind on any contracted work. Mrs. Simpson had heard through others in the community that it was when Mr. Griffith lost his job that he started to drink.

Casey's sister, Claudia, is now a fifth grader who is described by her teachers as a "real talker" and not well liked by her peers. She misses school when her parents' activities take precedence over the school schedule. Her transition from Clover Valley Elementary School to Midland Middle School was not easy, and her grades have dropped from A's and B's to mostly C's for no obvious reason.

Documentation from kindergarten prescreening over 2 years ago reveals that Casey's birth was typical. He had an at-birth **Apgar** of 8, weighed 9 pounds and 4 ounces, and was 21 inches long. According to his parents, Casey was a "fussy" baby prior to their realization during his third month that he was allergic to milk. When Mrs. Griffith finally found a free source of lactose-free formula, he began to sleep for longer periods of time and became "a quiet baby." Records from first-year well-baby checkups at the Midland City Health Department reported that he exhibited below-average reactivity to sensory stimulation and was above the 90th percentile in weight and below the 50th percentile in height.

Interview notes taken during kindergarten screening showed that Mr. and Mrs. Griffith were questioned about potentially traumatic events. The only ones they could remember were a series of five family moves that occurred over a 2-year period while Mr. Griffin tried to find a stable job. Several times Mrs. Griffith and the children stayed with extended family in crowded conditions while Mr. Griffith hunted for work. Each move left Casey less likely to interact with those outside his family and more likely to withdraw into "his own little world."

Casey's parents reported that during this period of time, he seldom played outside with Claudia, his cousins, or other neighborhood children. He preferred to watch TV or play alone with the few toys he had. With his mother and father focused on work and housing, they had little time for interactive play with him. Children's books were not viewed as important, with Mr. Griffith asking, "What difference does reading make anyway? I never learned to read, and you don't need to read to fix cars."

Notes included in Casey's permanent file indicated that during his kindergarten year, his attendance was irregular, he was slow to play and interact with other children in his class, and he was viewed by his teacher as more quiet and withdrawn than his classmates. His oral grammar and listening comprehension were typical for boys his age, but he had difficulty with shapes, letters, numbers, and **fine motor** tasks. Casey appeared to enjoy **gross motor** activities, but his response time and speed while playing games with other children was much slower, perhaps due at least in part to being considerably overweight.

Additional records showed that some of Casey's same behaviors continued in first grade. His attendance remained erratic, with 25 school days missed. Casey's first-grade teacher, Mrs. Simpson, noted that he followed oral directions, could give accurate and detailed retellings for stories read to him, and enjoyed hands-on math and science activities. However, Casey appeared unable to grasp **sound-symbol relationships**, had difficulties printing letters, and became frustrated with most paper-and-pencil tasks, sometimes responding to such tasks with refusals to do the work or by bothering other students.

Mr. Jones, Casey's second-grade teacher, has been concerned about both Casey's behavior and performance since the second week of school. Almost immediately, Casey began to exhibit inappropriate behaviors prior to his reading group time. Casey also is off task much of the time that he is supposed to be working independently. His behaviors include daydreaming, picking at other students, and responding with "I won't do it, and you can't make me." By the end of the first month of school, Casey has missed 5 days, and calls to his home have not been returned.

When Mr. Jones reviewed Casey's cumulative folder, he noticed that Casey's first-grade achievement tests showed that Casey scored at a preprimer level in reading and on grade level in math. When Mr. Jones has Casey read orally to him, he realizes that Casey does not discriminate among short vowel sounds and that he reverses many letters. Mr. Jones has seen similar reversals in Casey's written work, as well as a labored approach to printing, in which he presses down on the paper so hard with his pencil that he regularly tears the paper.

This information, coupled with the attendance patterns from the past 2 years, prompted Mr. Jones to persist in making contact with Mrs. Griffith to see if she can help him understand Casey's behavior and academic performance. When he finally reached Mrs. Griffith by phone, she indicated that, unlike when they were moving around, Casey is "talkative now" with family members and a few friends but remains shy around others. She also indicated that Casey "loves to follow his dad around at home," can take anything apart and put it back together, and avoids reading and writing tasks. She compares his reluctance to read or write to that of his sister. She dismisses his absences by saying, "Sometimes there are just places we have to go, and I want my kids with me."

During the first 2 months of school, Mr. Jones tried a variety of **multisensory approaches** to see if he could develop sound-symbol relationships. Casey made little progress, and his inappropriate behaviors escalated. Mr. Jones doesn't know what else to try. Casey appears even more frustrated than Mr. Jones and is beginning to take it out on his classmates.

# SIXTH GRADE

## Midland Middle School

Now 11 years of age and in sixth grade, Casey Griffith still lives with both parents and his 14-year-old sister, Claudia, in the same house he has been in since kindergarten, the longest time the family has lived in one place. Mrs. Griffith has taken on extra hours as an LPN just to make ends meet. According to Casey, Mr. Griffith still does handyman jobs he secures around town. However, one of Casey's cousins who works in food services at the middle school gossiped that Mr. Griffith's work tends to be late and shoddily completed.

The same cousin told the principal that Mr. Griffith is drinking more and more all the time and his wife occasionally accuses him of being "a drunk" and "needing help." Casey hates it when his parents get into a fight over his father's drinking. He likes to spend time puttering around with Mr. Griffith in the garage, now used as a makeshift workshop. Unfortunately, after the Griffiths fight about Sam's drinking, Mr. Griffith storms out of the house and will not let Casey help him for days. Casey's sister, Claudia, is now in ninth grade. Her grades now average D's in all subjects but art.

Despite the consistent efforts of Mr. Jones, Casey's second-grade teacher, Casey had made no significant progress in reading or writing by November. His inappropriate behaviors increased, and his attendance decreased. Mr. Jones asked that the building-level **Intervention Assistance Team (IAT)** convene to help him discuss other behavioral and instructional alternatives for Casey. Mr. Jones tried several of the team's suggestions throughout the remainder of the fall semester. However, Casey continued to make little, if any, progress in his basic reading skills and in written expression.

During January, Mr. Jones talked with Mrs. Griffith about referring Casey for a **multifactored evaluation (MFE)** to determine if Casey might have a **specific learning disability (SLD)**. Although she had to fight her husband to do it, Mrs. Griffith finally agreed to permit the schools to conduct the MFE. At one point she commented to Mr. Jones, "It was worth the fight," because she didn't want Casey to drop out of school like his father had done.

Casey's multifactored **evaluation team report (ETR)** indicated that Casey has a specific learning disability in the areas of basic reading skills, written expression, and math calculations.

According to the **Wechsler Intelligence Scale for Children III (WISC III)**, Casey has a verbal scaled score of 85, a performance-scaled score of 118, and a full-scaled score of 101. Additional tests indicated that he is a strong visual and simultaneous processor, has weak **auditory and visual discrimination** skills, and processes sequential information very slowly and not always accurately. The report indicated that Casey has strong oral communication and listening comprehension skills.

At the end of Casey's second-grade year, he was identified with a specific learning disability, and an **individualized education program** (IEP) was developed for him with academic goals in the areas where he has been identified with a learning disability. He began receiving special education services for reading and language arts instruction in third grade. Initially, special education support was provided for him in the general education classroom, but he still made little progress. Halfway through his third-grade year, he began to receive more intensive reading and language arts instruction in the resource room but remained in the general education classroom with special education support for his mathematics instruction.

Now, almost halfway through his sixth-grade year, he still is reading and writing on a second-grade level. Casey continues to exhibit many of the behaviors seen in students with **dyslexia**, for example, reversals, looking at the first letter of a word and then guessing, and sounding out words so slowly that he loses comprehension. He earns B's in his grade-level math class with no special education services other than extended time on math tests and a quiet place to work. His grades in science, social studies, and health last year and so far this year have been primarily D's. Even though he has grade-level or above comprehension of the actual content in these subjects, he does not complete homework, study for tests, or take any written objective tests seriously.

Casey has "learned" to avoid schoolwork (in and out of class) that he does not enjoy doing, and his attendance has become more and more irregular. Phone calls home regarding Casey's attendance are no more productive than in earlier years. When his days absent neared the level where the truant officer would be called, Mrs. Griffith seems to force the issue and make him go to school until the "fuss" dies down. Mr. Griffith remains uninvolved in Casey's schooling, and Casey has been heard saying, "Dad never finished school, so why should I?" Several cousins have already dropped out of school, and Casey begs to go with his father whenever Mr. Griffith is called in on a "family emergency."

Casey's social life at school appears no more rewarding than his academic performance. He wanted to play football this year but dropped it after 2 weeks because he was so much slower than the rest of the boys on his team. They teased him about his speed and his weight until he just quit going to practice. The teasing carried over to his sixth-grade classes, where the occasional "fat boy" or "lard butt" is heard. Although Casey works hard to disguise his challenges with reading and writing, his "baby printing" also is the brunt of many jokes. His reaction varies according to the individual or group calling the names, with responses ranging from "Go to hell" aimed at the football team to putting his head down in front of the girls. When his teachers are asked, they indicate that his only friends are a handful of other boys who also have special education services provided in a resource room setting.

Ms. Jasper is Casey's sixth-grade science teacher. Since the beginning of the school year, he has been included in her regular education science class with 27 other sixth graders, three of whom have been identified with mild disabilities. Aware of his attendance and other challenges, Ms. Jasper has seen just how well Casey understands what is happening in class while they complete a science experiment. She also has seen him take written tests over the material she is sure he knows and earn less than 60%. She notices that his performance also seems related to the composition of the group to which he is assigned for an activity. She vividly remembers how excited he was the one day in class when he "figured out" the experiment, and she wishes she could replicate his excitement on a regular basis. The question is how.

## TENTH GRADE

### Midland High School

Casey Griffith is now 15 years old and in 10th grade. Last year, his parents were evicted from their house when their rent was late 3 months in a row. During that period of time, Casey's mother, Mrs. Griffith, was off work with a back injury. After staying with an aunt and cousins for 2 months, the Griffiths found another rental in Midland, with fewer rooms and little workshop space. Mrs. Griffith has returned to work on a part-time basis, leaving the family with no medical benefits.

Although Casey's mother does not interfere with his coming to school, her focus is on her nagging back problems. Mr. Griffith's drinking continues to drain already limited family funds, and both his wife and daughter have given up on him. Casey knows his father needs help, but he will not do anything to strain the already tense relationship they have. While Mr. Griffith knows he needs Casey in the shop, he often resents his help, which results in many late night shouting matches.

Casey struggled throughout middle school, surviving ongoing taunts from boys in his classes and being ignored by girls. Although he experienced little success in most subjects in sixth grade, his performance in science consistently improved. His science teacher, Ms. Jasper, had noticed how much he enjoyed (and understood) the science experiments they were conducting and began to use him as a lab assistant. As Casey's confidence in his ability to "do science" increased, he began to study for his tests, accept the testing **accommodations** that were available to him, and listen to his paraphrased science text on tape.

By the time Casey entered seventh grade, Midland Middle School had hired a reading specialist, Mrs. Smith. Casey received 45 minutes of intensive reading instruction daily in a small group setting throughout seventh and eighth grades. By the end of eighth grade, he appeared to have "cracked the phonics code," and his silent reading comprehension improved from a second-grade level to a fifth-grade level. Just as important, for the first time in his life he did not shy away from all reading-related activities and began to spontaneously read in his spare time.

Casey's writing, however, has improved little, although his reading intervention teacher was able to write "use of a laptop computer for daily assignments and essay tests" into his eighth-grade IEP. Casey quickly developed his computer skills and used the laptop in class to complete assignments. Unfortunately, when Casey took the laptop home over his eighth-grade winter break, it was stolen when his cousins came over. No one admitted stealing the laptop, and he had to go without it until he started high school.

Casey continues to do well in his general education mathematics courses, earning a C in Algebra I in ninth grade and, to date, a B+ in geometry. This year in his ecology class, Casey has a strong B, with his only accommodations being use of a laptop and extended time on tests. He serves as a lab assistant for one of the sections of ninth-grade biology 3 days per week during his double-blocked study hall.

Casey's listening comprehension and oral expression skills remain strengths for him. He continues to work with Mrs. Smith the other 2 days per week during his study hall when he walks down to the middle school and joins the reading intervention group that is furthest along in the program. He spends half of the time in reading intervention and the other half serving as Mrs. Smith's assistant in one of her lower reading intervention groups. He ignored the jibes he received from a couple of students the first day he headed down to the middle school this year and responded to their comments with, "Hell, at least I'm learning something."

However, his 10th-grade year has not been without incident. Casey's first contact with his civics teacher, Mr. Parker, was when he turned in a handwritten essay, since the new laptops had not yet arrived. Mr. Parker's response was to crumple up the "scribbled" assignment, throw it in the trash can, and tell Casey that "until he was ready to take his work seriously, he could return to first grade since his work looked like a first grader had written it." It took weeks of work with Mrs. Smith to overcome such a negative start and to brave using the laptop in Mr. Parker's class.

Over the years, Casey had always enjoyed helping his father on projects. This year, Casey has begun to take over for his dad when he is too drunk to finish the few jobs he has. Casey has not received any recognition for his work, since he will not let anyone know his father has been too drunk to do it himself. However, recently with pride he has confided to the reading interventionist that he has picked up a couple of home repair jobs on his own.

This flicker of self-confidence has spilled over to his athletic performance. Although his football experiences had not always been positive, he once again tried out for the team and was added to the reserve roster. His attendance improved during football season, though it quickly dropped after the season. Likewise, his appearance during football season was much neater and cleaner than in previous years. Unlike his attendance, his improved appearance has continued. He is still a loner in school and has few close friends.

Casey's disciplinary infractions have been limited to tardiness and one office conference after he ran out of Mr. Parker's class the first day of school. Mrs. Rigley, the assistant principal, has heard via the grapevine that the "Griffith pattern" is to drop out in 11th grade. When she investigates the rumor, she finds out that in the past 8 years, four cousins and Casey's sister, Claudia, have all dropped out before their senior years. She does not want that to happen again.

It is nearing IEP time. Casey's parents receive a letter from his special education teacher, Mr. James, encouraging them to discuss with Casey what he plans to do for his last years of high school and after he graduates. When Mrs. Griffith questions Casey, he tells her that Mr. James said he has to include a **transition plan** in his next IEP. Casey says it's "about getting me ready for being an adult." Mrs. Griffith tells Casey that as long as he finishes high school and "stays out of trouble," she does not care what they write in the IEP. She is too busy to bother with another boring conference.

Mr. James knows that Casey has confided in both Mrs. Smith and his geometry teacher, Ms. Ames, and encourages them to talk to Casey about his "career goals." When Ms. Ames tries, Casey indicates he does not have plans for after high school. All he knows is that he likes helping his father in their "shop," his mother will kill him if he drops out, and he would rather be with his cousins riding four wheelers than anything else. Ms. Ames sees the potential Casey has and wishes she could encourage him to seek some type of technical or postsecondary training. What options are there for someone like Casey? She wishes she knew. Why didn't anybody talk about transition and **postsecondary options** in her teacher education classes?

Casey's Cumulative Folder

# REFERRAL FOR EVALUATION

## Identifying Data

Student's Name: Casey Samuel Griffith

Date of Birth: 8/31

Address: 6783 Container Road
Midland

Phone: 863-942-1548

Mother: Juanita Griffith

Address (if different than student): Same

Phone (if different than student): Same

Work Phone: 863-943-0500

Father: Samuel Alan Griffith

Address (if different than student): NA

Home Phone (if different than student): NA

Work Phone: at home

Legal Guardian (if different than parent): NA

Address (if different than student): NA

Home Phone (if different than student): NA

Work Phone: NA

Parents' Native Language (if not English): NA

Student's Native Language (if not English): NA

Student ID Number (as appropriate): 603-48-6971

Building of Current Attendance: Clover Valley Elementary School

Grade: 2    Present Teacher(s): Mr. Dan Jones (second grade teacher)
Mrs. Sue Roosevelt (Title One Reading teacher)

Reason for Referral: reading, writing and math interventions recommended by the
IAT team have not resulted in improved academic performance.

## Educational History

Indicate any current or past supplemental programs/services or interventions (e.g., Title 1, early intervention services, preschool, Reading Recovery, individualized interventions).

Reading: 1st grade - Reading Recovery   2nd grade - continued Title I reading intervention

Writing: Larger writing implements and larger lined paper, printing models

Math: Number line, free access to counting manipulatives, touch math strategies

Number of school districts attended: 1    Years at present school building: 3 (K through 2)

List schools/early childhood programs and dates:
No preschool programs attended.

Attendance: ☐ Regular   ☑ Irregular (explain)  Casey averages 5 absences
per month, usually for illness
or family emergencies. No
doctor's excuses provided
when requested.

Is this student age-appropriate for grade level? ☑ Yes ☐ No

If **No**, check all that apply
- ☐ Retained (specify grade)
- ☐ Enrolled late in school
- ☐ Held out of school by parent
- ☐ Unknown

Background Information

*A. Health Data*

Do you suspect problems with ☑☐ Vision ☐☐ Hearing ☐

Does the student ☐☐ Wear Glasses ☐ Use hearing aid(s)

Does the student take medication ☐☐ Yes ☑☐ No Not to my knowledge

If Yes, specify type and purpose:

Does the student have any health/developmental/physical problems of which you are aware? ☑☐ Yes ☐☐
No

If yes, please explain: Casey's weight appears to affect his response time and speed when playing outside at recess. He tires easily and acts tired most of the time.

*B. Environmental Factors*

Describe any specific home factors that might affect the student's performance in school:

_____

For Preschool Children Only *(please check the area(s) of concern)*:

- ☐ Eating
- ☐ Receptive Communication
- ☐ Cognitive
- ☐ Vision

- ☐ Dressing
- ☐ Expressive Communication
- ☐ Fine Motor
- ☐ Social/Emotional Behavior

- ☐ Toileting

- ☐ Play

- ☐ Attention
- ☐ Hearing
- ☐ Gross Motor

Other

Is there any other pertinent information not previously described?

| Signature of Person Initiating the Referral<br>Mr. Dan Jones | Signature of Person Receiving the Referral<br>Roy Stephens |
|---|---|
| Position or Relationship to Student<br>Second grade teacher | Title Principal |
| Date<br>1/15 | Date Received 1/21 |
| | Date District Suspects a Disability 1/21 |

(Initial Evaluation)
Reevaluation (if additional assessment is to be conducted)

# PARENT CONSENT FOR EVALUATION

**Part I: To Grant Consent**

I have received a copy of my procedural safeguards and I understand the information provided.

I HEREBY GIVE MY PERMISSION FOR _Casey Samuel Griffith_ to receive an evaluation(s) by designated personnel. I understand the evaluation information will be shared by teachers, principals, and other appropriate school personnel, and that the school district will forward educational records upon request to another school district or educational agency in which my child seeks or intends to enroll. I further understand that my granting of consent is voluntary on my part and I may revoke my consent at any time.

_Mrs. Juanita Griffith_

Signature of parent/legal guardian/custodian, or student (if age 18 or older) Relationship to Child     Date _2|3_

---

**Part II: To Refuse Consent**

**(Do Not complete Part II if you completed Part I)**

I have received a copy of my procedural safeguards and I understand the information provided.

I DO NOT GIVE MY PERMISSION for a multifactored evaluation for ___

Reasons: (It would be helpful to school personnel who are designing an educational program to meet your child's unique needs if you would share with us your reasons for not giving your permission for a multifactored evaluation.)

Signature of parent, legal guardian, custodian, or student (if 18 or older)    Relationship to Child    Date

---

**Part III: (To be completed by school)**

Information about the multifactored evaluation and a copy of the procedural safeguards notice were presented/sent by: _Mr. Ray Stephens, building principal_

_Ray Stephens_

Signature of school district representative     _2|3_ .   Date(s)

The parents' native language is _English_ . If not English, was the information provided in the native language or other mode of communication?   Yes    No

If no, explain: _NA_

If the native language or other mode of communication is not a written language, attach documentation of the steps taken to ensure that the notice was explained and that the parent understands the content of the notice. _NA_

# EVALUATION TEAM REPORT (Part A)

Name of Student: <u>Casey Samuel Griffith</u>      Date of Birth: 8/31      Age: 7

Evaluator: <u>Pamela Hawthorne, Ph.D., Midland City Schools School Psychologist</u>

Areas of Assessment: <u>General Intelligence/Cognitive Abilities, Academic Performance Communication</u>

<u>Status, Social-emotional/Behavioral Functioning or Status</u>

---

Summary of assessment(s), including results of the student's progress in the general curriculum and instructional implications to ensure progress.

Casey is in his third 9 weeks of second grade. In the general education classroom, he has an extremely difficult time completing any reading and writing tasks independently. Any math work that requires writing he also refuses to complete on his own. He was enrolled in Reading Recovery during most of his first grade year, but made little progress. Title I reading intervention continued during second grade. However, to date Casey is still reading at a pre-primer level and avoids all reading activities. If a second-grade story is read to him, he can accurately retell it. When asked what might happen next, he responds with "I don't know."

Casey's full scale intelligence quotient score, as measured by the Wechsler Intelligence Scale for Children III (WISC-III) was 101, with a verbal scale score of 85 and a performance scale score of 118. An analysis of the subscale scores showed stronger performance in visual and simultaneous processing tasks and weaker performance in auditory and visual discrimination skills. Across tests he tended to process sequential information very slowly and not always accurately. When given the Stanford Diagnostic Math Test, Casey's math skill scores ranged from well below average in mathematics calculations to average in math reasoning. Although he can group up to five objects to show the principles of addition and subtraction, he cannot represent single digit addition and subtraction problems with numbers. Casey can count to 25. He cannot count money or tell time using either type of clock.

When given the Woodcock-Johnson Reading Mastery Test (WJRMT), Derek's reading skill scores fell into the significantly below average across all domains. He independently recognized 18 upper-case and 12 lower-case letters and identified the sounds for 75% of the consonants, 80% of the long vowels and none of the short vowels. He appeared to have memorized approximately 15 of the most common single syllable sight words and used them randomly when he tried to read words he does not recognize in sentences. Casey's written language performance on the Test of Written Language-2 (TOWL-2) was judged to be typical for his age with the exception of his handwriting, which was significantly below average for his age. His printing is illegible, with the exception of his name and the numerals 1–9.

Observations of Casey in the general education classroom revealed a pattern of off-task behavior 90% of the time he was instructed to complete reading, writing, or mathematics activities independently. Off-task behavior was at its lowest during story time and activities in which students were out of their seats engaged in the manipulation of learning materials. Off-task behaviors include fidgeting with objects at his desk, making objects out of paper, putting his head down, and staring out the window. No inappropriate behavior was observed with peers, although he seldom initiated conversations or activities either in the classroom or on the playground.

Interventions provided by Casey's general education teacher and the reading interventionists to date have not successfully improved Casey's performance. His reading, writing, and mathematics deficits are significantly impacting his school performance. Based on the test results, there is a significant underachievement in the areas basic reading skill, written expression, and math calculation when comparing expected academic performance with actual academic performance in these areas.

According to both his parents and teacher, Casey enjoys working with his hands, especially helping his father in his garage workshop. No other interests were noted by the mother. Although he avoids independent reading activities, he will pick up picture books in free time if no one is watching.

Casey needs to substantially improve his basic reading skills, written expression skills, and skills in mathematical computations to benefit from large group instruction. A more intensive systematic phonics-based reading intervention program coupled with substantial opportunities to engage in rich literacy activities should be proved. Accommodations that include a reader, scribe, extended time on written tests, and the use of math manipulatives must be made available for all content areas. Casey's strong listening skills should continue to be enhanced through general education content instruction.

Signature of Evaluator: *Pamela Hawthorne, Ph.D.*　　　　　Date: 3/31

## EVALUATION TEAM REPORT (Part B)

**Disability Determination:** Specific Learning Disability

**Basis for Eligibility Determination:**

Casey was evaluated to have average intelligence as measured by WISC-R (101 full scale score). However he shows a consistent pattern of significant underachievement in the areas of basic reading skill, mathematics calculations, and written expression. Substantial and varied in-class interventions, Reading Recovery instruction, and additional Title I reading intervention have not improved his academic performance.

| Name | Title | Signature | Date |
|---|---|---|---|
| Mrs. Juanita Griffith | mother | Mrs. Juanita Griffith | 4/21 |
| Daniel Jones | second grade teacher | Mr. Dan Jones | 4/21 |
| Ray Stephens | building principal | Ray Stephens | 4-21 |
| Gloria Rose | special education teacher | Mrs. Gloria Rose | 4/21 |
| Pamela Hawthorne, Ph.D. | School psychologist | Pamela Hawthorne Ph.D | 4/21 |
| Susan Roosevelt | Title I Teacher | Susan Roosevelt | 4/21 |

# EVALUATION TEAM REPORT (Part C)

## Criteria for Determining the Existence of a Specific Learning Disability

Student's Name: <u>Casey Griffith</u>          Date of Birth: 8/31          Age: <u>7</u>

**A.** **When provided with learning experiences appropriate for his/her age and ability level, the student is not achieving commensurate with his/her age and ability levels in one or more of the following areas:**

Oral Expression                                  Reading Comprehension
Listening Comprehension                (Mathematics Calculation)
Yes
(Written Expression)                            Mathematics Reasoning
(Basic Reading Skill)

*Summarize assessment results and other data used by the team to support this determination*:
In-class interventions in reading, handwriting, and mathematics that were recommended by the IAT did not improve Casey's performance. Two years of reading intervention programs have not helped Casey to progress beyond the pre-primer reading level.

**B.** **The student has a severe discrepancy between achievement and ability that is not correctable without special education and related services in one or more of the following areas:**

Oral Expression                                  Reading Comprehension
Listening Comprehension                (Mathematics Calculation)
Yes
(Written Expression)                            Mathematics Reasoning
(Basic Reading Skill)

*Summarize assessment results and other data used by the team to support this determination*:
Casey's full scale score on the WISC III was 101, although his achievement scores in basic reading skills, mathematics calculations, and written expression were significantly below what would be expected for his intellectual potential. Neither Reading Recovery nor Title I reading intervention has had a substantial impact on the development of Casey's reading skills.

**C.** **The severe discrepancy between ability and achievement is not primarily the result of**

visual, hearing, or motor impairment
mental retardation
emotional disturbance
environmental, cultural, or economic disadvantage

*Summarize assessment results and other data used by the team to support this determination*:
Regular vision, hearing, and motor screenings showed no problems in these areas, Casey's intelligence quotient as measured by the WISC-III is within average range. Observations and interviews with teachers yielded no indications of emotional disturbance. Casey's excessive absences may have impacted his development.*

**D.** **Describe the relationship of the relevant behavior noted during observation(s) to the student's academic functioning.**

*Summarize assessment results and other data used by the team to support this determination*:
Observations of Casey in his second-grade class revealed a pattern of off-task behavior 90% of the time he was instructed to complete reading, writing, or mathematics activities independently. Behaviors included fidgeting, putting his head down, and staring out the window. His behavior was on-task most of the time.**

**E.** **Describe educationally relevant medical findings, if any.**

*Summarize assessment results and other data used by the team to support this determination*:

*of basic reading skills, his deficts in this area exceed those that might be anticipated.
**during story time and activities in which students were actively engaged with support.

(Additional information can be attached or written on back)

Services Plan

# INDIVIDUALIZED EDUCATION PROGRAM (IEP)

Name Casey Griffith  Date of Birth 8/31  Grade Level 2  ☑ Male  ☐ Female
Student Identification Number 643-48-6971
Child/Student Address 6783 Cankoter Rd, Midland  Parent/Guardian Samuel and Juanita Griffith
Parent Address same  Home Phone 963-943-1540 Work Phone 963-943-0500 (mother)
Effective IEP Dates from 8/25 to 6/4  Meeting Date 5/17  ☑ Initial IEP  ☐ Periodic Review
District of Residence Midland City Schools  District of Service Midland City Schools

**Step 1  Discuss future planning.**
*(Family and student preferences and interests)*

Mr. and Mrs. Griffith and Casey want Casey to be able to read as well as others his age. They want him to enjoy school more. Casey indicated he wished he had more friends. Casey also said he knows he needs to learn math because his dad uses math in his repair shop. Casey likes to work with his dad.

**Step 2  Discuss present levels of academic and functional performance.**
*(What do we know about this child, and how does that relate in the context of content standards, or for preschool children, in the context of appropriate activities and how the disability affects the student's involvement in the general education curriculum.)*

Casey can recognize 18 upper case and 12 lower case letters. He can identify the sounds for 75% of the consonants; long vowel sounds for a, e, i; & o; and none of the short vowel sounds. He reads 15 single syllable words in and out of context. He can print his name and numerals 1-9 legibly. He can count to 25 and explain addition and subtraction using manipulatives. He can accurately retell a story * after someone has read it to him. He enjoys listening to stories about cars and participates well in most hands-on activities. His difficulties in reading and writing make it difficult for him to access information from grade-level texts and express his learnings in writing.
                                                                    * on grade level

(Duplicate as needed)

# INDIVIDUALIZED EDUCATION PROGRAM (IEP)

## Annual Goals and Short-Term Objectives

---

**Step 3: Identify needs that require specially designed instruction**

Casey needs to develop his basic reading skills well enough to access the general curriculum in all content areas.

---

**Step 4: Identify measurable annual goals, including academic and functional goals**

**Goal #** 1    **Content area addressed:** Reading - basic reading skills

Casey will analyze and decode words found in third grade materials with 85% accuracy.

**Benchmarks or short-term objectives**

① I dentify and say all sounds.    ② Blend phonemes to read unknown words.    ③ Use letter-sound knowledge and structural analysis to decode words.    ④ Use knowledge of word families to decode words.    ⑤ Increase sight words by 5 each week

**Student Progress**

*(Include a description of how the child's progress toward meeting the annual goals will be measured and when periodic reports on the progress the child is making toward meeting the annual goals will be provided.)*

Casey's progress will be assessed at least weekly using CBM to document progress in use of decoding skills and sight word recognition. Casey's parents will receive a summary of progress every six weeks as an attachment to his report card.

---

**Service:** Specially designed instruction    **Initiation date:** 9/25    **Step 5: Identify services** (one school year)    **Expected duration:** 6/1    **Frequency:** (how often) 45 minutes, 5 days/week

*(Identify all services needed for the child to attain the annual goal and progress in the general education curriculum. Services may include specially designed instruction, related services, supplementary aids, or, on behalf of the child, a statement of program modifications, (testing accommodations, or supports for school personnel.)*

Casey will participate in specially designed reading instruction that uses an intensive systematic multi-modal phonics approach.

---

**Step 6: Determine least restrictive environment**

**Determine where services will be provided**

*(An explanation of the extent, if any, to which the child will not participate with nondisabled children in the regular class.)*

Casey will participate with nondisabled children in the regular classroom for all activities except one 45 minute period 5 days/week 5 days per week.

# INDIVIDUALIZED EDUCATION PROGRAM (IEP)

## Annual Goals and Short-Term Objectives

**Step 3: Identify needs that require specially designed instruction**

Casey needs to develop his reading fluency and comprehension of texts and other printed materials to be able to access the general curriculum in all content areas.

---

**Step 4: Identify measurable annual goals, including academic and functional goals**

Goal # **2**    Content area addressed: Reading - reading Comprehension

Given one minute 3rd grade reading fluency probes, Casey will increase his reading fluency by 2 words a minute each week, reaching a rate of 100 words per minute by the end of the school year. Given a 3rd grade reading passage, Casey will read it silently and answer comprehension questions at 85% accuracy.

**Benchmarks or short-term objectives**
① Use context clues to help identify unknown words. ② Use expression and pacing to increase comprehension. ③ Identify story components and/or main ideas, details, sequence, and cause/effect relationships as relevant to particular texts.

**Student Progress**
(Include a description of how the child's progress toward meeting the annual goals will be measured and when periodic reports on the progress the child is making toward meeting the annual goals will be provided.)

Casey's progress will be assessed at least weekly with fluency probes and comprehension activities. Casey's parents will receive a summary of progress every six weeks as an attachment to his report card.

---

**Step 5: Identify services** (school year)    accommodations as requested by Casey or teacher.

Service: accommodations   Initiation date: 8/25   Expected duration: 6/4   Frequency: (how often) Consultation as requested by teacher
(Identify all services needed for the child to attain the annual goal and progress in the general education curriculum. Services may include specially designed instruction, related services, supplementary aids, or, on behalf of the child, a statement of program modifications, testing accommodations, or supports for school personnel)

Casey will be permitted to have a reader for all content tests as well as books on tape or CD. He may also have extended time on tests and assignments that are completed in class and are reading based.

---

**Step 6: Determine least restrictive environment**

Determine where services will be provided
(An explanation of the extent, if any, to which the child will not participate with nondisabled children in the regular class.)

Casey will participate with nondisabled peers in the regular classroom for literature Circles and other comprehension-related activities.

Note: Casey would have a separate "annual goals and objective" page for each problem area identified in the evaluation team report; e.g., for written expression & math calculations.

# INDIVIDUALIZED EDUCATION PROGRAM (IEP)

## Special Factors

Based on discussions of the information provided regarding relevant special factors and other considerations as noted below, the following is applicable and incorporated into the IEP.

|  | Incorporated into IEP (Check box) |
|---|---|
| Behavior: In the case of a student whose behavior impedes his or her learning or that of others. | ☐ |
| Limited English proficiency (LEP) | ☐ |
| Children/students with visual impairments (See IEP page ___) | ☐ |
| Communication | ☐ |
| Deaf or hard of hearing | ☐ |
| Assistive technology services and devices | ☑ |

## Other Considerations

|  | |
|---|---|
| Physical education | ☐ |
| Extended school year services | ☐ |
| Beginning at age 14...transition service needs which focus on the student's courses of study [See IEP page ___] | ☐ |
| Transition services statement, no later than age 16 [See IEP page ___] | ☐ |
| Testing and assessment programs, including proficiency tests [See IEP page 4] | ☑ |
| Transfer of rights beginning at least one year before the student reaches the age of majority under state law (Ohio law is age 18) | ☐ |

Relevant Information/Suggestions (e.g., medical information, other information): Casey received Reading Recovery services in first grade and Title I reading intervention in second grade. He missed more days of school in first and second grade than 90% of his peers. No serious medical conditions documented.

Note: only IEP forms relevant to this IEP have been included in this sample.

# INDIVIDUALIZED EDUCATION PROGRAM (IEP)

## Statewide and Districtwide Testing

**Student Name:** Casey Griffith **Student Grade** (when scheduled to take this test): 3 **Student ID:** 603-48-6971

**School Year:** **IEP Meeting Date:** ___

| Areas of Assessment | Grade Level of Test to be Administered | STATEWIDE TESTING: Will Take Test without IEP Accommodations | STATEWIDE TESTING: Will Take Test with IEP Accommodations | STATEWIDE TESTING: Will Participate in Alternate Assessment | DISTRICTWIDE TESTING: Grade Level of Test to be Administered | DISTRICTWIDE TESTING: Will Take Test without Accommodations | DISTRICTWIDE TESTING: Will Take Test with Accommodations | DISTRICTWIDE TESTING: Will Participate in Alternate Assessment |
|---|---|---|---|---|---|---|---|---|
| Reading | 3 | | ✓ | | | | | |
| ★ Writing | 3 | | ✓ | | | | | |
| ★ Math | 3 | | ✓ | | | | | |
| Science | 3 | | ✓ | | | | | |
| Citizenship | | | | | | | | |
| Technology | | | | | | | | |
| ITAC | | | | | | | | |

★ The goals & objectives pages for math and written expression (not included in this sample IEP) would indicate appropriate accommodations.

A statement of why the child cannot participate in the regular assessment and will be taking alternate assessment: NA

Excused from the consequences associated with not passing the test (Graduation Test) in the following area(s) of assessment: NA

Met participation requirements Yes No Date ___ NA
(Graduation Tests)

| Area of Assessment | List Accommodations to Assessment | Area of Assessment | List Accommodations |
|---|---|---|---|
| Reading | extended time, reader as state allows | Other (Specify) | |
| ★ Writing | extended time, scribe, reader | Other (Specify) | |
| ★ Math | extended time, scribe, reader | Other (Specify) | |
| Science | extended time, reader | Other (Specify) | |
| Citizenship | | Other (Specify) | |

# INDIVIDUALIZED EDUCATION PROGRAM (IEP)

Name: Casey Samuel Griffith

IEP summary for effective dates 8/ - 6/        Date of next IEP review 5/

Check one of the following: This IEP team meeting was a ☑ Face to face meeting ☐ Video conference ☐ Telephone Conference/ Conference Call.

**IEP Team Meeting Participants**

| | | |
|---|---|---|
| parent | Melissa Griffith ☑ Participated ☐ Excused | _____ ☐ Participated ☐ Excused |
| sp. ed. teacher | Ms. Do. Jones ☐ Participated ☐ Excused | _____ ☐ Participated ☐ Excused |
| sch. psychologist | Dennis Matthews ☑ Participated ☐ Excused | _____ ☐ Participated ☐ Excused |
| the Gen. teacher | Susan Roscoe ☑ Participated ☐ Excused | _____ ☐ Participated ☐ Excused |

Summary of special education services:

## Initial IEP

☑ I give consent to initiate special education and related services specified in this IEP.*

☐ I give consent to initiate special education and related services specified in this IEP except for ___ **

☐ I do not give consent for special education services at this time.**

Parent Signature _M/H_  Date: 5/17  Mrs. Janice Griffith

* This IEP serves as prior written notice if there is agreement.

**If there is not agreement, the district must provide prior written notice to the parents.

## Consent for Change in Placement

☐ I give consent for the change of placement as identified in this IEP.*

☐ I give consent for the special education and related services specified in this IEP except for ___ **

☐ I do not give consent for a change of placement as identified in this IEP.

☐ I revoke consent for Special Education service.

Parent Signature _____  Date: _____

* This IEP serves as prior written notice if there is agreement.

**If there is not agreement, the district must provide prior written notice to the parents.

## Parent Notice of Procedural Safeguards/Copy of the IEP

☑ I have received a copy of the parent notice of procedural safeguards for the current year.

☐ Parent has requested and received a copy of the IEP

Parent Signature _Mrs. Janice Griffith_  5/17

Note: The student receives notice of procedural safeguards at least one year prior to his/her 18th birthday.

Student Signature _____  Date: _____

## Attendance Only

☐ I am signing to show my attendance/participated at the IEP team meeting but I do not agree with the special education and related services specified in this IEP

Signature _____  Date: _____

**Reason for Placement in Separate Facility (if applicable)**

Having considered the continuum of services and the needs of the student, this IEP team has decided that placement in a separate facility is appropriate because:

_____

Casey Griffith
6-B English
October 7

When I grow up I went to
be a mukenic lik my dad. He
cofiex carz real good. He
makz them run detter then when
they wher know. I whant to
pint carz two. when I gro up.

4-9

Attendence officer,

    Please quit stopping at our house about Caseys absences. His uncle had a heart atack and we had to be with him. Until we get back home, Casey has no way to get to school. He will be back.

                Mrs. Griffith

To: Mr. Holmes, Guidance Counselor
Fr: Mary Jasper, sixth-grade science teacher
Dt: 12/1
Re: Casey Griffith


When Miss Prentice met with the other sixth-grade teachers and me at the beginning of Casey's sixth grade year, she focused on how low of a reader and writer Casey was. I have watched Casey in my science class all fall and am amazed at how well he understands the science concepts he discovers during our laboratory activities. I have seen him very excited on several occasions about the experiments. The questions he has asked about the labs are equally as complex as most other students in my classes.


I request permission to take Casey out of study hall during second semester to serve as a laboratory assistant in the 6B section of sixth-grade science that meets last period of the day. I think it will help him feel better about himself. He already will have completed the experiments, and, after helping me set up for the later class, can assist groups that are having difficulty with the lab procedures. If you approve of this arrangement, I will contact both Miss Prentice to see if she sees any problems with this change. If not, I will talk with Casey about it and then make sure it is OK with Mrs. Griffith. If you can think of any potential problems or know of any other steps I should take, please let me know.


Thanks.

11968 Sherwood Drive
Midland, USA 67321
April 12

Mr. Jack Roberts, Principal
Midland High School
68331 Lucas Drive
Midland, USA 67321

Dear Mr. Roberts:

Please accept this letter in your role as district representative for Casey Griffith's IEP meeting later this month. I am the reading specialist for the adolescent literacy/reading intervention grant we received 3 years ago at the middle school. I have worked with Casey one period daily for the past 2 years using an intensive systematic phonics reading intervention program. Casey's silent reading grade-level equivalent scores have improved from second to fifth grade in 2 years and he is, for the first time in his life, reading magazines that interest him without prompting. His grades have begun to improve and he appears to no longer dread school every day.

I have talked with Miss Prentice about the possibility of keeping reading intervention as a goal on his IEP. I told her I would continue to service Casey next year in my highest reading intervention group at the middle school, since, even though he is a year ahead of all of them, they will all be working on the same sequence of skills. I will try to arrange for that group of students to come to my room at a time that Casey has a study hall at the high school. Our guidance counselor, Mr. Holmes' is willing to adjust the eighth- grade schedules of the other students because he sees how far Casey has progressed and knows that no similar program is available at the high school. Since the high school periods are double-blocked and I only serve my students for ½ block each day, I would like Casey to stay for the second half of the block and "assist" me with one of the lowest reading intervention groups. I will contact both Casey's parents and the parents of the children in the group in which he would be assisting me to ensure that all parties agree to the arrangement.

Miss Prentice indicated to me than there is no precedent for a high school student on an IEP to receive instruction at the middle school. She encouraged me to contact you to see what next steps I or she needs to take to see if this arrangement can be worked out and suggested to Casey's parents prior to his IEP conference, pending acceptance of the arrangement by other parties involved and compatible schedules.

Mr. Roberts, Casey has made more progress than any student with whom I have worked in my 18 years of teaching. I am beginning to get glimpses of the Casey that I know is buried beneath years of failures and name-calling. To curtail this intervention when he is finally making sense of the printed work would be down-right criminal.

I am available at your earliest convenience to discuss this matter further. I can be reached at ssmith@ midlandms.edu or (863) 942-1300. I look forward to talking with you further about Casey's future.

Sincerely,

Sara Smith
Reading Specialist, Midland Middle School

March 30

Dear Mr. James,

Yesterday I talked with Casey after class for a little while. I tried to get him to think about what he wants to do after high school. He started to talk about taking over his dad's business, but when I began asking questions about the business, he seemed to shut down.

I am worried about Casey. During football season his attendance was good and his appearance improved. He understands the content so well that his more and more frequent absences have not significantly impacted his course grade — still a B. I think he has more potential in math and science than his grades or past interest show. What are some options we can provide for him to help these interests and abilities develop? I've heard the rumors that Griffith never graduate. Let me know what else I can do.

Thanks,
Anne Ames

# Clover Valley Elementary

## CUMULATIVE RECORD

**Name:** Griffith (Last)  Casty (First)  Samuel (Middle)

**Date of Birth:** 8/31 (Month) (Day) (Year)   **Sex** F ( ) M (✓)

**Place of Birth:** Pleasant Valley (City) (State)   **Document of Birth:** certificate (Certificate, Passport, etc.)

**Date Entered:** 9/04 - K

603   S.S. No. 6171

**Date Withdrew:** NA

No. Brothers: Older ___ Younger ___
No. Sisters: Older 1 Younger ___
Father Deceased ( )  Mother Deceased ( )

**Father:** Griffith (Last)  Samuel (First)  Occupation mechanic (Middle)  Address 6783 Container Rd., Midland (in pencil)

**Mother:** Griffith (Last)  Juanita (First)  Occupation LPN (Maiden) (in pencil) (Middle)  Address 6793 Container Rd., Midland (in pencil)

Guardian (First) (Last) (Occupation) (Middle)  Address (in pencil)

Stepparent(s) (First) (Last) (Middle)  Address (in pencil)

Stepparent(s) (First) (Last) (Middle)  Address (in pencil)

## Annual Summary of Grades    Kindergarten - Eighth

| School | Grade | Year | Teacher | Days Present | Days Absent | Times Tardy | Reading | Writing | Spelling | English | Math | Social Studies | Science | Health | Phys. Ed | Art | Music | Life Skills | Tech-nology | Gifted | Music General | Music Inst. |
|---|---|---|---|---|---|---|---|---|---|---|---|---|---|---|---|---|---|---|---|---|---|---|
| CV | K | | Williams | | 21 | 17 | S-NI | | 1 | 1 | S | | 1 | 1 | 1 | S | S | | 1 | | | |
| CV | 1 | | Simpson | | 25 | 12 | U | NI | D | 1 | S | S | S | S | | S | S | | 1 | | | |
| CV | 2 | | Jones | | 19 | 9 | U | NI | D | 1 | S | S | D | S | | S | S | | 1 | | | |
| CV | 3 | | Ashauer | | 13 | 14 | D | D | D | C- | C | D | D | D | | A | B | | 1 | | | |
| CV | 4 | | Mitchell | | 22 | 8 | D | D | D | O- | C | D | C- | D | | B | B | | 1 | | | |
| CV | 5 | | Reed | | 16 | 11 | D | D | O | F | B- | D | Q | Q | | A | C | | 1 | | | |
| MMS | 6 | | Jasper (CH2) | | 22 | 15 | O | F | F | D- | B- | D- | B-D | B-D | | B | C | | C | | | |
| MMS | 7 | | Lemon (CH2) | | 16 | 3 | C | C | D | C | CJ | C | C | C | | B | C | | C | | | |
| MMS | 8 | | Sears (CH2) | | 9 | 9 | B | C | D | C | B- | F | B | C | | C | D | | B | | | |

### Assignment for next year — Teacher notes

- 1st: slow to play w/ other children, quiet, withdrawn
- 2nd: irregular attendance
- 3rd: irregular attendance
- 4th:
- 5th:
- 6th: if participates in Summer School will promote to 7th

parents difficult to reach
much potential in science
reading intervention (see notes in file)
reading intervention (see notes in file)

K - PP
1 - PP
2 - PP

Grades 9 - 12

**Name** Griffith (Last)  Casey (First)  Samuel (Middle)

**Birthdate** 8/31  **Birthplace** Pleasant Valley

**Address** 2182 Old Falls Rd., Midland

**Date Entered** 8/28  **Date Withdrew**  **Transferred To**

**Home Phone** 863-943-0701  **Work Phone** 863-943-0500 (mother)

**Parent or Guardian** Samuel and Juanita Griffith

**S.S. No.** 603-48-6971 (in pencil)

ADDITIONAL INFORMATION

### NINTH — School Year / Grade 9 H.R. 104

| Subjects | marks 1 sem. | 2 sem. | yr. | units credit | days pres. | days absc. |
|---|---|---|---|---|---|---|
| Eng I | C- | C | | 1 | 161 | 19 |
| Alg | C | C | | 1 | | |
| WHist | D | D-D | | 1 | | |
| P.E. | A-A | A | | 1 | | |
| Health | C | C+C | | 1 | | |
| Con Science | B | B B | | | | |

credits this yr. 6
credits total 6
class rank 187/203

### TENTH — School Year / Grade H.R.

| Subjects | marks 1 sem. | 2 sem. | yr. | units credit | days pres. | days absc. |
|---|---|---|---|---|---|---|
| | | | | | | |

credits this yr.
credits total
class rank

### ELEVENTH — School Year / Grade 10 H.R. 203

| Subjects | marks 1 sem. | 2 sem. | yr. | units credit | days pres. | days absc. |
|---|---|---|---|---|---|---|
| Ecology | B | | | | | |
| Geometry | B+ | | | | | |
| Eng II | C- | | | | | |
| Civics | C- | | | | | |
| WAlt | B+ | | | | | |
| P.E. | B | | | | | |
| Health | C+ | | | | | |

credits this yr.
credits total
class rank

### TWELFTH — School Year / Grade H.R.

| Subjects | marks 1 sem. | 2 sem. | yr. | units credit | days pres. | days absc. |
|---|---|---|---|---|---|---|
| | | | | | | |

credits this yr.
credits total
class rank

### OTHER — School Year / Grade H.R.

| Subjects | marks 1 sem. | 2 sem. | yr. | units credit | days pres. | days absc. |
|---|---|---|---|---|---|---|
| | | | | | | |

| Enrollment Checklist | Services Checklist | Other Information |
|---|---|---|
| **Enrollment Checklist** | **Services Checklist** | **Other Information** |
| ✓ Health Department Birth Certificate (Form 5111 F3) | ___ Attended a Preschool Program | Prescreening for K (5/27) |
| ✓ Social Security Number | ___ Received Speech Services | −Family moved frequently |
| ✓ Immunization Records Complete | ✓ Received Title I Services (2nd) | − child appears overly shy |
| ___ Court orders allocating parental rights and responsibilities or other documents allocating custody or guardianship, if applicable. | ✓ Special Education (3rd − current) | −allergies |
| ___ Proof of residency consisting of a deed, or building permit, or rental agreement, or tax statement, or voter registration card. (Form 5111 F2) | ___ Gifted Education | |
| ___ High School Transcript if transferring in to JGHS | ✓ Reading Recovery (1st) | |

# Chapter 3

## SARAH BROWN

*Supporting Intellectual Giftedness*

## SECOND GRADE

### Clover Valley Elementary School

Sarah Elizabeth Brown is a 7-year-old European American girl who has lived in Midland since birth with her parents, both of whom work at the local box factory. Mr. Brown is the third-shift foreman, and Mrs. Brown works in the human resources office as an administrative assistant.

Sarah's sister, Bethany, who is 3 years older than she, has recently qualified for the district's **talented and gifted** (**TAG**) program by scoring above the 95th percentile on the reading portion of the state's achievement test. The girls are close friends, as well as sisters, and spend much of their free time together. They like to play make-believe and have elaborate scenarios in which they are pioneers on the frontier, missionaries in South America, or orphans who are surviving on their own. Both girls play soccer on the box factory's team at the local park. They love every kind of school trip, especially to the art museum and the science center in the large city about an hour from Midland.

Sarah was born full-term, after an easy pregnancy. She weighed 7 pounds 6 ounces and had an Apgar rating of 10. As a toddler, she was very active and slept little, giving up her nap at 10 months. She spoke early, and by 2 was making up rhymes in language games with her older sister. At 3 and 4, she entertained her family at the breakfast table with accounts of her vivid dreams.

She has some mild reactions to certain foods, including citrus and chocolate, and occasionally has severe bronchitis. Her mother considers her a "picky eater," and she is currently at the 50th percentile for height and 35th percentile for weight for her age.

Her mother reports that she got a library card when Bethany was born and read constantly to the children from the time they were born until they started reading for themselves. Both girls got their own library cards as soon as they could sign their names. All the family members have reading lights attached to their beds, and there are stacks of books on every available surface. By the age of 4, Sarah was reading much of the printed material around her—cereal boxes, menus, and store signs—although she was never taught to read. In kindergarten and first grade, she dutifully filled out scores of phonics worksheets; at home she read chapter books, including everything by E. B. White and Madeleine L'Engle. The head librarian at the local library waived the restrictions on the number of books that could be borrowed, and Sarah was limited only by the number of books she could carry. She often writes imaginative stories, which are almost always based on things she has read rather than on her own original ideas.

During first grade, Sarah was reprimanded several times for "reading ahead" in the basal reader and for rolling her eyes or prompting other students when their responses were delayed. Her written work was usually correct although often sloppy. She did not always follow directions and twice received a zero on a paper for marking something other than the correct response. When she was finished with her work, she was allowed to read or to help the other children.

Second grade has been pretty much the same as the previous 2 years. She is in the highest group in reading but finds it pretty boring. It is more fun to talk with Bethany about books than to answer the questions the teacher poses. In math, the class still begins with "math meeting," and Sarah wonders how long it will take them to get to the 100th day of school—and the 100th popsicle stick in the cup. At home, she is decorating her room with three-dimensional geoforms she copied from a library book.

During recess, Sarah plays happily with Susan Mitchell, her best friend. They enjoy playing in a wooded section of the playground and often bring in leaves, sticks, and insects they have found. The girls have compiled scrapbooks of their nature collections, which they are willing to share with anyone who is interested. Sarah has other scrapbooks at home, filled with stamps, postcards, pictures of horses, and the science experiments she talks her mother into helping her with at home.

Sarah and Susan spend a lot of time at each other's homes, and often Sarah is invited to spend Friday night with the Mitchell family. Susan's parents are both doctors in Midland, and their home is full of artwork and books on science, arts, and history. After playing board games at Susan's, Sarah runs home to duplicate the games using cardboard and crayons so that she and Bethany can play the same games—with a few creative changes—at their own home.

In response to a commercial they saw on TV, Sarah, Susan, and Bethany decided to raise money to send to St. Jude's Hospital to help in pediatric cancer research. Last summer they held a carnival and raised $43 by selling refreshments, providing entertainment, and organizing games. They are sure that their contribution made the sick children happy.

Sarah has an impressive repertoire of jokes that she dips into often—and not always appropriately. Several times at school and at church she has gotten into trouble for telling a joke or making a flippant comment that only she thinks is funny. At age 7, she has already developed a reputation for being something of a smart aleck.

Although Sarah has done well in school so far, she has not been challenged to do her best work. She has learned that it takes very little effort to get A's and impress her teachers. She feels confused sometimes by the reactions of adults and children to her comments, and she thinks sometimes that there must be something wrong with her.

# EIGHTH GRADE

## Midland Middle School

Sarah Brown, now 13, is in the eighth grade at Midland Middle School. Sarah's sister, Bethany, is a junior at Midland High School, a straight A student and soloist in the show choir. The girls have grown apart over the past couple of years as their interests have taken them in different directions. Bethany thinks her sister is a little weird and wonders why she hangs around with those nerdy friends of hers. Sarah was recently grounded for calling Bethany "narrow minded and shallow" once too often within their mother's earshot.

At the end of third grade, Sarah was identified as "superior cognitive" based on her **IQ** score on the **Woodcock-Johnson Test of Cognitive Ability**. In fourth through sixth grades, she attended a **"pull-out" program** for gifted children one day a week at the middle school. Her teacher, Mr. Haines, provided the students with a wide array of activities, including creative writing, problem solving, and critical thinking. Most important, as Sarah told her mother, Mr. Haines's room was a "safe place to be smart." She made friends with several of the students in her gifted class and sought out their company after school. These classmates have continued to be her closest friends.

In Mr. Haines's class, Sarah began to write stories that were based on her own ideas rather than on those of the books she read. She also began to write poetry. Although she would readily share her stories with her classmates, she was more reluctant to share her poetry and kept her poetry journal in the bottom of her backpack so that she could keep it private.

Life in her regular class wasn't always comfortable. Her third-grade teacher, Mrs. Kettering, gave her an especially hard time about being in the gifted program. Mrs. Kettering insisted that Sarah complete her regular assignments as well as assignments for her gifted class and penalized her when she missed class work on the days she was in TAG. Some days she missed things she already knew; other days, she really did miss important parts of the topic the class was studying. Now, in the eighth grade, she still feels that there are parts of the curriculum that are just blanks for her; and as much as she knows about some things, there are others that just don't make sense.

There are no services for gifted children after sixth grade in the Midland district, but Sarah has been placed in an advanced math program. She took prealgebra in seventh grade and is currently taking Algebra I for high school credit. Her other classes are heterogeneous, and most of her teachers use teacher-directed strategies that address the class as a whole. A notable difference is Mrs. Sands, her science teacher, who has divided up the class into teams. Sarah has noticed that her team often does more challenging work than the others, although they are all studying the same topic. During this 9 week class, they are working independently on different projects, and she is currently working on an aerospace project for the science fair.

Science fair has been a high point in Sarah's academic work for the past several years. Based on work she'd done as a young child in their kitchen and garage, her projects routinely won at the school and district level and last year won third place at the state competition. She has been begging her father to send her to Space Camp next summer, but he doesn't know if they will have the money to send her. She and a friend have started painting house numbers on curbs for donations from friendly neighbors.

Now that all the kids from her TAG classes are at the middle school, her social life is great. All the kids sit together at lunch. The conversation is really fun, and everyone laughs at her jokes.

Susan is still her best friend, and the girls often spend weekends together. Sarah was invited to go with the Mitchells on vacation last summer, and she enjoyed visiting the Smithsonian Institution, especially the National Air and Space Museum, in Washington, DC. She wonders what it would be like to be a poetry-writing astronaut.

Her relationships with her teachers run the gamut from horrible to wonderful. Her Ohio history teacher has the students read **round-robin** around the room, and she is frequently reprimanded for not knowing where to start when it is her turn. There is a great deal of cheating on her multiple-choice tests, and she is incensed when someone who she thinks knows nothing gets a 100. Her history teacher begins class with a pile of worksheets, and when the pile is gone, the class is over. She has been in trouble twice for talking and served detention once for writing "creative" answers on her worksheet. Her computer science teacher told her that she "ruined" his class with her smart-aleck remarks. Her English teacher talks with her about the latest novels and encourages her to write her own stories. She secretly works on her poetry in her room at night.

Sarah's grades are still exceptional. She almost always gets straight A's, except when she doesn't follow directions and gets a zero for one or more assignments. The only class she has to work really hard in is science. Mrs. Sands gives her an A only if she achieves the high standard she sets for herself at the beginning of each grading period. About half the time, her grade report includes such comments as "Talks too much," "Doesn't follow directions," or "Doesn't focus on the work at hand."

Sarah is on the eighth-grade volleyball team. Although she is tall and well coordinated, she is not particularly aggressive. She frustrates her coach, who wishes Sarah would be more serious about sports. Sarah insists that she wants to play just for fun.

Her parents wish she were a bit more like Bethany, and lecture her about how important it is to get along with others. They tell her she needs to try her best at everything she does. They tell her it is more important to be nice than to be smart.

# TWELFTH GRADE

## Midland High School

Sarah Brown is now 17 and a senior at Midland High School. Her sister, Bethany, a junior in college, is majoring in music and English, on a full scholarship arranged by a guidance counselor at school and her colleague, who is a music professor at a good private college located about 2 hours from Midland.

During high school, the tightly knit group that had formed in her TAG days started to drift apart. One of the boys moved, and a couple of the girls started dating outside the group. Most of the kids took part in the state's postsecondary option, in which they attended classes at the local college. Sarah took several courses, and although she enjoyed talking with the professors, she did not really get to know her fellow students. They did not seem that interested in what they were studying, and she had little in common with them outside the class.

Sarah and Susan continue to be friends, but their busy schedules make it hard to spend as much time together as they used to. Susan is dating a boy from a nearby school and usually is busy on Friday and Saturday nights. One weekend, Susan invited Sarah to join her and some of her boyfriend's friends at a church youth group picnic. Although Sarah was excited about going, she didn't have a very good time. The other students all knew each other and didn't seem very interested in talking with her. After a few embarrassing moments of standing alone, she was invited by the adult group leader to help set up the dessert table. She spent the rest of the evening talking with the adult chaperones.

Sarah decided not to pursue interscholastic sports in high school but has been fairly active in intramurals. She played in the volleyball and softball tournaments set up through the physical education department and was happy just to be in the gym and on the field playing with other students who played for the sheer enjoyment of it.

In the ninth grade, Sarah talked with Mr. Haines about getting a high school team together for a critical problem-solving competition. Although some of the former TAG students showed initial interest, there was no support from the high school teachers or from the school. The idea soon faded away, and the students got caught up in other activities.

All of Sarah's classes at the high school were in the college prep track, in which about two thirds of the students were enrolled. In most classes, the teacher covered a portion of the textbook, then asked the students to answer a few questions for homework. Sarah usually finished her work before class was over and began reading one of the novels she always carried in her book bag. Her science classes remained her favorite, and a succession of interesting and dedicated teachers helped her pursue her passion. She attended Space Camp one summer on a partial scholarship, and the summer before her senior year she was a teen counselor at a science camp. She continued to pursue her own projects and won science fairs in biology, chemistry, and physics as she progressed through high school. Her physics teacher excused her from the regular lectures and labs so that she could pursue her own independent projects.

Now, as a senior, it appears that Sarah has stopped playing the game. She dropped an advanced placement English class and has decided not to compete in this year's science fair. She turns in enough work for a B or low A, calculating how little she can do and still have a decent average. Applications for colleges lie on her desk at home. The envelope from the Educational Testing Service with her **ACT** scores is still unopened. When confronted by her mother, she said, "I'm doing just fine. My grades are better than just about anyone's. I know I can get into State U. at the last minute. And it's about time I had some fun."

Encouraged by her parents to talk with someone outside the family about her future, she made an appointment with the school guidance counselor. The counselor told her that she was fed up with students who are intelligent but don't have any plans for the future. She said that Sarah could be anything she wanted to be—she just needed to "get her act together." Sarah knew that there were lots of things she couldn't be—or wouldn't want to be—but was having a hard time picturing just what it was that she was supposed to be. When she received a note from the counselor asking that she make an appointment to discuss scholarship opportunities, Sarah dropped it into the nearest wastebasket.

The students Sarah is hanging around with are mostly good students who are beginning to show up at school with new body piercings, tattoos, and creative haircuts. Sarah has taken a job at the local convenience store after school and on weekends so that she can make some spending money. She studies the magazines in the convenience store to see how people look in places far away from Midland, and she and her friends struggle to look more cosmopolitan, buying clothes at the local thrift shop rather than at the local discount store. They have weekly—or biweekly—parties, usually with beer and sometimes marijuana. Occasionally someone brings something more interesting for them all to try. Sarah finds their conversations about books and music and politics and life "out there" endlessly fascinating. She continues to write poetry and is anxious to share it with her friends, who are impressed with the depth of her emotion and the seriousness of her work.

Sarah's parents see a smart young person who is throwing away opportunities for her future. They know that her intelligence, once harnessed, can open doors for her and that she is capable of doing so much for herself, for her family, and for society. They wonder if they have done enough to make sure that Sarah reaches her full potential. They wonder if her teachers have seen her potential and have cared enough to challenge her.

Sarah wonders what all the fuss is about.

August 27

Dear Parents,

Last spring your child took an Otis Lennon Ability Test and a Stanford Achievement Test. On these tests, a Student Ability Index (SAI or IQ) of 126 or above and a 95% on the achievement composite is required to meet the Midland gifted service eligibility criterion. Your child did very well on one or both of these tests and may qualify for our gifted program. In order to determine this, further evaluation must be done by our school psychologist, school psychologist intern, or gifted intervention specialist. This involves your child meeting with one person for one or more assessments. You will be notified of all results.

Please do not make a big deal out of this with your child. He or she is very talented regardless of how well they do on these assessments. Should your child qualify for the program, you will still have the option of turning down the services. Your child may then be looked at again for placement in the program the following school year.

If you agree to allow further evaluation of your child, please sign the form enclosed and return it by August 31. If you have any questions, please contact me at 555-3452.

Thanking you,

*S. Haines*

Mr. Haines
Talented and Gifted Teacher

# Midland School District

## Educational Report

Sarah Brown
Grade 4
Clover Valley Elementary

D.O.B. September 21
C.A. 9 years, 3 months

Reason for referral: An individual ability measure was requested to assist with determining gifted eligibility in the area of Superior Cognitive.

Observations: Sarah was very focused and task oriented. She was personable and cooperative. Her level of conversational proficiency appeared above average for her grade.

Test Administered:

Woodcock-Johnson III—Test of Cognitive Abilities

|  | Standard Score (Mean=100, SD=15, SEM=3) |
| --- | --- |
| Verbal Ability | 128 |
| Thinking Ability | 133 |
| Cognitive Efficiency | 116 |
|  |  |
| General Intellectual Ability | 130 |

Sarah earned a GIA of 130 on the WJ-III, placing her in the Superior classification of cognitive ability. In this respect, her performance equaled or exceeded 98% of the standardization group. The chances that her IQ lies between 124 and 136 are ninety out of one hundred. Sarah's relative strength is in pulling together information to solve a problem.

Sarah's ability score of 130 meets the eligibility requirement for Superior Cognitive identification.

Written Educational Plan (WEP) for Gifted Students

Student ___Sarah Brown___     Grade Level __6__     School year_____-_____

Area(s) of Identification (check all that apply)  Serve in these areas:
- ✔ Superior Cognitive      ✔ Science            ___ Visual Art
- ✔ Reading/Writing         ✔ Social Studies     ___ Music (vocal)
- ✔ Mathematics             ✔ Creative Thinking  ___ Music (instrumental)

| Service Providers | | | | | |
|---|---|---|---|---|---|
| Re | Reading/Language Teacher | C | Consulting Teacher | I | Intervention Specialist |
| Ma | Math Teacher | L | Librarian/Media Specialist | G | Guidance Personnel |
| Sc | Science Teacher | GS | Gifted Specialist | P | Parent |
| So | Social Studies Teacher | M | Mentor | V | Volunteer     O Other |

The following individuals have participated in this Written Educational Plan:

| | | | | | |
|---|---|---|---|---|---|
| Re | Rqizk | C | | I | |
| Ma | Saunders | L | | G | |
| Sc | Jasper | GS | Haines | P | M/M Brown |
| So | | M | | V | |
| O | | O | | O | |

| Service Options | Re | Ma | Sc | So | C | L | GS | M | _ | G | P | V | O | O |
|---|---|---|---|---|---|---|---|---|---|---|---|---|---|---|
| Acceleration | | | | | | | | | | | | | | |
| Advanced Placement Classes | | | | | | | | | | | | | | |
| Career Counseling | | | | | | | | | | | | | | |
| Classroom Intervention | ✔ | ✔ | ✔ | ✔ | | | | | | | | | | |
| Cluster Grouping | | | | | | | | | | | | | | |
| Differentiated Instruction | ✔ | ✔ | ✔ | ✔ | | | | | | | | | | |
| (Extra-curricular Academic Involvement) | | | | | | | | | | | | | | |
| Gifted Pull-Out Program | ✔ | | | | | | ✔ | | | | | | | |
| Guiding Independent Studies for content enrichment | | | | | | | ✔ | | | | | | | |
| Guiding Independent Studies for skill development | | | | | | | | | | | | | | |
| Honors Classes | | | | | | | | | | | | | | |
| Intervention Specialist | | | | | | | | | | | | | | |
| Mentorship Networking | | | | | | | | | | | | | | |
| PSEO Post Secondary Enrollment Option | | | | | | | | | | | | | | |
| Visual/Performing Arts Instruction | | | | | | | | | | | | | | |
| Other: | | | | | | | | | | | | | | |
| Notes: | | | | | | | | | | | | | | |

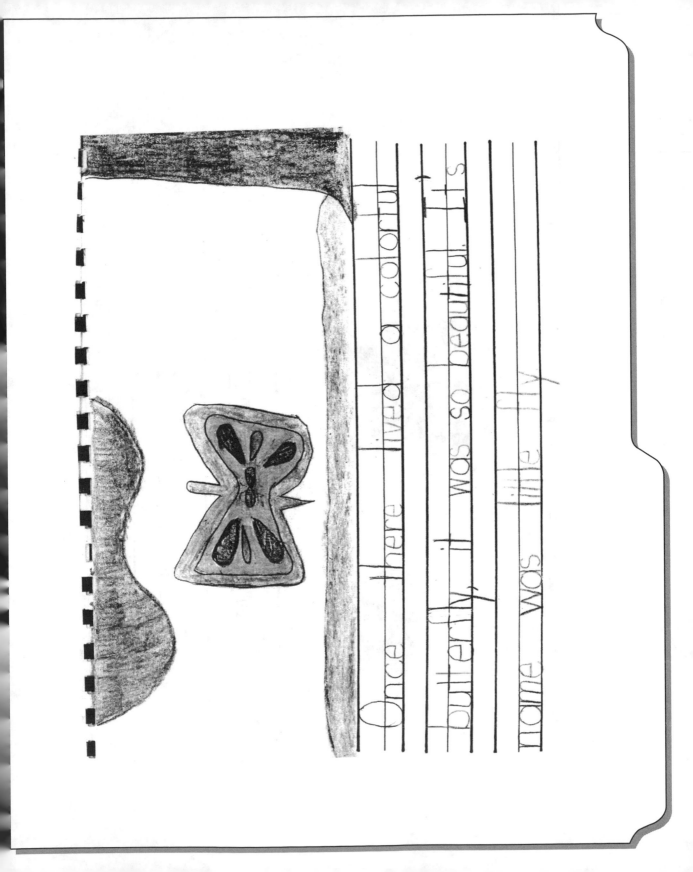

Once there lived a colorful butterfly, it was so beautiful. Its name was little fly

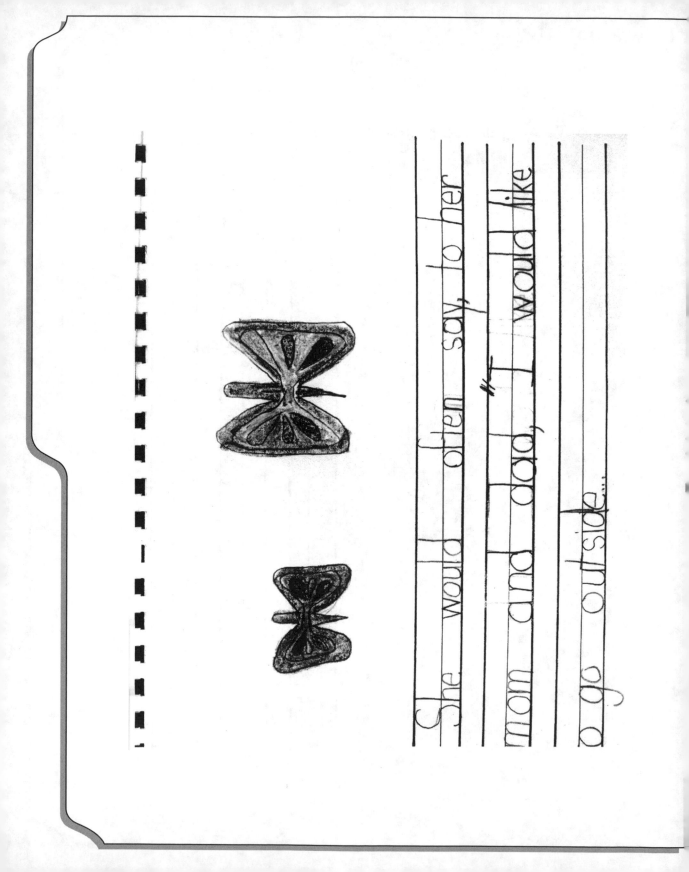

She would often say to her

mom and dad, "I would like

to go outside..."

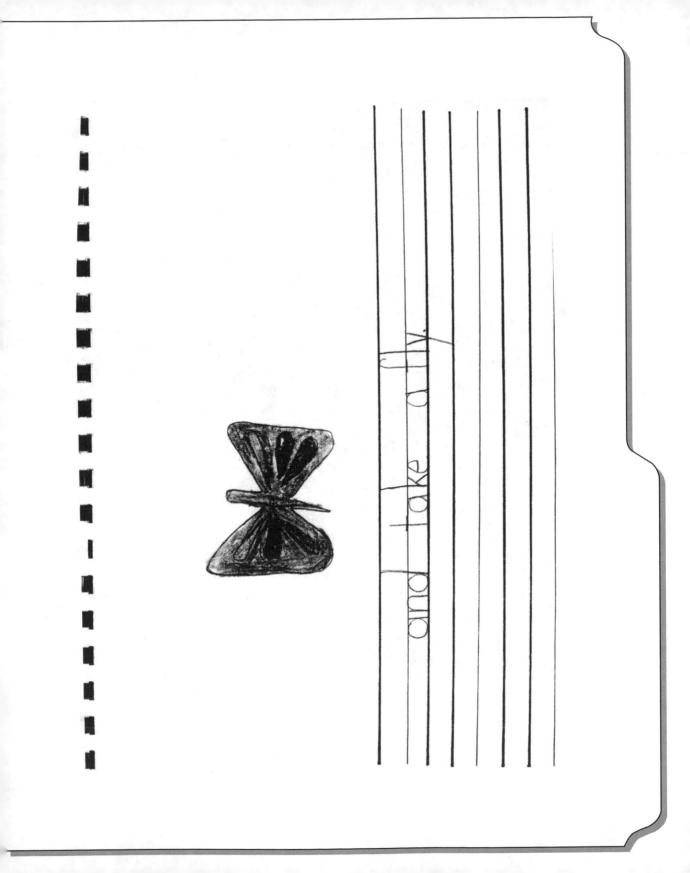

and take a fly.

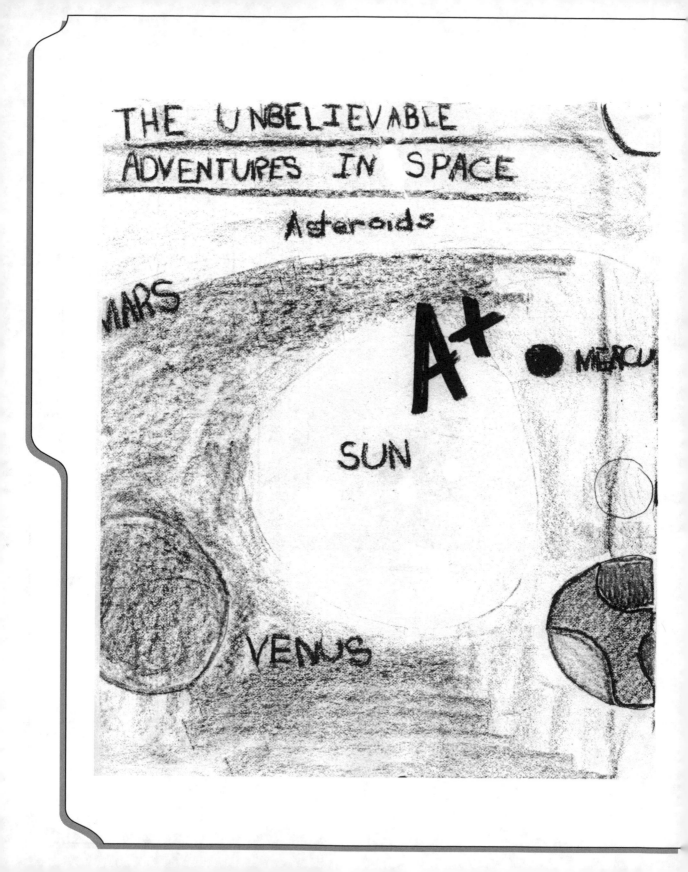

# The Mystery Of Life

Why does the sun rise,
and the earth spin,
and the seasons change
regular
as clockwork.

Why does the moon
control the tides,
as they wash in
and out
in a never-ending pattern.

And why are there wars fought,
and battles engaged,
when we should be
working,
reaching,
striving toward common goals.

These questions remain,
unanswered,
as the mystery
of life.

Sarah
Grade 8

Source: Reprinted with permission.

# CUMULATIVE RECORD

VALLEY Elementary

|  | | |
|---|---|---|
| BROWN (Last) | SARAH (First) | E (Middle) |
| 9 (Month) | 21 (Day) | (Year) |
| | Sex F (✓) M ( ) | Document of Birth: Birth Certificate (Certificate, Passport, etc.) |
| MIDLAND (City) | (State) | |
| 8-25 | | |

| Relation | Name | Occupation | Address |
|---|---|---|---|
| Father | Brown Richard | Foreman (in pencil) | 113 Hilton Ave. (in pencil) |
| Mother | Brown Emily | Secretary (in pencil) | Same (in pencil) |
| Guardian | | | From |
| | | | From |
| Stepparent(s) | | | Address (in pencil) |
| Stepparent(s) | | | Address (in pencil) |

From _____ To _____
From _____ To _____

Father Deceased ( )  Mother Deceased ( )

No. Brothers: Older ____ Younger ____
No. Sisters: Older 1 Younger ____

S. No. _____   N _____

## Annual Summary of Grades — Kindergarten - Eighth

| School Year | Teacher | Days Present | Days Absent | Times Tardy | Reading | Writing | Spelling | English | Math | Social Studies | Science | Health | Phys.Ed | Art | Music | Life Skills | Tech-nology | Gifted | General Music | Music Inst. | Assignment for next year |
|---|---|---|---|---|---|---|---|---|---|---|---|---|---|---|---|---|---|---|---|---|---|
| Preschool | Prewar | | | | | | | | | | | | | | | | | | | | Promoted to 1st |
| | Hunt | 1160 | 3 | 2 | S | S | S+ | S+ | S | S | S | S | S | S+ | S+ | | | | | | Promoted to 2nd |
| | Scott | 1732 | 13 | 0 | S+ | S+ | O+ | O | S+ | O | O | O | S+ | S+ | S | | | | | | Above grade level in reading |
| | Toons | 168 | 3 | 0 | B | A | A | A- | A | A+ | S+ | S+ | S+ | O+ | S+ | | | | | | promoted to 4th |
| | Fitzpatrickson | 166 | 2 | 0 | A | S | A+ | A | A | A | A- | S | O | O | O | | | | | | promoted to 5th |
| | Franklin | 168.5 | 2.5 | 0 | O | | | A+ | A | A | A- | A- | A | S | S | | | | | | Promoted to 6th |
| | Osman | 1169 | 1 | 0 | | | | A | A | A | A | A | A | A | A | A | A | | | | Promoted to 7th |
| | Yoder | 165.5 | 5 | 0 | | | | A | A | A | A | A | A | A | A | A | A | | | | promoted to 8th grade |

# Grades 9 - 12

**Name:** Brown, Sarah E. (Last) (First) (Middle)

**Birthdate:** 9-21  **Birthplace:** Midland

**Address:** 113 Hilton

**Date Entered:** 8-21  **Date Withdrew:** _____  **Transferred To:** _____

**Home Phone:** 555-0305  **Work Phone:** 555-4390

**Parent or Guardian:** Richard/Emily

**S.S. No.:** _____

## NINTH

**School:** MHS  **School Year:** _____  **Grade** 9  **H.R.** 106

| Subjects | marks sem 1 | sem 2 | yr. | units credit |
|---|---|---|---|---|
| ENG | A | A | A | 1 |
| SS | A | A | A | 1 |
| ALG II | A | A- | A | 1 |
| SCI | A | A | A | 1 |
| SP I | A-B | B | A | 1 |
| ART | B | B | A | 1 |
| PE | A | A | A | 1/4 |

credits this yr: 1315
credits total: 6 1/4
class rank: _____

## TENTH

**School:** _____  **School Year:** _____  **Grade** 11  **H.R.** 101

| Subjects | marks sem 1 | sem 2 | yr. | units credit |
|---|---|---|---|---|
| ENG | A | A | A | 1 |
| HIST | A | A | A | 1 |
| PHY | B | B | A | 1 |
| CHEM | A | A | A | 1 |
| SP III | A | A- | A- | 1 |
| FR | A | A | A | 1 |

credits this yr: 6
credits total: 18 3/4

## ELEVENTH

**School:** _____  **School Year:** _____  **Grade** 10  **H.R.** 110

| Subjects | marks sem 1 | sem 2 | yr. | units credit |
|---|---|---|---|---|
| ENG | A | A | A | 1 |
| SS | A | A | A | 1 |
| GEOM | A | A | A | 1 |
| BIO | A | A | A | 1 |
| SP II | A-A | A- | A | 1 |
| CT | A | A | A | 1 |
| HEALTH | A | A | A | 1/2 |

credits this yr: 6 1/2
credits total: 12 3/4
class rank: _____

## TWELFTH

**School:** _____  **School Year:** _____  **Grade** _____  **H.R.** _____

| Subjects | marks sem 1 | sem 2 | yr. | units credit |
|---|---|---|---|---|
|  |  |  |  |  |

## OTHER

**ADDITIONAL INFORMATION** (in pencil)

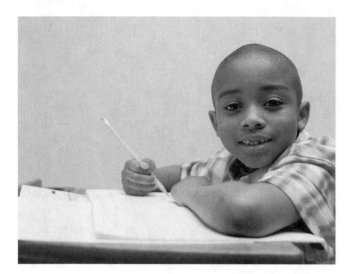

# Chapter 4

## MALCOLM SINGER
### *Addressing the Challenges of ADHD*

## FIRST GRADE

### Clover Valley Elementary School

Malcolm Singer is a 6-year-old African American boy who has recently moved from Philadelphia to Midland with his mother, grandmother, and two teen-age aunts following the death of his grandfather. Malcolm's grandmother grew up in Midland and has relatives in the area. She has returned to Midland with her family to reestablish a home in familiar surroundings.

Malcolm's cumulative folder shows that he attended kindergarten at Fairlawn Elementary in inner-city Philadelphia last year. There is a recommendation from his kindergarten teacher, Ms. Renzulli, that Malcolm be retained for a second year in her kindergarten class. She cites his late August birthday, immaturity, impulsivity, clumsiness, failure to follow directions, and general lack of attentiveness as the reasons for her recommendation. She reports that Malcolm has a difficult time remembering how to return to the kindergarten room from the playground and lunchroom. A note to the file records that Malcolm once unscrewed the lid to his glue in his desk and then glued all his books together in his attempt to clean up the mess. She felt that an extra year of maturity would benefit Malcolm before he moved on to first grade. But except for some notes from home, no one had come in to talk to her until she recommended retaining Malcolm in first grade.

After a note home about the retention request, Mrs. Singer became very adamant about not "holding" Malcolm back. She and her mother, Mrs. Barnett, both came to meet with Ms. Renzulli about their concerns. Mrs. Singer told Ms. Renzulli that if they continued to insist on keeping him in kindergarten, she was pulling him out of the school and putting him in a charter school. This, however, did not happen.

There is no evidence in the file that Malcolm's father, DeShawnto Singer, was consulted about the retention recommendation. Mrs. Singer stated that her husband had a drug addiction problem and that he is no longer part of the family. He does not appear to have custody rights.

At the end of kindergarten, Mrs. Singer still refused to allow Malcolm to be retained, and he was assigned to first grade in a transitional step-up unit that was a small class with a few other children who were struggling to learn the skills needed for first grade. As each child made progress, they were transferred to a traditional first-grade classroom.

Malcolm attended the transitional first-grade program at Fairlawn Elementary sporadically during the fall semester. His teacher, Mrs. Gatten, requested several conferences to discuss her concerns about Malcolm's frequent truancy, academic failure, aggressiveness, low test scores, generally disheveled appearance, and a growing problem of **enuresis** and **encopresis.** She received two notes from Mrs. Barnett stating that she could not come in because she had no way to get to school. In addition, the family was dealing with the terminal illness of Malcolm's grandfather. Mrs. Gatten continued to work individually with Malcolm when he attended school but reported that little progress was made.

Malcolm's health records show no obvious signs of ill health even though he is in the lower 20% of the growth chart. He was born 3 weeks prematurely as the first child of his 17-year-old mother. While he had a low birth weight of 5 pounds 3 ounces, his Apgar rating was 7. Aside from a milk intolerance as a baby, his medical records show no abnormal health problems, and his immunization records are up to date.

At Fairlawn, Malcolm was frequently absent from school and complained regularly about stomachaches. The school offered both a comprehensive free breakfast and lunch program for all of its students. However, Mrs. Gatten had frequently noted that Malcolm did not eat much of his breakfast or lunch and was distracted by other children during meal periods. She began sending him to the office when he complained, where he would sit until it was time to go home. His regular "accidents" necessitated keeping an extra set of clothes in the main office, but he would cry until his grandmother was called. By the beginning of November, Malcolm had made no academic progress and was unable to make the anticipated transition to a traditional first-grade class.

Shortly after Thanksgiving, Malcolm's grandfather died, and the family moved to Midland. Malcolm is now living a few blocks from the school with his mother, grandmother, and his two aunts. His aunts are enrolled in Midland High School, and his mother has recently taken a job at the deli counter of a Wal-Mart store working the 3 to 11 shift.

When Malcolm's grandmother, now his primary caretaker, brought Malcolm to school to register him, she expressed concern about his troubles in his previous school. Mrs. Barnett feels that Malcolm is a very sensitive child and that Fairlawn Elementary did not encourage him to reach his full potential. She believes that he was picked on by other students at Fairlawn and that the teachers and principal did not protect him from that behavior. She is concerned that something similar may happen at Clover Valley. She is particularly concerned about his walking alone to and from school each day. She is concerned about older students bullying him and also about Malcolm losing his way. She has decided to walk with him in the mornings to prevent problems but, because of her health problems, is concerned she will not be able to do this twice a day. She requests that the school place him on a bus that passes their home and drops him off in the afternoons. The principal explains that no child living within a mile of the school is eligible for transportation.

Malcolm has a difficult time making friends and overwhelms them with his demands for attention. He does not wait his turn well and frequently interrupts others. Mrs. Barnett admits that he has a short fuse and sometimes resorts to hitting other children when frustrated. Even at home, he has become increasingly intolerant of any changes in his environment and throws things when upset. His teenage aunts are complaining that he breaks their possessions. He is sleeping less and less, and he frequently falls or has other accidents, resulting in increasingly serious injuries. Both Mrs. Singer and Mrs. Barnett believe that his behavior became more difficult as he progressed in school. Mrs. Barnett is concerned that he will have a hard time coming into a new classroom. She has asked the school to call her if Malcolm experiences any problems. Malcolm will be entering a regular first-grade classroom in Clover Valley Elementary School in Midland right before winter break.

## SIXTH GRADE

### Midland Middle School

Malcolm is now 12 years old and is part of the sixth-grade class at Midland Middle School. Malcolm and his mother, now Monique Males, have their own home with Malcolm's stepfather, Anthony Males, whom she met at church, and his twin half-sisters, Debraysha and Keisha, who are preschoolers. Mr. Males wanted to adopt Malcolm, but the cost of adoption is prohibitive for the family. Nonetheless, Mr. Males has stepped into the role of father for Malcolm and tries continuously to engage Malcolm in some of his pastimes such as fishing and baseball. Both Mr. and Mrs. Males work different shifts to trade off child-caring chores. Mrs. Males works at Wal-Mart from 7 a.m. to 3 p.m., and Mr. Males works from midnight until 8 a.m. at a local asphalt plant. The family shares one car, making it difficult for Mr. Males to attend parent-teacher conferences during the school day. He met with Malcolm's teachers at the open house held in September and stays in touch by phone. He is very interested in regularly communicating with Malcolm's teachers to ensure he is getting the attention he needs in school. Mr. Males appears to have a positive and influential relationship with Malcolm.

Malcolm has had academic and social problems at school since he entered kindergarten. Although he was marginally successful in first grade, he was retained in second grade for failing to demonstrate required skills in reading. Because of increasing aggressiveness and short attention span during his second year in second grade, Mrs. Briggs, his teacher, recommended that he be evaluated by a committee for testing for learning problems. The committee agreed he should undergo multifactored testing. The school counselor administered the **Wechsler Intelligence Scale for Children**, Revised (WISC-R), and then recommended that a local pediatric neurologist examine Malcolm. Dr. Harry Longert, the neurologist, completed the **DSM III-R** (*The Diagnostic and Statistical Manual of Mental Disorders)* and asked both Malcolm's mother and teachers to fill out observational forms, including the **Conners Rating Scale**, **Social Skills Assessment** teacher form, and the **Goldstein Behavioral Observation Checklist.** The neurologist gave Malcolm a complete physical, and except for an unusually high tolerance for pain, Malcolm was in perfect health. All indicators pointed to not a learning problem but a high probability for having **attention-deficit/hyperactivity disorder (ADHD)**. Dr. Longert prescribed 20 milligrams of **Ritalin** a day for Malcolm to take during the school year.

Malcolm's behavior seemed to improve for the remainder of this year, and his academic performance showed some improvement. Soon, however, he began to complain of a variety of health problems. He couldn't eat, and his grandmother reported to Dr. Longert that Malcolm had irregular sleep patterns and severe headaches. After a summer without the drug,

Dr. Longert switched his medication, and Malcolm began taking **Adderall**. During his third-grade year, the medical complaints seemed to lessen. He was delighted when his mother married Anthony Males and was happy to be gaining a new father and, within the year, new baby sisters.

The next year, however, Malcolm began to display some of his old behavioral symptoms. He became increasingly agitated, lost or did not turn in assignments, and became generally noncompliant. Notes and phone calls home seemed to affect his behavior positively for only a short time. Mr. Barnard, his fourth-grade teacher, became frustrated after repeated attempts to keep Malcolm on-task and to keep him from disrupting the rest of the class. After a group conference with Mr. and Mrs. Males, counsel teachers, it was decided that Malcolm could benefit from an **individualized education program (IEP)** with a specific **Cognitive Behavior Modification** component. Even with the additional help, Malcolm barely passed fourth grade.

Fifth grade was a disaster. In October, the family had moved to Florida for part of the year because Malcolm's stepfather had an opportunity to get a job in construction. The school records from Florida have not been sent, and there is no way to determine if further intervention was given during his stay. It is not even clear if Malcolm attended one or two different schools during the 6-month stay. Upon returning in the late spring, Malcolm seemed to have given up on school. He spent more time in the principal's office for misbehavior than he did in his classroom. According to his discipline slips, he had also begun to lie and steal. As Mr. Males became increasingly involved in parenting and disciplining Malcolm, Malcolm seemed to resent him more. More and more tension between the two began to create stress within the whole family.

Surprisingly, despite his aggressiveness and his increasing attraction to risk-taking behavior such as climbing to the roof of the school and sneaking alcohol into the classroom, he had become quite popular among his peers. By the end of fifth grade, he was a leader among the other boys and a much sought-after prize boyfriend of the girls. He was beginning to develop the social skills that attracted the attention of some of the older students with track records in court and discipline problems. In an attempt to forestall anticipated problems with the older boys, his parents have limited his contact with them. He seems particularly angry at being told with whom he can hang out. At school, without the watchful eye of his stepfather, he seeks the company of the forbidden friends.

Concerned with his aggressiveness with his younger sisters, his parents took Malcolm back to Dr. Longert. This fall, Malcolm began a new medication, **Clonidine**, to see if this can control his impulsive and increasingly dangerous behavior. Malcolm displays some of the typical behaviors of many adolescent boys, but he seems to take everything to the extreme. He is enjoying the popularity his outrageous behavior brings him from his peers. When directly engaged by the teacher, Malcolm will stay on-task, but he does not complete assignments once left to work individually. Still, he seems to like math, and he exceeds in physical education, where he can be on the move during most of the class. Attempts to have him work in small groups have failed. Malcolm typically gets the whole group off-task enjoying his entertainment. When engaged in the lesson, Malcolm performs at an average or above-average level. Unfortunately, he is beginning to miss some essential concepts as he tunes out more and more frequently. Mr. and Mrs. Males worry that he will fail his state achievement test at the end of sixth grade and be retained again. They are hoping that he will be motivated by the prospect of failing to take his schoolwork seriously. At this point, that doesn't seem to be happening.

# TENTH GRADE

## Midland High School

Malcolm is now 16 years old in 10th grade at Midland High School. He has just failed the first tests of the semester, and several homework assignments are missing in every class. During class, Malcolm is off-task much of the time. Although he is personable and popular with students, he is increasingly becoming a distraction. He constantly tries to divert the classroom discussion to interesting but irrelevant subjects. Unable to concentrate for very long, he drums and hums during work periods and engages other students in conversation. He frequently asks for the bathroom pass, and he is often tardy to class. The odor in his clothing smells suspiciously of marijuana. When isolated in the classroom, he goes to sleep.

Citing difficulties in getting along with his stepfather, Malcolm recently chose to move back in with his maternal grandmother, Mrs. Barnett. Because she does not have legal custody, the school must still contact his mother, Monique Males, each time he is suspended or put in In-School Suspension (ISS). Mrs. Males and her husband, Anthony Males, have spent years trying to encourage Malcolm, and they are exhausted. Attempts by Mr. Males to engage Malcolm in building projects and hobbies have been rejected. They have taken him to court for unruly behavior, and like several of his friends, he is on probation from the juvenile courts. To further complicate matters, Malcolm has been contacted from Philadelphia by his biological father, DeShawnto Singer. Although Malcolm has never met his father, who is suspected of drug trafficking, he wants to return to Philadelphia to live with one of his aunts who returned to the old neighborhood shortly after her graduation from Midland. His main purpose is to begin a relationship with his father. Mrs. Males says that she is afraid that Malcolm will end up in serious trouble. She has not had contact with her ex-husband in 16 years and fears he has not changed. Mr. Males, naturally, feels rejected but has tried desperately to maintain a good relationship with Malcolm, hoping that he will change his mind.

Mrs. Barnett is concerned about Malcolm but has no control over his behavior. She has reported to the probation officer and to the school that he is often gone all night and, when confronted about it, becomes violent, punching holes in the walls. Malcolm is scheduled back in court for failing to comply with the court orders; he is also scheduled to show up for meetings with his probation officer. There is a real possibility that he will be placed in foster care or ordered to a group home. Because he is repeating several courses that he failed his freshman year, there is no chance of his graduating on time. He has mentioned several times that as soon as he turns 18, he will drop out of school.

Although he was scheduled for all remedial classes in the ninth grade, his math grades were high enough to enter algebra this fall. He is doing well in this class, and his standardized test scores indicate above-average performance in mathematics. His teachers are surprised when they note from his cumulative file that his intelligence tests indicate average or above-average ability in all subjects, not just math.

He has confided to his grandmother that he feels he cannot succeed. Unfortunately, he has created a niche for himself as the comic relief in most classes. To give up that role will mean that he will not only take a chance in finding out that he really is stupid but that he will lose the admiration of his peers. He also feels bad that he has rejected his stepfather's attempts at a relationship, but he thinks that he cannot live up to his expectations.

He has lost all interest in organized sports because of the self-discipline required, and his only alternative as he sees it is to hang with the "druggies." Besides, drugs have become part of his life. He has been on Ritalin, Adderall, and more recently, Clonidine. Unsatisfied with the side effects and embarrassed at being forced to go to the school nurse before lunch each day for medication, Malcolm took himself off the medication last year. Some of his teachers still ask him in class if he "forgot" to take his medication that day when he is in a particularly rambunctious mood. Not only does Malcolm seem to have lost all interest in school, but he also appears angry at being forced to attend. More recently, this anger turned to aggression, and Malcolm was suspended for yelling obscenities at a teacher. While he has never physically attacked a teacher, the possibility seems to exist if he is pushed too aggressively.

Out of school, Malcolm's behavior has become more risk-seeking. He smokes, experiments with drugs, and has unprotected sex. He believes that marijuana actually works better than the prescribed drugs to curb his impulsiveness and anger. He sees himself as functioning better and being happier smoking dope. Unfortunately, his life seems to be falling apart. He currently is under license suspension for reckless operation, which, combined with his problems already in court, means that he may lose control of his life altogether. He has held and lost two part-time jobs, one at a local fast-food restaurant and another at a car wash, for failure to show, and now he is considering illegal means of making money.

Besides seeing Philadelphia as an opportunity to leave the area and his troubles, he is also curious to meet his father. He has built up a fantasy life of becoming successful in the city learning from the street smarts of his father. While he loves his stepfather, he sees him as "boring and generic." Malcolm and Anthony are so different. Mr. Males works hard, spends time with his family, and has interests in fishing and sports. Malcolm dreams of a more exciting life. When Mr. Males wants Malcolm to follow the house rules, he rebels. He respects his stepfather but cannot see himself being like him. He doesn't understand Anthony's concern with following rules and respecting authority. Malcolm feels a real man would stand up to the law. He has no other real plans for the future except a vague notion about enlisting in the military.

Despite his dim prospects, Malcolm is a likeable person with above-average intelligence who has fallen through all the safety nets in the system. At his age, this is the last chance the school system or a teacher has to help him direct his future on a more positive course.

# Fairlawn Elementary

Oct. 28
Dear Mrs. Barnett,

This is my third request for a conference and I really need to see you about Malcolm. He is continually getting more aggressive and non-compliant. He has missed more days than he has attended. He continues to soil his pants in class and when I've sent him to the office for a change, he does not return. His test scores show that he has made little improvement throughout the term.

I am really worried about his health. When he does come to school, he seems tired and in disarray. Please contact me as soon as possible. I have tried to call you at home, but the number is no longer in service. If I do not get a response to this letter, I will contact the school counselor for advice.

Sincerely,

Audrey Gatten

## Fairlawn Elementary School

January 10

Dear Ms. Barnett,

I am very concerned about Malcolm's behavior in my class. He is not finishing his work, he is easily distracted, and he is constantly interrupting me and the other children. Yesterday, he lost both his worksheets and his pencil. Malcolm has a difficult time waiting in line and often runs to the front of the class. I have repeatedly tried to get him to follow the rules, but he doesn't appear to remember them.

I had another parent complain today that Malcolm had hit her child while waiting for the bus yesterday. His behavior is disrupting the class and his own education. He is making very little progress in learning to read, and he doesn't listen well.

Please contact me for a parent teacher conference at your convenience. Thank you.

Sincerely,

Amanda Renzulli

**Fairlawn Elementary School**

March 13

Dear Ms. Barnett,

Thank you and Mrs. Rosella Barnett for coming in for our conference last week. Since you were here, Malcolm's behavior has improved somewhat. He is trying hard to keep track of his belongings and has only had to be reminded twice to return to his seat. He is still having a hard time getting along with the other students and I am concerned that he is beginning to "borrow" without asking. Several students have reported missing items that have disappeared while Malcolm was near their desk.

While his math seems to be improving, he is still not reading. I would like to talk to you about having him repeat kindergarten. He is a very young and immature student, and given his other problems this year, I believe it would benefit Malcolm to spend another year in kindergarten before moving on to first grade.

Sincerely,

Amanda Renzulli

# FAIRLAWN ELEMENTARY SCHOOL

Philadelphia City Schools
June 1, 2006

Monica Barnett
3142 5th Ave.
Philadelphia, PA

Dear Ms. Barnett,

It has been recommended by myself and Ms. Renzulli that Malcolm Singer, your son, be retained in kindergarten for the school year. You have verbally indicated that you do not wish Malcolm to be retained. If this is still your intent, please sign and return the attached document.

Sincerely,

Mr. Joseph Cummmigs

Principal, Fairlawn Elementary

# Release

**To:**      Monica M. Barnett

**From:**   Joseph Cummings

**CC:**      Ralph Sizemore, Superintendent

**Date:**

**Re:**       Retention Refusal

_____

I refuse to have my child, <u>Malcolm Singer</u>            , retained in his present grade of <u>kindergarten</u> for the school year. I understand my rights as custodial parent to refuse the recommendation of the teacher and principal of Fairlawn Elementary School and will not hold the personnel responsible for my decision.

Signed _____     Date_____

# Iowa Tests of Basic Skills

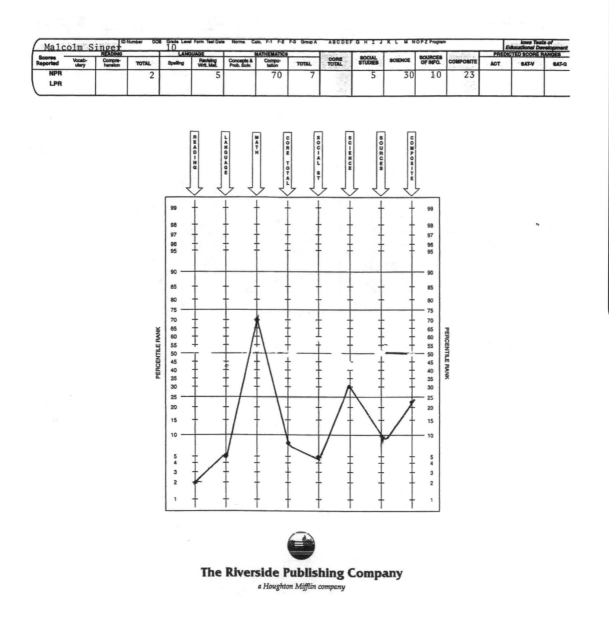

| Scores Reported | READING Vocab-ulary | READING Compre-hension | TOTAL | LANGUAGE Spelling | LANGUAGE Revising Writ. Mat. | MATHEMATICS Concepts & Prob. Solv. | MATHEMATICS Compu-tation | TOTAL | CORE TOTAL | SOCIAL STUDIES | SCIENCE | SOURCES OF INFO. | COMPOSITE | PREDICTED SCORE RANGES ACT | PREDICTED SCORE RANGES SAT-V | PREDICTED SCORE RANGES SAT-Q |
|---|---|---|---|---|---|---|---|---|---|---|---|---|---|---|---|---|
| NPR | | | 2 | | 5 | | 70 | 7 | | 5 | 30 | 10 | 23 | | | |
| LPR | | | | | | | | | | | | | | | | |

Malcolm Singer — Grade Level 10

Iowa Tests of Educational Development

**The Riverside Publishing Company**
*a Houghton Mifflin company*

# Iowa Tests of Basic Skills

| Malcolm Singer | ID Number | DOB | Grade Level | Form | Test Date | Norms | Calc. F-1 F-2 F-3 Group A | A B C D E F G H I J K L M N O P Z Program | | Iowa Tests of Educational Developm |
|---|---|---|---|---|---|---|---|---|---|---|

| Scores Reported | READING | | | LANGUAGE | | | MATHEMATICS | | | CORE TOTAL | SOCIAL STUDIES | SCIENCE | SOURCES OF INFO. | COMPOSITE | PREDICTED SCORE RANGES | | |
|---|---|---|---|---|---|---|---|---|---|---|---|---|---|---|---|---|---|
| | Vocab-ulary | Compre-hension | TOTAL | Spelling | Revising Writ. Mat. | Concepts & Prob. Solv. | Compu-tation | TOTAL | | | | | | | ACT | SAT-V | SAT |
| NPR | 54 | 70 | 62 | | 26 | | 83 | 68 | 70 | 25 | 45 | 42 | 68 | | | |
| LPR | | | | | | | | | | | | | | | | |

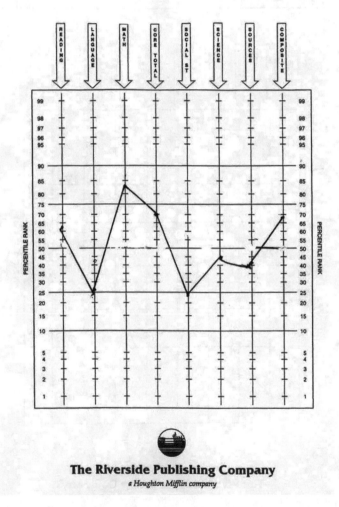

The Riverside Publishing Company

*a Houghton Mifflin company*

# Iowa Tests of Basic Skills

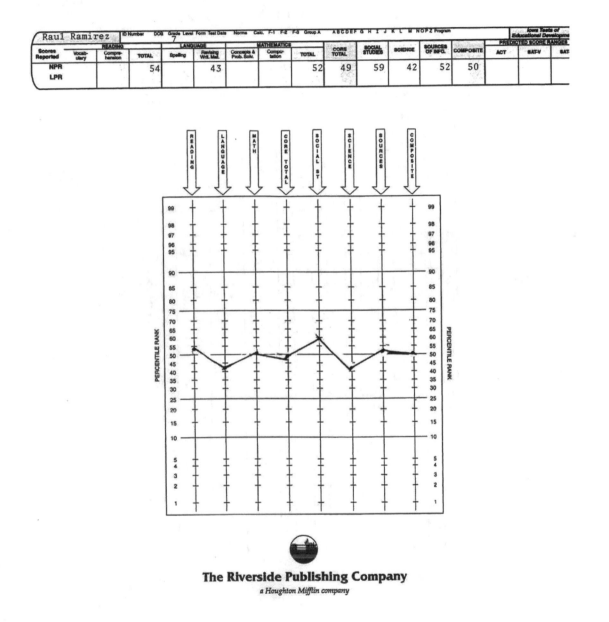

| Raul Ramirez | ID Number | DOB | Grade Level | Form | Test Date | Norms | Calc. F-1 F-2 F-3 Group A | A B C D E F G H I J K L M N O P Z Program | | | | Iowa Tests of Educational Development | | |
|---|---|---|---|---|---|---|---|---|---|---|---|---|---|---|

| | READING | | | LANGUAGE | | MATHEMATICS | | | | | | | | PREDICTED SCORE RANGES | | |
| Scores Reported | Vocabulary | Comprehension | TOTAL | Spelling | Revising Writ. Mat. | Concepts & Prob. Solv. | Computation | TOTAL | CORE TOTAL | SOCIAL STUDIES | SCIENCE | SOURCES OF INFO. | COMPOSITE | ACT | SAT-V | SAT |
| NPR | | | 54 | | 43 | | | 52 | 49 | 59 | 42 | 52 | 50 | | | |
| LPR | | | | | | | | | | | | | | | | |

The Riverside Publishing Company

*a Houghton Mifflin company*

NAME                  GRADE

# Tests of Achievement & Proficiency

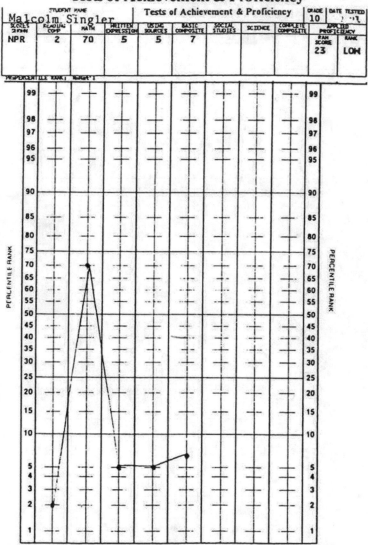

| STUDENT NAME | Tests of Achievement & Proficiency | | | | | | | GRADE | DATE TESTED |
|---|---|---|---|---|---|---|---|---|---|
| Malcolm Singler | | | | | | | | 10 | |

| SCORES 2-PRM | READING COMP | MATH | WRITTEN EXPRESSION | USING SOURCES | BASIC COMPOSITE | SOCIAL STUDIES | SCIENCE | COMPLETE COMPOSITE | APPLIED PROFICIENCY | |
|---|---|---|---|---|---|---|---|---|---|---|
| | | | | | | | | | RAW SCORE | RANK |
| NPR | 2 | 70 | 5 | 5 | 7 | | | | 23 | LOW |

PR/PERCENTILE RANK | RANK=1

PERCENTILE RANK

| 99 | | | | | | | | | 99 |
| 98 | | | | | | | | | 98 |
| 97 | | | | | | | | | 97 |
| 96 | | | | | | | | | 96 |
| 95 | | | | | | | | | 95 |
| 90 | | | | | | | | | 90 |
| 85 | | | | | | | | | 85 |
| 80 | | | | | | | | | 80 |
| 75 | | | | | | | | | 75 |
| 70 | | | | | | | | | 70 |
| 65 | | | | | | | | | 65 |
| 60 | | | | | | | | | 60 |
| 55 | | | | | | | | | 55 |
| 50 | | | | | | | | | 50 |
| 45 | | | | | | | | | 45 |
| 40 | | | | | | | | | 40 |
| 35 | | | | | | | | | 35 |
| 30 | | | | | | | | | 30 |
| 25 | | | | | | | | | 25 |
| 20 | | | | | | | | | 20 |
| 15 | | | | | | | | | 15 |
| 10 | | | | | | | | | 10 |
| 5 | | | | | | | | | 5 |
| 4 | | | | | | | | | 4 |
| 3 | | | | | | | | | 3 |
| 2 | | | | | | | | | 2 |
| 1 | | | | | | | | | 1 |

PERCENTILE RANK

Note: Many different norms (ranks) are available with the Tests of Achievement and Proficiency. Each school decides for itself which norms are most meaningful to students and parents. Some schools desire more than one type of ranking. If a label showing ranks has been affixed near the top of this page, the type of norms used is printed on it (NPR = percentile rank among students in the nation, LPR = percentile rank in the local school system, etc.)

**The Riverside Publishing Company**
8420 Bryn Mawr Avenue, Chicago, IL 60631

# PENNSYLVANIA DEPARTMENT OF HEALTH
## DIVDISION OF VITAL STATISTICS

Reg. Dist. No. **9401**  
Primary Reg. Dist. No. **8401**

Registrar's No. **177**

| CHILD-NAME | First | Middle | Last | SEX | DATE OF BIRTH | HOUR |
|---|---|---|---|---|---|---|
| | Malcolm | DeShawnto | Singer | Male | Aug. 23, 1996 | 1:14 am |

| HOSPITAL-NAME | CITY LOCATED | COUNTY OF BIRTH |
|---|---|---|
| Shaw | Philadelphia | |

REGISTRART -SIGNATURE

*Nova Lee Ahart*

DATE RECEIVED BY LOCAL REGISTRAR

9-02-96

I certify that the above named child was born alive at the place and time and on the date stated above

SIGNATURE *[signature]*

DATE SIGNED 9-24-96 ATTENDANT (MD, DO, MIDWIFE)

ATTENDENT NAME John Halliday

890 Seneca St., Monroeville, PA

| MOTHER-MAIDEN NAME | First | Middle | Last | Age at birth | State of Birth |
|---|---|---|---|---|---|
| | Monique | Rae | Barnett | 17 | Ohio |

| RESIDENT-STATE | COUNTY | CITY | RESIDENCE |
|---|---|---|---|
| Pennsylvania | | Philadelphia | |

| FATHER-NAME | First | Middle | Last | Age at birth | State of Birth |
|---|---|---|---|---|---|
| | DeShawnto | Lee | Singer | 27 | PA |

Informant's signature *Monique Barnett*

Relation to child *mother*

**THIS IS TO CERTIFY THAT**

**THIS IS A PHOTOSTATIC**

**COPY OF THE OFFICIAL**

**BIRTH CERTIFICATE**

# GOLDSTEIN BEHAVIORAL OBSERVATION CHECKLIST

Name  Malcolm Singer                     Age  10    Date _____

Size _____ small _____        Appearance _____ disheveld _____

Apprehension accompanying E _____   Entering Room ___ distracted ___

Alert __yes__      Attention ___no___     Concentration __no__

Cooperation _____ no _____        Attempt _____

    Eye Contact __yes__          Tearfulness __no__

Startle Response __strong__ ✓           Tremulousness __no__

Expression: Anxious ✓        Sad _____      Miserable _____

    Unhappy ____   Calm ✓   Concerned about performance ____

    Lack of Affect _____   Labile _____   Other _____

Preoccupation with topics of: Anxiety _____

    Depressive _____   Aggressive ✓

Muscular tension: Clinching jaw __no__

    Sitting stiffly in chair __no__

    Gripping Table of Chair __no__

    Gripping hands together __no__          Other _____

Habitual mannerisms: Tics __no__          Rocking ✓

    Twisting hair __no__       Facial mannerisms _____

    Sucking __no__          Flapping arms __no__

Activity:  Underactive, little spontaneous movement _____

    Normal _____   Tendency to increased activity _____

    Markedly overactive relative to situation ✓

    Extremely overactive, tempo of activity increases _____

Fidgetiness:  Normal _____   Occasional squirming or wriggling ____

    Marked fidgetiness ✓

Persistence:  Normal _____   Needs occasional prompting _____

    Needs continuous examiner praise and encouragement ____

    Inconsistent effort ✓

Motivation __low__          Maturity __low__

Emotional Stability __low__

Distractibility:  not distracted _____   occasionally distracted ____

    easily distracted ✓          seeks distraction _____

Orientation to purpose of testing: _____

Self-Confidence:  Extremely confident _____   Overly confident ____

    Moderately confident ____   Inclined to distrust abilities ✓

    Very Insecure _____

Speech and Language: Receptive _____   Expressive Syntax _____

    Expressive Articulation _____   Maintains Conversation ✓

    Initiates Conversation _____

Comprehension _____

Relationship with Examiner _____

Emotional Responsiveness to Examiner _____

Smiling:  Smiles appropriately _____   Smiles only occasionally ✓

    No, or very little smiling _____

Orientation to Testing: _____

Final Adjustment: _____

Thought Processes: Logical _____   Focused _____   Relevant ____

NOTES: _____

_____

_____

Mrs. Gatten,

I have left a clean sack of clothes for Malcolm in the office in case he has an accident. He says the kids are picking on him. I don't think that should go on in a class. Please make them stop

Also, he has been sick all week. He should be back to school next week.

Rosella Barnett

Ms. Renzulli;

Please call me if Malcolm is sick and I will come and get him. Do not keep him at school if he is sick.

Monique Barnett

Initial Evaluation

Reevaluation (if additional assessment is to be conducted)

# PARENT CONSENT FOR EVALUATION

**Part I: To Grant Consent**

I have received a copy of my procedural safeguards and I understand the information provided.

I HEREBY GIVE MY PERMISSION FOR_____Malcolm Singer_____ to receive an evaluation(s) by designated school personnel. I understand the evaluation information will be shared by teachers, principals, and other appropriate school personnel, and that the school district will forward educational records upon request to another school district or educational agency in which my child seeks or intends to enroll. I further understand that my granting of consent is voluntary on my part and I may revoke my consent at any time.

___*Monique Burnett*_____  ___mother___  ___November 1___
Signature of parent, legal guardian, custodian, or student (if 18 or older)  Relationship to Child  Date

---

**Part II: To Refuse Consent**

**(Do Not complete Part II if you completed Part I)**

I have received a copy of my procedural safeguards and I understand the information provided.

I DO NOT GIVE MY PERMISSION for a multifactored evaluation for _____.

Reasons: (It would be helpful to school personnel who are designing an educational program to meet your child's unique needs if you would share with us your reasons for not giving your permission for a multifactored evaluation.)

_____

_____

_____  _____  _____
Signature of parent, legal guardian, custodian, or student (if 18 or older)  Relationship to Child  Date

---

**Part III: (To be completed by school)**

Information about the multifactored evaluation and a copy of my procedural safeguards were presented/sent by:

___*Dr. Roberta Smith*_____  ___November 1___
Signature of school district representative  Date(s)

The parents' native language is ___English___. If not English, was the information provided in the native language or other mode of communication?  ☐ Yes  ☐ No

If no, explain:_____

_____

If the native language or other mode of communication is not a written language, attach documentation of the steps taken to ensure that the notice was explained and that the parent understands the content of the notice.

# WISC-R RECORD FORM

**Wechsler Intelligence Scale for Children—Revised**

NAME *Malcolm Singer* AGE ___ SEX *M*
ADDRESS *Midland USA*
PARENT'S NAME *Monique Singer*
SCHOOL *Clover Valley E.S.* GRADE *2*
PLACE OF TESTING *school* TESTED BY *B. Levy*
REFERRED BY *Naomi Briggs, teacher*

## WISC-R PROFILE

Clinicians who wish to draw a profile should first transfer the child's *scaled* scores to the row of boxes below. Then mark an X on the dot corresponding to the scaled score for each test, and draw a line connecting the X's.*

*See Chapter 4 in the manual for a discussion of the significance of differences between scores on the tests.

| | Year | Month | Day |
|---|---|---|---|
| Date Tested | | | |
| Date of Birth | | | |
| Age | 7 | 5 | 16 |

| | Raw Score | Scaled Score |
|---|---|---|
| **VERBAL TESTS** | | |
| Information | ___ | 8 |
| Similarities | ___ | 8 |
| Arithmetic | ___ | 12 |
| Vocabulary | ___ | 10 |
| Comprehension | ___ | 9 |
| (Digit Span) | (___) | (13) |
| Verbal Score | | 47 |
| **PERFORMANCE TESTS** | | |
| Picture Completion | ___ | 12 |
| Picture Arrangement | ___ | 9 |
| Block Design | ___ | 12 |
| Object Assembly | ___ | 13 |
| Coding | ___ | 15 |
| (Mazes) | (___) | (14) |
| Performance Score | | 61 |

| | Scaled Score | IQ |
|---|---|---|
| Verbal Score | 47 | 96 |
| Performance Score | 61 | 115 |
| Full Scale Score | 108 | 105 |

*Prorated from 4 tests, if necessary.

**NOTES**

Retained?:— 2nd grade - Referred in K — (M) refused. Somewhat fidgety + impulsive but attempted all tasks - Rapport was easy to establish — Responded well to positive feedback - Results should be considered valid + reliable —

# EVALUATION TEAM REPORT (Part A)

Name of Student: Malcolm Singer    Date of Birth: August 29    Age: 8

Evaluator: Dr. Robert Young

Summary of assessment(s), including results of the student's progress in the general curriculum and instructional implications to ensure progress.

Malcolm Singer, grade 2, has been identified as having Attention Hyperactivity

Deficit Disorder. He has been tested with WISC-R, assessed by a pediatric

neurologist, Dr. Martin Longer, and observational forms by parent and teacher.

Malcolm has had academic and social problems affecting both his progress in

reading and writing and his classroom behavior.

Malcolm will be taking 20 mg of Ritalin a day and will see the school counselor

weekly. Additionally, classroom adaptations include not sitting by the window

or door and having a contract with reward activities for completing in-class work.

Malcolm will be formally assessed on his progress by his IEP team twice yearly.

Signature of Evaluator: _Dr. Roberta Smith_    Date: _Nov 9_

## EVALUATION TEAM REPORT (Part B)

**Disability Condition(s) for which Child is Eligible**

        Attention hyperactivity
        Deficit disorder

**Basis for Eligibility Determination**

        Full assessment, multifactor

| | |
|---|---|
| _(signature)_ | November 1 |
| Signature/Title | Date |
| _(signature)_ | November 1 |
| Signature/Title | Date |
| _(signature)_ | November 1 |
| Signature/Title | Date |

Agree with disability determination   Yes ☒     No ☐

**Statement of Disagreement**

| | |
|---|---|
| Signature/Title | Date |

# EVALUATION TEAM REPORT (Part C)

## Criteria for Determining the Existence of a Specific Learning Disability

Student's Name: __Malcolm Singer__ Date of Birth: __08__ / __29__ / _____ Age: __8_____

**A.** When provided with learning experiences appropriate for his/her age and ability level, the student is not achieving commensurate with his/her age and ability levels in one or more of the following areas:

| | | | |
|---|---|---|---|
| Oral Expression | [X] | Reading Comprehension | [X] |
| Listening Comprehension | [X] | Mathematics Calculation | [ ] |
| Written Expression | [X] | Mathematics Reasoning | [ ] |
| Basic Reading Skill | [X] | | |

*Summarize assessment results and other data used by the team to support this determination:*

**B.** The student has a severe discrepancy between achievement and ability that is not correctable without special education and related services in one or more of the following areas:

| | | | |
|---|---|---|---|
| Oral Expression | [ ] | Reading Comprehension | [X] |
| Listening Comprehension | [ ] | Mathematics Calculation | [ ] |
| Written Expression | [X] | Mathematics Reasoning | [ ] |
| Basic Reading Skill | [X] | | |

*Summarize assessment results and other data used by the team to support this determination:*

**C.** The severe discrepancy between ability and achievement is not primarily the result of

| | |
|---|---|
| visual, hearing, or motor impairment | [X] |
| mental retardation | [X] |
| emotional disturbance | [X] |
| environmental, cultural, or economic disadvantage | [X] |

*Summarize assessment results and other data used by the team to support this determination:*

**D.** Describe the relationship of the relevant behavior noted during observation(s) to the student's academic functioning.
*Summarize assessment results and other data used by the team to support this determination:*

**E.** Describe educationally relevant medical findings, if any.
*Summarize assessment results and other data used by the team to support this determination:*

      allergy test results attached

(Additional information can be attached or written on back)

Ms. Renzulli,

I can not come in for a
conference because my
father is very ill.

Monique Barnett

TEACHER CHECKLIST

STUDENT NAME: _Malcolm Singer_ TEACHER _B. Barnard_

Progressive Discipline Plan for Classroom Disruptions

Definition: Behavior that interferes with:

    A.    the teaching/learning process
    B.    student learning
    C.    teacher's ability to teach or carry out responsibilities
    D.    safety of others
    E.    respectful behavior toward others and property

Step 1:    **Polite Reminder** - reteach appropriate behavior(s)
           Teacher's choice of:

| Date Initiated | Other dates/on-going efforts | |
| --- | --- | --- |
| 9-3 | | a. moved to workstation by teacher |
| 9-3 | 9-18  9-20 | b. nonverbal cues |
| | | c. proximity |
| | | d. disapproving look |
| | | e. positive reinforcement/recognition of students with appropriate behavior - verbal recognition of positive behavior change |
| 9-3 | 9-18 | f. redirection to task |
| | | g. other: please list _____ |

           Teacher then gives a choice: either positive behavior changes occur or Step 2 alternatives will be used. Teacher may show student the above list.

Step 2:    **Polite Reminder** - Time Out/Verbal Plan - Consequences/Forfeit
                   Recess/Optional Parent Contact

| Date Inititated | Other dates/on-going efforts | |
| --- | --- | --- |
| | | All students will have: |
| 9-4 | | a. **TIME OUT** 1: classroom/work station/recess - verbal G-PAR/Plan |
| 9-4 | 9-18  9-20 | b. **FORFEIT RECESS**: (portion or all) supervised by a teacher. Recess may be increased/progressive as incidents reoccur. Verbal plans are to be discussed at each incident. |

Teacher then gives student a choice: either positive behavior changes occur or Step 3 alternatives will be used. Teacher will show this form to student.

    c. other logical consequences, if applicable

**Step 3:**   **Time Out/Written Plan - Parent Conference - Consequence**

Date Initiated        Other dates/on-going effort

All students will have:

_____    _____ _____    a. **TIME OUT 2:**  classroom/work station/other classroom/recess - G-PAR/written plan

9-3
(attempted)    _____ _____    b. **PARENT CONFERENCE** (face to face, phone)  teacher will share this form with parent

c. **CONSEQUENCE** - required

_____    _____ _____        1. forfeit recess/may be progressive
_____    _____ _____        2. restitution
_____    _____ _____        3. public apology
9-20       _____ _____        4. after-school time out
_____    _____ _____        5. letter of apology
_____    _____ _____        6. other_____
_____    _____ _____        7. other_____

Teacher then gives student a choice:  either positive behavior changes occur or Step 4 alternatives will be used.  Teacher will discuss this form with the student.

**Step 4:**   Direct Referral to Principal
Time Out/Written Plan/Parent Conference/Consequence from principal's list/other
Referral will include:  teacher checklist, written plan(s), other

Date:_____        Action Taken:_____

Date:_____        Action Taken:_____

Date:_____        Action Taken:_____

# EVALUATION PLANNING FORM

Name of Student: **Malcolm Singer**    Date of Birth: **Aug 23**    Student ID Number: **286-43-8111**

[1] Area of Disability or Suspected Disability: **EMOTIONAL DISTURBANCE (ED)**    Date of Referral: **Nov. 10**

                 (Initial Evaluation Only)

Initial Evaluation ✓    Reevaluation ____    Preschool Evaluation: ____    School Age Evaluation: ✓

STEP 1 In the appropriate box, document the source and date of existing data that the team determines will be a part of the evaluation.
STEP 2 If additional data is needed, indicate in the appropriate box which method(s) will be used and the position of the person assigned to collect the data.

| Assessment Areas | Methodology[1] | | | |
|---|---|---|---|---|
| | Interview/Records Review | Observation[2] | Standardized Test | Criterion Referenced /Curriculum Based |
| Background Information | DEV 3 AND PR VP | | | |
| Health/Medical Status | DEV 3 AND PR OV | | | NURSE Y/N |
| Vision Abilities[1] | DEV 3 AND PR OV | | | NURSE Y/N |
| Hearing Abilities[4] | DEV 3 AND PR OV | | | |
| General Intelligence/ Cognitive Abilities[5] | DEV 3 | | SCHOOL PSYCHOLOGIST | |
| Adaptive Behavior[5] | DEV 3 | | | |
| Academic Performance or Pre-academic Skills | DEV 3 | | G. COUNSELOR (ELEM) TEACHER (MRS E.MILK) | |
| Communication Status | DEV 3 | | | |
| Motor Abilities or Sensori Motor Functioning | DEV 3 | | | |
| Social-Emotional /Behavioral Functioning or Status | DEV 3 AND DEV 2 | G. COUNSELOR AND TEACHER | BES (TEACHER) | |
| Other (Specify) VOCATIONAL ASSAY (10 YRS & OLDER) | COUNSELOR OR TEACHER | | | |
| CONNERS ADHD | | TEACHER AND PARENT Y/N | | |
| RATING SCALE | | | | |

[1] All 4 methodologies must be used for Preschool in area of suspected deficit. [2] Required for Specific Learning Disability. Multiple Observations Required for Preschool. [3] Full Vision Exam Required for Visually Impaired.
[4] Full Audiological Exam Required for Hearing Impaired. [5] Standardized Test Required for Cognitive Disability. [6] Standardized Test Required for Multiple Disability

Team Members:
S. Hess
B. Barnard    B. Leonard
M. Singer - Males    J.B. Cotten

_____ Signature of Evaluation Team Chairperson      Date of Plan: **Dec. 3**

SOCIAL SKILLS ASSESSMENT
(Teacher Form)

Student's Name ___Malcolm Singer_____ Date _____

Individual Completing this Form ___J. Barnard_____ Grade ___4_____

Description of Child: Please check any statements which you feel describe this student
in interaction with peers. If parts of these statements apply to
this student, please qualify your response by specifically
underlining those parts.

| Not True | Sometimes True | Frequently True | This Student: |
|----------|----------------|-----------------|---------------|
| ___ | ___ | ✓ | appears socially isolated. A large proportion of school time is spent in solitary activities. isolation appears to result from the student's withdrawal as opposed to rejection by classmates. |
| ✓ | ___ | ___ | interacts less with classmates due to shyness or timidity. |
| ___ | ___ | ✓ | appears anxious in interactions with classmates and adults. |
| ___ | ___ | ✓ | spends less time involved in activities with classmates due to a lack of social skills and/or appropriate social judgment. |
| ___ | ___ | ✓ | appears to have fewer friends than most due to negative, bossy or annoying behaviors which alienates classmates. |
| ___ | ✓ | ___ | appears to spend less time with classmates due to awkward or bizzare behaviors. |
| ___ | ___ | ✓ | disturbs classmates by teasing, provoking, fighting or interrupting. |
| ___ | ___ | ✓ | will openly strike back with angry behavior if teased by classmates. |
| ___ | ___ | ✓ | is argumentative with adults and classmates. This student must have the last word in verbal exchange. |
| ___ | ___ | ✓ | displays physical aggression towards objects or persons. |

-over-

Name **Malcolm Singer** Case No. **91-12884**

## ADMINISTRATIVE SUPERVISION

You are hereby under the supervision of the probation department of this court upon the following terms and conditions:

1. You shall live at home with your parents;

2. ~~You shall obey your parents;~~

3. You shall attend school regularly;           *AND BUS*

4. You shall obey the rules and regulations of your school;

5. You shall obey the instructions of your teacher and other school officials *(INCLUDING BUS DRIVERS)*;

6. You shall obey the laws and be of good behavior generally;

7. You shall not unless accompanied by a parent, be outside your place of residence after *9:30 SCHOOL NIGHTS; 10:30 WEEKENDS (PARENTS MAY MODIFY FOR SPECIAL ACTIVITIES)*

8. You further agree to *LIMIT YOUR CONTACT W/ NATHANIEL HANSON TO SCHOOL UNTIL FURTHER NOTICE. SUPERVISION*

9. You shall obey the rules and regulations imposed by the probation department of this court and shall follow the instructions of the probation department;

10. You understand that you are fully responsible for arranging your community service schedule with any non-profit organization and/or senior citizens. You also understand that your community service time-sheet(s) must indicate where you performed your service and be signed by yourself and countersigned by your supervisor or the senior citizen for whom you worked;

11. You understand that if you do not perform the consequences required or if you do not follow instructions concerning restitution or other requirements assigned, then the Juvenile Probation Department will initiate action to have your case transferred to formal status leading to hearings with the Judge.

Date **9-23-**          *Malcolm Singer*
                              Juvenile's signature

We have read these conditions, fully understand them, and will do everything in our power to insure that our child abides by their provisions and to otherwise cooperate with the Court and Probation Staff.

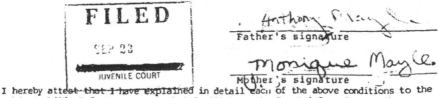

**FILED**

SEP 23

JUVENILE COURT

*Anthony Mayle*
Father's signature

*Monique Mayle*
Mother's signature

I hereby attest ~~that I have explained~~ in detail each of the above conditions to the subject child. I further attest that I will keep the Court informed as to the progress of said child.

NOTICE OF INTENT FOR PLACEMENT IN
ALTERNATIVE LEARNING


Date _____September 24_____          Grade _____9_____
Student Name ___Malcolm Singer_____

The reason(s) you may be suspended is/are:

   smoking

_____

_____

_____

I have received a copy of this placement in Alternative Learning. I understand that all
work assigned will be completed, that academic grades/credit will be assigned to the
quality of work I perform and that I may be suspended from school for refusal to do the
assigned work or displaying work at a quality which is adjudicated to be insubordinate to
the task.

                                            _Malcolm Singer_____
                                               (Student Signature)

Parent/Guardian Contact:
Phone No. _____
Time/Date _____                _____
Comments:_____                (Authorized School Official)
_____
_____

Appeal Hearing Requested: YES_____ NO __✓__
cc:    Student File
       Principal

# Record of Immunization

*Malcolm Singer 286-43-8111*

DPT

10-12
12-24
02-22
08-18

MMR

02-24
08-18

Chicken pox
04-12

Name **Singer    Malcolm    DeShaunte**
(Last)        (First)        (Middle)

Birthdate **08/23**   Birthplace **Philadelphia, PA**

Address **710 Holiday Ave, Apt. 23**

| Date Entered | | Home Phone | | Work Phone |
|---|---|---|---|---|
| Date Withdrew | | | | |
| Transferred To | | | | |
| | | Parent or Guardian | | |
| | | S.S. No. | | |
| | | ADDITIONAL INFORMAT | | (in pencil) |

## NINTH

School **Midland HS**   School Year ____   Grade **9**   H.R. **304**

| Subjects | marks 1 sem | 2 sem | yr | units credit | days pres. | days absc. |
|---|---|---|---|---|---|---|
| Eng. | D | D | D | 1 | 158 | 26 |
| Alg. | C | B | C | 1 | | |
| Sci. | F | F | F | 0 | | |
| SS | D | F | D | 1 | | |
| Key.B | D | D | D | 1/2 | | |
| Phy.Ed. | A | A | A | 1/4 | | |
| Art | F | F | F | 0 | | |

credits this yr: 4 3/4
credits total: 4 3/4
class rank: 301

## ELEVENTH

School ____   School Year ____   Grade ____   H.R. ____

| Subjects | marks 1 sem | 2 sem | yr | units credit | days pres. | days absc. |
|---|---|---|---|---|---|---|
| | | | | | | |

credits this yr:
credits total:
class rank:

## TWELFTH

School ____   School Year ____   Grade ____   H.R. ____

| Subjects | marks 1 sem | 2 sem | yr | units credit | days pres. | days absc. |
|---|---|---|---|---|---|---|
| | | | | | | |

credits this yr:
credits total:
class rank:

School ____   School Year ____   Grade ____   H.R. ____

| Subjects | marks 1 sem | 2 sem | yr | units credit | days pres. | days absc. |
|---|---|---|---|---|---|---|
| | | | | | | |

**Singer     Malcolm     D.**
(Last)      (First)      (Middle)

of Birth  Aug.   23    _____        Sex  F ( )  M ( )
(Month)  (Day)  (Year)

of Birth  Philadelphia   PA           Certificate Passport, etc.
(City)        (State)      Document of Birth

Entered _____  From _____

Withdrew _____  To _____

S.S. No.  386  42  811        Father Deceased ( )   No. Brothers: Older ____ Younger ____
                              Mother Deceased ( )   No. Sisters: Older ____ Younger  2

| | | |
|---|---|---|
| Father | Singer | DeShawnto  R. |
| | (First) | (Middle) |
| Address | unknown (in pencil) | Occupation |
| Mother | Males   Monique  B (in pencil) | Occupation |
| | (First) | (Maiden) |
| Address | 1436 Front St. (in pencil) | Occupation  clerk |
| Guardian | mother | (in pencil) |
| | (Last) | (First)  (Middle) |
| Address | From | (in pencil) |
| Stepparent(s) | Males   Anthony  J. (in pencil) | Occupation |
| | (Last) | (First)  (Middle) |
| Address | 1436 Front St. | (in pencil) |
| Stepparent(s) | (Last) | (First)  (Middle) |
| Address | | (in pencil) |

Assignment for next year

## Annual Summary of Grades    Kindergarten - Eighth

| Grade | School Year | Teacher | Days Present | Days Absent | Times Tardy | Reading | Writing | Spelling | English | Math | Social Studies | Science | Health | Phys.Ed | Art | Music | Life Skills | Tech-nology | Gifted | General Music | Inst. Music |
|---|---|---|---|---|---|---|---|---|---|---|---|---|---|---|---|---|---|---|---|---|---|
| K | | A. Ramelli | 180 | 60 | 5 | U | U | U | U | S | U | U | S | S | S | S | | | | | |
| 1 | | A. Cotten | 40 | 13 | 13 | F | F | F | F | D | F | F | F | S | S | S | | | | | |
| 2 | | N. Briggs | 168 | 12 | 14 | C | C | C | C | D | C | B | C | S | S | S | S | | | | |
| 3 | | N. Briggs | 172 | 6 | 8 | C | C | C | B | B | B | C | B | S | S | S | | | | | |
| 4 | | J. Barnard | 167 | 12 | 8 | D | C | C | D | C | C | C | C | | | | | | | | |
| 4 | | E. Barnard | 162 | 28 | 13 | C | C | C | D | J | J | D | D | S | | | | | | | |
| 5 | | M. Short | 132 | 38 | 11 | D | D | D | D | C | D | D | F | S | S | S | | | | | |
| 7 | | R. Cottrell | 142 | 26 | 14 | C | D | D | F | E | E | F | F | A | F | F | | | | | |
| 8 | | M. Buckley | 158 | 32 | 12 | F | F | F | F | D | F | F | F | A | D | F | | | | | |
| 9 | HR | S. Hess | 114 | 66 | 46 | | | | | | | | | | E | | | | | | |

# Chapter 5

## RAUL RAMIREZ
### *Bridging Cultural Gaps*

## KINDERGARTEN

### Clover Valley Elementary School

Raul Ramirez was born 5 years ago into a working-class home in Mexico City. Earlier this year, his parents, Carmen and Jorge, had the opportunity to be sponsored by Jorge's brother, who immigrated to Midland 2 years ago, with the hope of making enough money in just a few years to buy a farm in Mexico. They know that their U.S. wages will quickly allow them to become landowners in Mexico.

Raul was a healthy baby who had the advantage of being the first son of a young couple with two older and doting sisters, Angelina, then 5, and Diana, then 2. While Mr. and Mrs. Ramirez loved their daughters, Mrs. Ramirez often repeated to family and friends that "God has blessed us with a son to carry on the family name." Raul does not seem spoiled by his family's coddling. He does, however, expect that he will have privileges his sisters may not have because it is his birthright. Every subtle message he gets from his family and community is that he is special and will go far. The sisters, in turn, do not expect as much, because, after all, they are "just girls." Raul appears to be a very happy child, surrounded by a loving extended family. He assumes that his life in the United States will be much the same as it was in Mexico.

Upon arrival in Midland, Mrs. Ramirez quickly found a job as a salad maker at a local chain restaurant on the 3-to-11 shift. She is a hard worker and very proud of her ability to contribute to the financial security of her family. Mr. Ramirez discovered a group of Mexican men who work for a salsa manufacturer in the nearby city. Getting a job was easy, but the pay is in cash and unreported. The men do not seem to mind that they are making less than the required minimum wage in the United States. They are relieved each day to receive cash in hand for their work. Each day they are picked up by a van at 11 p.m. and delivered home at 7 a.m. Mr. Ramirez has also acquired some odd jobs on local farms in the afternoons. The family tells one another that they are "blessed" to be able to save most of their earnings.

The family was able to move into a rented house to live with Jorge's brother, Michael Carlos, his wife, Maria, and their new baby. Thomas, an unrelated single man, also rents a spare bedroom in the house. Together they are able to afford an older home in a residential neighborhood. Raul and his parents share a bedroom, and the girls sleep on a couch in the living room. The house is in a lower-income section of Midland inhabited by many recent immigrants from Mexico. They have met with some subtle prejudice as the neighborhood changed in this small town. Some locals call the three-block area "South of the Border" and refer to their neighbors as "beaners."

At first it was difficult for the family to find food to which they were accustomed. The large supermarket with Mexican products is across town, and the Ramirez family shares one vehicle with the other residents in the household. They can usually make only one trip to the store each month. A new corner market with Mexican imports has just opened in the neighborhood. Because many of the neighbors also speak Spanish, the Ramirezes have a comfortable but isolated feeling about living in the United States.

Mrs. Ramirez enrolled the children in the neighborhood school, Clover Valley Elementary. She had no trouble enrolling the children in school even without previous transcripts, but a month after school began, she was contacted by the principal. The school had no immunization records for the children, and the school nurse insisted on having the children immunized within 2 weeks or they would not be permitted to continue attending Clover Valley. Because of the language barrier and confusion over what was required, the children were suspended from school. The children missed 2 weeks of school before the family was assigned a Spanish-speaking social worker, who explained the school requirements, including the immunization requirements. She set the family up with access to a health clinic, food stamps, and legal services. The town has just begun to respond to the growing number of Mexicans in the community, and services are scarce.

Mrs. Ramirez comes regularly to school to meet with the teacher despite the language barrier. She is embarrassed that she cannot help her children more, but she trusts the school to do what is best for her children. She rarely questions any suggestions by the teachers and respects the authority of the institution.

Raul picks up skills quickly and gets along with the other students. He has no other Spanish-speaking students in his class, but through nonverbal signals he communicates on a basic level with other students. One of the school's parent volunteers speaks some Spanish and is able to work with Raul one morning a week. Raul looks forward to the parent volunteer coming and eagerly waits to have content explained in Spanish. Each week he is able to do a little more because of the support he is receiving in his first language.

Raul is viewed as a novelty among his peers, and students ask to sit with him and invite him to play on the playground. While he wants to speak English, he recognizes that his Spanish makes him special among his classmates, and he likes the attention. The only problem he has had with his peers is that the friendships do not extend beyond the school day. Because of his parents' work schedules, he does not participate in Little League or other weekend activities except for a mass in Spanish at the local Catholic church. Because he is Mexican and the parents of the other children do not know his family, Raul is never invited to their homes. Ms. Buell, his kindergarten teacher, has worked hard to integrate him into the classroom, but she noticed that one student invited all of the classmates to his birthday party except for Raul. Fortunately, Raul didn't fully comprehend the situation and knew only that the other children seemed to share something from which he was excluded.

Raul seems to like school and spends a lot of time looking at pictures in books. He likes to draw and frequently chooses to draw answers to questions instead of attempting to write words. His frustration with not speaking English is only apparent when he asks his teacher questions and she doesn't know what he is asking. He is beginning to notice that the other children do not look like his family and Mexican friends and that he does not see many pictures in his books of people who look like him or live in homes like his. He has learned during the fall to pretend that some of the new ways of his new country are all familiar to him. He is uncomfortable being different. He is beginning to be ashamed about things his family does differently and does not talk about those things with his classmates. At the beginning of the year, he sat quietly during meals and did not eat breakfast or lunch. While the food on the lunch trays at first was tasteless and unfamiliar to him, he now eats some of it and pretends that he eats this kind of food at all meals.

Thanksgiving was a surprise to him, and he still remains confused about the holiday. His family is very religious, and as Christmas approaches, he again feels the chasm between his family's celebration and that of his classmates. He is forbidden at home to talk about Santa Claus. Presents are brought by angels. He has overheard his parents criticize American ways that seem frivolous and, in their view, anti-Catholic. His class makes secular decorations depicting some aspects of Christmas that his family looks down upon in their new country, so he destroys his decorations before he gets home.

His parents are very strict about his learning and ask him every day to show them what he has learned in school. When he feels lost and frustrated, he makes up things to tell his parents so that they will be proud of his success. He worries that somehow, despite the language barrier, his parents will discover at a parent-teacher conference that he is lying. He is learning that he needs to keep school and home very separate to be successful at both. He has noticed that his older sisters are not as much fun as they used to be. They are absorbed in making their own ways in their new environment. As the Christmas holiday is only a week away, Raul looks forward to being at home. He likes school, but even as young as he is, he feels exhausted pretending to be "American" in school and "Mexican" at home.

# EIGHTH GRADE

## Midland Middle School

Raul is now truly bilingual. He speaks Spanish at home and almost fluent English in school. He is secretly disgusted that his parents still have not learned much English even though they have been in the United States for 7 years. At times, he ignores them when they speak Spanish. He feels more American than Mexican and rarely hangs with the other Mexican boys in his neighborhood, instead preferring to spend more time in after-school activities and sports that align him with his Anglo friends. Because of this, he is ostracized by the other Mexican boys for "acting White." Some of these boys have started running with gang members from the nearby city. His sisters hooked up with boys from out of town to avoid dating the local Anglo boys, and dating the city boys gave them more status in their own neighborhood. Raul's older sister, Angelina, has dropped out of school and is pregnant by a boy from the nearby city. She is proud of her baby's father, who is a leader in a Latino gang. Much to her parents' distress, she has moved in with his family and rarely communicates with her own.

Mr. and Mrs. Ramirez feel that they are losing Raul and Diana as well. Diana struggles in school and is aloof and noncommunicative at home. She still helps with the housework but expresses resentment that Raul is not expected to help around the house. The Ramirezes have raised their children as they were raised and cannot understand why the children do not share their values. They have been strict parents, but it doesn't seem to keep their children from disobeying. They are most concerned about the children leaving the Catholic Church. The first time Raul refused to go to church, Mr. Ramirez used the belt and threatened damnation. This tactic did not work and resulted only in driving a bigger wedge between him and his son. Raul has refused to go back to church and will not tell them why. Secretly, he feels that he cannot live up to the expectations of his religion and cannot face thinking about the consequences. Raul spends most of his time alone in a separate room or goes off to be by himself at the library or wandering the streets.

Despite their concern over his attitude toward their culture and their religion, Raul's parents are still proud of his success in school. He has always gotten above-average grades, and they hope that he will graduate from high school. They have devoted much more time and energy to Raul's school success than to Diana's, and they are angry when they feel he is not living up to their expectations. They get frustrated when they find him doodling in a notebook instead of doing his homework. They constantly stress the importance of his getting his high school degree.

Raul began the year doing well in most of his classes. He tried very hard, and his teachers recognized his effort. His math and science grades were outstanding, but his English and social studies grades were just average. Raul tries to relate to the literature, language, and history of his adopted country, but he feels a disconnect. He has lost his own Mexican heritage as his parents assimilated to U.S. ways, and he cannot find a connection to the things he is learning in his texts. Despite his success in some classes, he finds that he is frequently sad. He has a strange feeling of not belonging, not being like anyone he knows. As his schoolmates and teammates joke about sex and girls, he feels embarrassed and isolated. He is very uncomfortable with his peers.

On occasion, he has thought about college when his peers talk about the assumption that they will continue their education, but he knows that his only ticket will be financial aid. He fears his grades probably will not be good enough for an academic scholarship. His family's dream of going back to Mexico has grown more distant. They speak of the future in terms of staying in the United States. He becomes depressed thinking that he will end up working two menial jobs like his father while other less talented students may be able to go to college because they can afford it. His teachers see inconsistency in his work and moodiness in his demeanor. Originally, they thought that he could benefit by having a Spanish major from the nearby college meet with him. They assumed that the need to speak his native language was the problem. He resented the effort and refused to cooperate with the tutor.

Raul desperately wants to fit in, but he is accepted socially only by his classmates at school. He is not included in parties. Girls from his school do not seem interested in him, nor he in them. This is compounded by the problem that his parents are constantly asking why he doesn't have a girlfriend. The message from home is that he should be "breaking hearts" with his good looks, and the message from school is that he is too different to be a serious boyfriend. Raul likes hanging out with the girls, but as friends, not as potential dates. This confuses him, and he tries not to think about it. Instead, he blames his heritage for the disconnect. Raul thinks that if he had been born Anglo, he too could have everything.

Not being able to be Anglo after years of trying in school has left Raul ashamed of his family, neighborhood, and himself. He thinks he will never be what he wants to be: popular, accepted, and admired. He is angry every day at his parents, his friends, his teachers, and his situation. He is angrier every day with himself. He is beginning to be seen by his teachers as a resistant learner. He only cooperates enough in class to get by and not to be singled out as a troublemaker. By the end of the year, he is making C's and D's in all his classes. At 14, he is at a crossroads.

## TWELFTH GRADE

### Midland High School

By 12th grade, Raul speaks fluent English. In fact, he has forgotten any complex Spanish and never dreams in anything but English. His parents are bilingual but are more comfortable speaking Spanish at home and with their friends and extended family. Raul can no longer join in any meaningful conversations with his parents or his Mexican community. He feels sad that something in his relationship with his parents is missing. When he visited his grandmother last year in Mexico City for the first time, it was as if he was a tourist. He did not understand the language or the customs, and he did not like the food. He thought he would starve until he found a McDonald's a few miles from his grandmother's house.

Raul is finishing his high school career. His family has just purchased their first home, and for the first time it is a single-family dwelling in a mixed middle-class neighborhood. Raul's oldest sister, Angelina, has moved back into the home with her two children, so the small home is still filled with people. Diana graduated from high school and is living at home and attending a local vocational program to get her nurse assistant license.

Raul is a senior with no clear plans for the future. His grades are just average, and he knows that his family cannot afford a 4-year college. He is not sure that he even wants to continue in school. School has often been a battleground for him. As a young immigrant, he had difficulty catching up with his classmates because of the language barrier. As he grew older, he worked very hard to please his parents and teachers but could never really relate to some of the subjects. English and social studies could not hold his interest. The textbooks and teachers did not talk about him or his heritage. When he did run across a story with Latinos, it depicted them as migrant farmworkers or people still in Mexico. He found more success in math and science. But he found his passion in art. Taking it as an elective in ninth grade, he found it to be an outlet for the anger that had been inside him for so long. He had found a niche. He could forget everything when he was drawing, and his work was admired by both the teachers and his fellow students. His art teacher was amazed and for 4 years encouraged him to enter contests. He never did. Art was his private salvation. When he drew, he could forget the disappointment that he could never be what he wanted, what his family wanted, and what society wanted.

He was not the macho young man his father had so desperately wanted him to be. He was not the successful young Anglo man he desperately wanted to be. At school his classmates were always friendly, but distant. At first he assumed this was only because he was Mexican. As he grew older, he realized that he was different in other ways. Raul had stuffed a secret inside him that ate at him until he could no longer deny it to himself. At first he did not even have words for it, but then he overheard others talking about "fags" and "homos" and the words came. Raul suddenly had another reason for shame. The anger that had separated him from his family, classmates, and community began to separate him from himself. He desperately wanted to talk to someone whose sexual orientation was the same as his. He could no longer deny to himself who he was, but he felt there was no one with whom he could reveal his true self. He had formed no close personal bonds with his classmates, and he felt his family would never understand or accept him. He longed for a normal loving relationship and acceptance. He felt he could never be who he was where he was.

Standing on the brink of his adult life at the beginning of his senior year, Raul is alone. What he wants more than anything now is not to be alone. He feels that if he could continue his art and find a community of his own where no one had to try to be something they weren't, he could be happy. He sees no way to find this in Midland. He has no knowledge of how to go about finding this. College is a mystery to him and his family, he knows no other community but Midland, and he feels no support from family, school, or friends. At this point, he is burdened with knowledge he cannot share, talent he cannot use, and separation that he feels will never end.

Raul is beginning his final journey in his senior year. This is the last opportunity anyone from the Midland educational system can help him. He is depressed and lost. To his family, classmates, and teachers, it may seem as if he has chosen to be alone and to work in solitude. Nothing could be further from the truth.

Raul's Cumulative Folder

This record must be completed by school and child care personnel from an immunization record provided by parent or guardian. See reverse side for instructions.

Student Name **Raul Ramirez**

Sex: M ☑  F ☐     Birthdate **09/02**     Place of Birth **Mexico City, Mex**

Name of Parent or Guardian **Jorge and Carmen Ramirez**

Race/Ethnicity:
☐ White, not Hispanic
☑ Hispanic
☐ Black
☐ Other: _____

Address **125 Barbar St.**

Telephone **706-3939**     Daytime _____ Nighttime _____

City **Midland** _____ ZIP _____

| VACCINE | | DATE EACH DOSE WAS GIVEN | | | | | |
|---|---|---|---|---|---|---|---|
| | 1st | 2nd | 3rd | 4th | 5th | Booster |
| POLIO (OPV or IPV) | 09/14 | 11/12 | 03/17 | | | |
| DTP/DTaP/DT/Td (Diphtheria, tetanus and [acellular] pertussis OR tetanus and diphtheria only) | 09/14 | 11/12 | 03/17 | | | |
| MMR (Measles, mumps, and rubella) | 09/14 | 11/12 | | | | |
| HIB (Required only for child care and preschool) | | | | | | |
| HEPATITIS B | 09/14 | 11/12 | | | | |
| VARICELLA (Chickenpox) | 09/14 | 11/12 | | | | |
| HEPATITIS A (Not required) | | | | | | |

| TB SKIN TESTS | Type* | Date given | Date read | mm Indur | Impression | CHEST X-RAY (Necessary if skin test positive) |
|---|---|---|---|---|---|---|
| | ☑ PPD-Mantoux ☐ Other | 09/17 | 09/21 | | ☐ Pos ☐ Neg | Film date: _____ Impression: ☐ normal ☐ abnormal |
| | ☐ PPD-Mantoux ☐ Other | | | | ☐ Pos ☐ Neg | Person is free of communicable tuberculosis: ☐ yes ☐ no |

*If required for school entry, must be Mantoux unless exception granted by local health department.

Midland School District

1/16

Dear Mr. and Mrs. Ramirez,

It has come to our attention that Raul is experiencing academic difficulty in several subjects this year. He was referred to the Midland Middle School Academic Intervention Committee by several of his teachers.

After reviewing his grades and his file, we discovered that he has not had any English language support since early elementary school. We are concerned that he may be falling behind because he lacks competency in English. Beginning in February, with your permission, we will arrange to have a tutor from the local college work with him on English language skills during his study hall.

If you agree to this, please sign on the permission slip below and return it to the main office. Thank you.

John H. Haberman
Midland Middle School Principal


Name of child: Raul Ramirez


____✓____ Yes, I give permission for my child to be tutored during study hall.

_____ No, I do not want my child tutored during study hall.

Signature of parent (s) _Jorge Ramirez_____ Date__12-13__

# Iowa Tests of Basic Skills

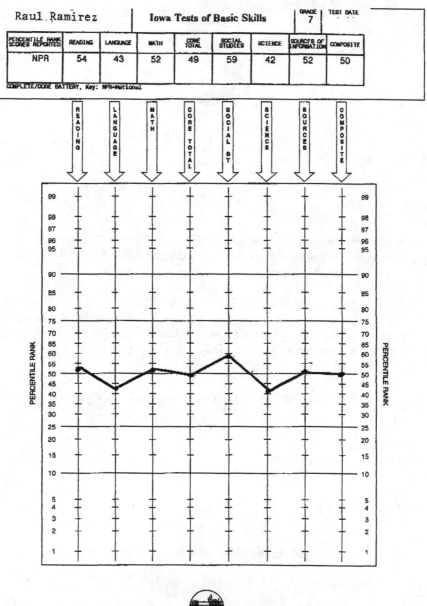

| PERCENTILE RANK SCORES REPORTED | READING | LANGUAGE | MATH | CORE TOTAL | SOCIAL STUDIES | SCIENCE | SOURCES OF INFORMATION | COMPOSITE |
|---|---|---|---|---|---|---|---|---|
| NPR | 54 | 43 | 52 | 49 | 59 | 42 | 52 | 50 |

Raul Ramirez — Iowa Tests of Basic Skills — GRADE 7 — TEST DATE

COMPLETE/CORE BATTERY, Key: NPR—National

**The Riverside Publishing Company**

*a Houghton Mifflin company*

Raul Ramirez

# Tests of Achievement

| | Test 1 Reading Comp. | Test 2 Math | Test 3 Written Expression | Test 4 Using Sources of Info | Test 5 Social Studies | Test 6 Science | BASIC COMPOSITE | | | APPLIED PROFICIENCY SKILLS |
|---|---|---|---|---|---|---|---|---|---|---|
| GRADE EQUIVALENT | 44 | 128 | 48 | 54 | | | 63 | | | Raw Score |
| | 2 | 70 | 5 | 5 | | | * | | | 23 LOW |
| NATIONAL PERCENTILE TILE & STANINE | 2  1 | 6 | 5  2 | 5  2 | | | 7  2 | | | |

**READING COMPREHENSION**
- Textbook
- Everyday
- Fact
- Inference
- Generalization

**MATHEMATICS**
- Operations (Form & Order)
- Equivalent Applications
- Algebra Applications
- Geometry & Measurement
- Statistics, Graphs & Tables
- Basic Mathematical Principles
- Computation
- Concepts
- Problem Solving

**WRITTEN EXPRESSION**
- Capitalization/Punctuation
- Grammar & Usage
- Sentence/Paragraph Structure
- Organizing Ideas
- Writing Conventions
- Knowledge/Information
- Comprehension
- Application and Analysis
- Synthesis and Evaluation

**USING SOURCES OF INFO**
- Maps
- Tables
- Table of Contents and Indexes
- Dictionaries
- General Reference Materials
- Knowledge/Information
- Comprehension
- Application and Analysis
- Synthesis and Evaluation

**HIGHER ORDER THINK. SKILL**
- Reading Comprehension
- Mathematics
- Language Usage/Expression
- Work Study Skills

**SOCIAL STUDIES**
- Historical Perspective
- Patterns & Systems
- Higher Order Thinking Skills
- Economic
- Geographic
- Political
- Social & Anthropologic
- Related Social Sciences
- Knowledge/Information
- Comprehension
- Application and Analysis
- Synthesis and Evaluation

**SCIENCE**
- Nature of Science
- Life Science
- Earth/Space Science
- Chemistry & Physics
- Higher Order Thinking Skills
- Knowledge/Information
- Comprehension and Analysis
- Synthesis and Evaluation
- Experimental Methods/Techniques

**APPLIED PROFICIENCY SKILLS**
- Obtaining Information
- Primarily Verbal Materials
- Visual Materials
- Communicating Ideas in Writing
- Applied Mathematics

## Midland School District
## Home Language Survey

Student's Name___Raul Ramirez_____

School (Circle one) CE (MMS) MHS

Parent (s) or Guardian (s) name (s)___Carmen Ramirez_____

Jorge Ramirez_____

Address:

Phone:

1. What was the first language your child learned to speak?

   Español

2. What language (s) does your child speak at home?

   Both

3. What language(s) is spoken most often at home?

   Español

4. What language(s) does your child speak most often with friends?

   Both

5. Has the student received any English Language Learner services in the past?
   If yes, # of years___✓ Where___school_____

6. How long has your child lived in the USA?

   6 years

7. What language do the parents speak? Español   Read? Español

Dear Parents:

**ACCORDING TO STATE LAW, A STUDENT WHO HAS EARNED THE REQUIRED NUMBER OF CREDITS BUT DID NOT PASS THE NINTH GRADE PROFICIENCY OFICIENCY TEST WILL AWARDED A CERTIFICATE OF ATTENDANCE BUT WILL NOT RECEIVE A DIPLOMA.**

Our district is committed to the goal of providing a sound education for each student entrusted in our care. We will be offering extra help for those students who do not pass all sections of the test on the first trial so they can be successful when they take the test again. We will also be addressing instruction in kindergarten through eighth grade so that our students have the skills they need to pass the test when they reach the ninth grade.

Attached are the results for your child. Unfortunately, the scores are not provided; this report only states whether your child passed or failed each of the form areas.

**NAME:** Raul Ramirez
**SCHOOL:** Midland High School        Grade: 09
**DISTRICT:** Midland School District

| MATHEMATICS | READING | CITIZENSHIP | WRITING |
|---|---|---|---|
| PASSED | PASSED | PASSED | PASSED |

We look forward to working with you to help your child achieve the goal of receiving a high school diploma.

Sincerely,

*Jane L. Carr*

Jane L. Carr
Superintendent
Midland School District

Querida Señorita Buell,

Muchas gracias para consiguiendo Señortta Manning a ser la tutora de Raul en Inglés. Querem. muchisimo que él aprenda en la escuela. Quiero que sepas que mi esposa y yo lo vamos a ayudarlo a él en todo posible. Sabemos que el es inteligente y que va a aprender rápido.

Sinceremente,

Jorge Ramírez

10-27

Dear Mrs. Buell,

Thank you for getting Mrs. Manning to tutor Raul in English. We want very much for him to learn in school. Please know that my wife and I will help him all we can. We know he is smart and will learn fast.

Sincerely,

Jorge Ramirez

Elementary _____

# High School   Grades 9 - 12

**Last:** Ramirez  **(First)** Raul  **(Middle)** Jorge

**Birthplace:** Mexico City, Mexico

| Date Entered | 9-38 |
| Date Withdrew | |

Transferred To _____

| Home Phone | 706-3939 |
| Work Phone | — |

Parent or Guardian: Jorge Ramirez (in pencil)

S. S. No. _____

ADDITIONAL INFORMATION

### Grade 9 — H.R. 23 — days pres. 174 — days absc. 6

| School Year Subjects | marks 1 sem. | marks 2 sem. | yr. | units credit |
|---|---|---|---|---|
| Alg. | A | A | | 1 |
| Eng | B | B | | 1 |
| G. Science | A | B | | 1 |
| Geography | B | B | | 1 |
| Art | A | A | | 1 |
| Phy. ed. | A | A | | 1/4 |
| Spanish | A | A | | 1 |

credits this yr. 6 1/4
credits total 6 1/4
class rank

### Grade 10 — H.R. 18 — days pres. 177 — days absc. 3

| School Year Subjects | marks 1 sem. | marks 2 sem. | yr. | units credit |
|---|---|---|---|---|
| Geometry | A | B+ | A | 1 |
| Bio | B | B | | 1 |
| Eng | B | B | | 1 |
| Art | A | A | | 1 |
| Phy ed | A | A | | 1/4 |
| Spanish | A | A | | 1 |
| World Hist | B | B | | 1 |

credits this yr. 6 1/4
credits total 12 1/2
class rank

ELEVENTH

### Grade 11 — H.R. 14 — days absc. 6

| School Year Subjects | marks 1 sem. | marks 2 sem. | yr. | units credit |
|---|---|---|---|---|
| Alg II | A | A | | 1 |
| Eng | B | B | | 1 |
| Am Hist | C | C | | 1 |
| Sp III | A | A | | 1 |
| Art III | A | A | | 1 |
| Soc. | A | A | | 1 |

credits this yr. 6
credits total 18 1/2
class rank

### Grade 12 — H.R.

| School Year Subjects | marks 1 sem. | marks 2 sem. | yr. | units credit |
|---|---|---|---|---|
| | | | | |

credits this yr.
credits total
class rank

TWELFTH

### Grade — School — H.R.

| Subjects | marks 1 sem. | marks 2 sem. | yr. | units credit |
|---|---|---|---|---|
| | | | | |

credits this yr.
credits total
class rank

### Grade — School Year — H.R.

| Subjects | marks 1 sem. | marks 2 sem. | yr. | units credit |
|---|---|---|---|---|
| | | | | |

credits this yr.
credits total
class rank

Name **Ramirez** (Last) **Raul** (First) **J** (Middle)

| | | |
|---|---|---|
| Date of Birth **69** (Month) **02** (Day) ____ (Year) | | Sex F ( ) M (X) |
| Place of Birth **Mexico City** (City) ____ (State) | Document of Birth | (Certificate, Passport, etc.) |
| Date Entered **8-28** | | |

S.S. No. ____ 

No. Brothers: Older ____ Younger ____
No. Sisters: Older **2** Younger ____

Father Deceased ( )
Mother Deceased ( )

Date Withdrew ____ To ____
____ To ____

|  |  | |
|---|---|---|
| Father | **Ramirez** (Last) **Jorge** (First) **M** (Middle) | Occupation **Swim Instructor** |
| Address | **125 Barbar St.** | |
| Mother | **Carmen** (First) **Ramirez** (Last) **Melina** (Maiden) | |
| Address | **125 Barbar St** | Occupation **Red Lobster** |
| Guardian | (First) (Last) | Occupation |
| Address | (in pencil) | (in pencil) |
| Stepparent(s) | (First) (Last) | (in pencil) |
| Address' | (in pencil) | |
| Stepparent(s) | (First) (Last) | (Middle) |
| Address | | |

Assignment for next year

## Annual Summary of Grades — Kindergarten - Eighth

| Grade | School Year | Teacher | Days Present | Days Absent | Times Tardy | Reading | Writing | Spelling | English | Math | Social Studies | Science | Health | Phys. Ed | Art | Music | Life Skills | Tech-nology | Gifted | General Music | Inst. Music |
|---|---|---|---|---|---|---|---|---|---|---|---|---|---|---|---|---|---|---|---|---|---|
| K | | J. Buell | 177 | 3 | 0 | S | S | S | S | S | S | S | S | O | O | O | | | | | |
| 1 | | A. Gatten | 179 | 1 | 0 | B | B | B | 5 | B | B | A | O | O | O | O | | | | | |
| 2 | | B. Leonard | 176 | 4 | 0 | B | B | B | B | A | B | A | O | | O | O | | | | | |
| 3 | | K. Miller | 179 | 1 | 0 | A | B | B | B | B | B | A | O | O | O | O | | | | | |
| 4 | | E. Barnard | 178 | 2 | 0 | A | A | B | B | A | B | A | O | | O | O | | | | | |
| 5 | | M. Short | 180 | 0 | 0 | A | A | B | B | B | B | B | B | O | A | B | | | | | |
| 6 | | R. Cottrell | 178 | 2 | 0 | A | A | A | A | A | A | A | A | A | A | B | | | | | |
| 7 | | T. Shorts | 177 | 3 | 1 | C | C | B | C | B | A | A | B | A | B | I | | | | | |
| 8 | | S. Hess | 172 | 6 | 3 | C | C | C | C | B | B | D | C | B | A | B | | A | | | |

# Chapter 6

## LESLIE CARR

### *Accommodating Physical Disabilities*

## FIRST GRADE

### Clover Valley Elementary School

Although John and Carolyn Carr consider themselves middle class, most of Midland considers them rich. John is executive vice president at the Midland Chrysler plant, where Carolyn worked as director of human resources. Mrs. Carr and Mrs. Brown, who is Sarah's mother (see Chapter 3), are former colleagues and good friends.

At birth, Leslie Marie Carr, a European American female, weighed 8 pounds, 2 ounces and measured 19 inches long. Leslie was an active, cheerful baby who even at a young age did not like to take naps, much to her parents' chagrin. She sat, crawled, walked, and spoke at the anticipated times, and as she grew older, loved to ride her tricycle and play with her two cats. She enjoyed going to children's events at the museums and concerts in the nearby city and had an extensive collection of toy cats, cat pictures, and cat figurines. She also loved the Breyer horses and had a stable, ring, and all the pieces needed to run a busy horse establishment. At 4, she began taking gymnastics and ballet lessons and, according to her mother, was "quite the ham" in productions.

Just before Leslie's fifth birthday, the Carrs were returning from a party when the family's car was struck by a drunk driver who had run a red light. Leslie had just begun using an adult seat belt and was sitting in the back on the driver's side of the car. When the other driver's car hit her side of the car, the impact drove her under the seat belt and into the far side of the vehicle. The force of the impact damaged her spinal column, causing a burst fracture and bruising resulting in an incomplete (spinal column not completely severed) injury at the C8 through T7 spinal region. The left side of her spinal column suffered the most damage. Because the impact was to the rear of the car, her parents were not injured.

Leslie's spinal cord injury left her with control of her arms and right hand but limited use of her left hand, which up to that time of the accident had been her dominant hand. In the days following the accident, doctors and therapists cataloged her condition in her growing medical file: "Leslie can spread the fingers of her right hand but not the fingers of her left hand. She can grasp with both hands, but the left hand grasp is weaker than the right. She has some hand dexterity, but dexterity is limited in both hands, especially in the left. Leslie has some trunk control but it is relatively poor due to limited control of her abdominal muscles. She can still sense a light touch, pain, and temperature on her left side, since these senses are controlled by the right side of the spinal column that suffered the less severe damage. Her sense of touch, pain, and temperature are reduced on the right side, since this is controlled by the left side of the spinal column. She has no use of her legs. She will be able to use an electric wheelchair by using her right hand on the controls."

Mrs. Carr immediately quit her job to take care of Leslie. Instead of attending kindergarten as planned, Leslie—along with her parents—spent the year learning to deal with and adapt to her physical disability. There was much to learn and to do. The entire family felt as if their lives had been turned upside down. Mrs. Carr, who hated cleaning skinned knees, had to learn overnight to deal with catheters and pressure sores and bowels that wouldn't move or would move at the wrong time. It was especially distressing to try to explain to their child that all their lives were changed forever.

The Carrs decided to homeschool Leslie that year in hopes that she could be ready to join her classmates the following year. By 5, Leslie had already learned most of the content expected of a child ready to enter first grade, but Mrs. Carr borrowed a set of workbooks from one of her friends who taught kindergarten at Clover Valley to, as she told her friends, "make sure we haven't missed something." Leslie and her parents were thrilled when it became clear after a thorough evaluation of her physical health that she would be able to attend first grade at Clover Valley Elementary.

Now 6, Leslie can feed herself again. Her mother, with the help of an occupational therapist, is working with her to increase her bathing and grooming independence. Leslie is learning to deal with catheterization and bladder control and knows that she can ask for assistance from the school nurse if necessary. Bowel control has been practiced at home and should not be a problem at school. She needs to be reminded often to shift her weight frequently to avoid pressure sores. If there are problems, Mrs. Carr would be contacted immediately.

Leslie has a laptop computer that attaches to her wheelchair. It can be used for writing, drawing, and looking up information. The computer has a voice recognition program, and Leslie can use it to improve her ability to get her thoughts into words. She can also type, but typing is a much slower process than the voice recognition program. The other children are fascinated with this technology and wish that they could use such "cool stuff."

Leslie gets angry when she struggles to use the crayons, pencils, and books or cannot maneuver around an obstacle. Her teacher, Mrs. Clawson, has found that a quiet comment can help Leslie deal with her frustration, and she makes it clear that Leslie is not to take her frustration out on the other children. Twice Mrs. Clawson has removed Leslie from her group's table for speaking rudely to the other children.

Mrs. Clawson held a "disability etiquette" workshop for the class so that students in the class understand Leslie's disabilities and what she can and cannot do. Once the other children understood more about Leslie's disabilities, they became much more helpful and considerate. In fact, Mrs. Clawson sometimes has to remind the other children to let Leslie get her own materials and do things for herself. Leslie occasionally takes advantage of the situation and lets classmates do what she is quite capable of doing for herself.

With accommodations for her disabilities, Leslie is able to easily keep up with the class. The aisles between tables and desks need to be wide enough for Leslie's wheelchair, and the sink, tables, and workstations need to be low enough for her to reach from her wheelchair. Mrs. Clawson has been quite inventive in coming up with ways of incorporating the necessary accommodations so that they are hardly noticeable. Some are as simple as having books on CD so that Leslie can read them using her computer. To her surprise, Mrs. Clawson has found that when she makes accommodations for Leslie, other students benefit as well. One of the attention-deficit/hyperactivity disorder (ADHD) students in the class finds it easier to focus on reading when the book pages are presented on the computer. Leslie is performing at grade level in all subjects, and her favorites are math, science, and art. Her art takes the form of graphics and Web pages, and she is in charge of the class Web page.

Leslie is actively involved in activities outside of school. Although gymnastics and ballet are no longer options, she is enrolled in a horseback riding program for children and adults with disabilities and in a swimming program at the local YMCA. Grooming and tacking up the horse helps Leslie work with her hands. The horseback riding helps her by mimicking how her body moved when she was able to walk, keeping her muscles working and supple. The horse's body heat helps relax Leslie's muscles as well. Since Leslie loves horses, riding has also helped keep her spirits up. Swimming helps strengthen Leslie's upper body and arms and stretch her tight muscles. She works with a physical therapist twice a week to work her muscles and prevent contraction of her hands and legs. The physical therapist has suggested purchasing walkabout calipers that enable people who are paraplegic or partially quadriplegic to walk, but Leslie isn't sure she's ready for that.

According to Mrs. Carr, two girls who were Leslie's special friends before the accident, Anna and Terri, have continued their friendship. Both girls are in Mrs. Clawson's class too and are careful to include Leslie in their play times, both at school and at home. Her other special friend, Kate, has had a hard time dealing with Leslie's paralysis. After several attempts to talk to her, Leslie has given up trying to be friends with Kate. Mrs. Carr tells Mrs. Clawson that Leslie is hurt by Kate's behavior and does not understand her former friend's attitude. Both Mrs. Carr and Mrs. Clawson have tried to explain to Leslie that some people just cannot handle it when people change. To counter some of this hurt, Leslie has made several new friends through her riding and swimming classes.

# SIXTH GRADE

## Midland Middle School

As Leslie enters sixth grade at Midland Middle School, she struggles with respiratory infections caused by a weak cough reflex but is completely responsible for her own feeding, bathing, and elimination with limited help from her mother. Her trunk stability has improved due to her years of riding and swimming exercise, and she easily controls her wheelchair with a right-hand joystick.

Although Leslie's work has been average or slightly above in all subjects, her mother is concerned that she is beginning a downward trend in both her schoolwork and her social interactions with her friends. In a parent-teacher conference with Ms. Jasper, Leslie's sixth-grade science teacher, Mrs. Carr expressed concern that Leslie no longer seems to be excited about coming to school and that she seems much less interested in her favorite activities, including swimming, which she now claims is "just for babies." She also noted that Anna and Terri, who had been Leslie's friends since they were in preschool together, no longer come to the house to visit as often. According to Mrs. Carr, Leslie complains that the girls are leaving her out of their activities—going to the mall, shopping for clothes, and meeting up with boys. She is no longer invited to the girls' slumber parties. The parents of the girls had apologized to Mrs. Carr, explaining that they were the ones who were worried since they did not know how to handle the special care they thought Leslie would need. The parents were concerned about stairs and emergencies, and although Mrs. Carr tried to allay their fears, Leslie is still not included in the sleepovers.

Ms. Jasper acknowledged that she had noticed that Leslie appears angry and sullen and suggested that Mrs. Carr talk with the school counselor about her concerns. In a meeting with the school counselor the following week, Leslie and Mrs. Carr talked with the counselor about how they could help Leslie develop some grown-up interests and activities. They discussed the disability etiquette workshop that was held for Leslie's homeroom class and each of her course classes, and Leslie reported that most of her classmates were helpful and considerate. But as Leslie grumpily explained to her mother and the counselor, "It isn't the school stuff; it is the girl stuff." Instead of the swimming classes, the counselor suggested **hydrotherapy**, and Mrs. Carr said she would look into that option. Leslie, slumped in her wheelchair, muttered that she couldn't wear all the cool clothes and she felt stupid going to the dances. And how could you hang out at the mall in a wheelchair? None of her friends were still going to swim classes and riding horses—they were buying makeup and talking about seventh-grade boys. Mrs. Carr, who appeared surprised at Leslie's comments, promised to try to treat Leslie in a more grown-up way and to see if there were ways to meet some of her more grown-up needs.

Although Leslie seemed encouraged for a few days, she soon became withdrawn and quiet, almost sullen, further isolating herself from her peers. She grew increasingly careless about taking care of herself, and some of her classmates chided her about her slovenly appearance. She developed several urinary tract infections and a severe respiratory infection and soon began having serious problems with pressure sores. By the end of the year, she had quit hydrotherapy and riding, claiming that she was too sick to participate. She began to be late for classes, saying that her wheelchair was hard to maneuver in the hallways. She did not complete in-class or homework assignments, claiming that the work took too much time when you couldn't use a pencil or marker like everyone else. She refused to join any of the expanded activities and clubs available at the middle school, saying that she just wasn't interested.

To Ms. Jasper, it felt like Leslie was daring her teachers to make her participate, to make her perform, and she was pushing her classmates away. She wondered how she could push Leslie to perform when she seemed so physically fragile. Leslie's classmates wondered how to include her or help her when she was always so rude and moody.

## TWELFTH GRADE

### Midland High School

After an abysmal sixth-grade year, which she barely passed, Leslie was forced by her desperate parents to attend a month-long summer camp for adolescents with physical disabilities. Much to her parents' relief, the camp proved to be a turning point for Leslie as she grappled with the dual challenges of a physical disability and puberty. Sally, a 17-year-old counselor with a similar disability, took an instant liking to the troubled but capable Leslie and quickly befriended her and became her role model. When Sally asked, Leslie would ride horses, swim, lift weights, and take an active part in every activity. For the first time, Leslie saw many other young people with physical disabilities—pushing themselves, trying and failing, and encouraging each other to try again. In 4 weeks, she felt something she hadn't felt for a long time—acceptance of who she was and the confidence to interact with friends, old and new.

During the next year, Sally continued to communicate with Leslie, providing friendship and support. They returned to camp the following summer. Again, Leslie had a wonderful experience, and she returned to eighth grade ready to take an active part in her school's activities and to reenroll in riding and swimming classes. Her experiences with the boys at camp gave her the confidence to talk with the boys at her school, and she discovered that not all of them were bothered by the fact that she was in a wheelchair. Some, in fact, were fascinated by the technology that helped her move quickly through the hallways and turn her speech into written words.

By ninth grade, Leslie was performing above grade level in all subjects and made the honor roll. She joined the science club and was elected secretary. She also maintained records for the girls' basketball team. She helped decorate the gym for school dances and learned that she had a flair for being a disk jockey. Leslie continued to go to camp in the summer and went from being a camper to a camp counselor. She enjoyed working with others and doing for them what Sally had done for her.

Leslie took the **PSAT** during her sophomore year and did well, paving her way for college entrance. She took a full schedule of biology, literature, social studies, Algebra II, and art. She continued to work on graphic designs for Web pages.

Later that year, a boy in her class asked her to go to the movies with him. After some awkward discussion of the driving arrangements and much eye rolling on Leslie's part, the logistics were sorted out and the date was a success. Leslie's social life became more hectic, and she began begging her parents to drive her to the mall and school activities and events. All of a sudden Leslie's parents were facing the same worries as other children's parents. And they thought that was just fine.

A major event of Leslie's junior year was getting her driver's license. A certified driver rehabilitation specialist evaluated Leslie's ability to drive and provided a list of recommendations and necessary vehicle **modifications**. Although Leslie had strengthened her arms and upper body, it was decided that it was necessary to purchase a van that she could drive from her wheelchair. The big day arrived, and her red minivan with hand controls, steering assist, reduced effort braking and steering, wheelchair lift and tie down, and automatic door openers was delivered with much fanfare. After 3 months of hard practice, she passed her driver's test on her first try. She no longer has to beg her parents to take her places, and she picks up and does the driving on dates.

When Leslie enrolled in chemistry during her junior year, the school purchased a handicapped mobile laboratory unit that accommodated Leslie's wheelchair. She performed all the experiments that the other students did. This required some ingenuity on the part of the chemistry teacher, who designed a system of boards with rubbery bottoms of drink containers nailed to them to hold beakers firmly. Plastic items were used whenever possible to avoid breakage. A large apron was used to prevent spills from landing in her unprotected lap, and goggles were used to protect her eyes. A study hall scheduled right after chemistry class gave Leslie the extra time she needed to do some of the experiments and to work on chemistry problems using the computer.

Now in her senior year, Leslie looks forward to coming to school. Her left hand, her dominant and most disabled hand, still cannot hold a pencil well, and writing with her right hand is laborious. She much prefers using her computer to do written work. She prefers her voice recognition for writing, but teachers often prefer the quieter use of the keyboard. She still enjoys science, math, and the arts. She is taking physics this year but claims she likes chemistry better. The chemistry teacher is also the physics teacher and is becoming quite good at figuring out creative **adaptations** that allow Leslie to experience as much hands-on science as possible.

As Leslie thinks about her future, she thinks about going to college and majoring in forensic science. She has read the Lincoln Rhymes books by Jeffrey Deaver and figures she can solve problems like Lincoln, a quadriplegic who has much less motion than she has. She has taken the **SAT** and is looking into colleges with good wheelchair accessibility and forensics programs. Life still isn't easy, and she has to be careful about what she eats and drinks and has to work hard to maintain her mobility and strength. But she is looking forward to the challenges of college and a career—and a life.

Leslie's Cumulative Folder

# Midland School District

## Physical Exam Form

**Name:** Leslie Marie Carr        **Home Phone#:** 555-4555

**Address:** 118 West Cherry Hill Drive

**City:** Midland        **State:** _____        **Zip Code:** _____

**Gender:** F        **Date of Birth:** Feb. 6        **Age:** 6        **Grade:** 1

**Father's Name:** John Carr

**Place of Employment:** VP - Midland Chrysler Plant

**Daytime Phone Number:** 555-4455

**Mother's Name:** Carolyn Carr

**Place of Employment:** Homemaker

**Daytime Phone #:** 555-4555

**Alternate Emergency Contact Person:** ___ Jennifer Shumaker _____

**Relationship:** Aunt        **Daytime Phone:** 555-4444

## PHYSICAL EXAM – TO BE COMPLETED BY PHYSICIAN

Height 3 ft 10 in

Weight 50 lb

Percent body fat (optional) _____

Pulse 70

Blood Pressure 100/60

Vision: R 20/ 20        uncorrected R___/___corrected L   20/ 20   uncorrected

|  | Findings |
|---|---|
| 1. Eyes | *Normal 20/20* |
| 2. Ears, Nose, Throat | *Normal/Slight tendency toward ear infections* |
| 3. Mouth & Teeth | *Normal* |
| 4. Neck | *Normal* |
| 5. Cardiovascular | *Normal* |
| 6. Chest & Lungs | *Respiratory weakness due to spinal cord injury/respiratory infections common* |

| | |
|---|---|
| 7. Abdomen | *Normal* |
| 8. Skin | *Normal/No pressure sores* |
| 9. Genitalia-Hernia (female) | *Normal* |
| 10. Musculoskeletal: ROM, strength, etc. | |
| • Neck | *T1 Vertebra injury resulting in limited use of hands especially dominant left hand, some respiratory problems, limited trunk control and no use of legs quadriplegic* |
| • Spine (Scoliosis) | *Normal* |
| • Shoulders | *Some weakness due to injury* |
| • Arms/hands | *Turns mobile, hands have weakened grip and mobility, especially in left, no curling of fingers observed* |
| • Hips | *Quadriplegic* |
| • Thights | *Quadriplegic* |
| • Knees | *Quadriplegic* |
| • Ankles | *Quadriplegic* |
| • Feet | *Quadriplegic with some trouble with in-grown toenails* |
| 11. Neuromuscular | *Loss of neuro-motor function due to SCI T-1 injury* |

| | YES | NO |
|---|---|---|
| 12. Diabetes – **check appropriate answers** | | √ |

| **IF YES.** | YES | NO | NON-INSULIN DEPENDENT | YES | NO |
|---|---|---|---|---|---|
| INSULIN-DEPENDENT | | | | | |

Comments re: Abnormal Findings

| **Please Print/Stamp** |
|---|
| Physician's Name: *Dr. Sheila Clayton, MD* |
| Street Address: *Midland Medical Center* |
| City, State, *Zip Code: Midland* |
| Telephone: *555-555-5555* |

Physician's Signature: *Dr. Sheila Clayton, MD*　　　　Date: *Feb 5*

# Midland School District
## Transcript

### Student Information

| | |
|---|---|
| Name (Last, First, Middle) | Carr, Leslie Marie |
| Address | 118 West Cherry Hill Drive |
| City/State/Zip | Midland |
| Parents | John and Carolyn Carr |
| Telephone | 555-4555 |
| Gender | Female |
| Place of Birth | Midland |
| Date of Birth | Feb. 6 |

### Health Information

| Immunization | Form | Date |
|---|---|---|
| Hepatitis B | HepB # 1 | March 1 |
| | HepB # 2 | April 2 |
| | HepB # 3 | Feb. 6 |
| Diptheria, Tetanus, Pertussis | DTaP#1 | April 2 |
| | DTaP # 2 | June 10 |
| | DTaP # 3 | August 6 |
| | DTaP # 4 | June 15 |
| Tetanus, Diptheria | Td | Feb. 15 |
| Inactivated Poliovirus | IPV # 1 | April 2 |
| | IPV # 2 | June 10 |
| | IPV # 3 | Feb. 6 |
| Varicella | Varicella | June 15 |
| Measles, Mumps, Rubella | MMR # 1 | June 15 |
| | MMR # 2 | Feb. 15 |

Services Plan

# INDIVIDUALIZED EDUCATION PROGRAM (IEP)

Name _Leslie Carr_ Date of Birth _2/6_     Grade Level _6th_    ☐ Male   ☑ Female

Student Identification Number

Child/Student Address _118 W Cherry Hill Dr., Midland_

Parent Address _same_    Home Phone _555-_   Parent/Guardian _John and Carolyn Carr_
                          _4555_   Work Phone _555-4455_

Effective IEP Dates from _4/21_ to _5/31_   Meeting Date _4/21_   ☐ Initial IEP   ☑ Periodic Review

District of Residence _Midland_     District of Service _Midland_

## Step 1  Discuss future planning.
*(Family and student preferences and interests)*

Leslie's parents hope that Leslie will be prepared for college work by the time she graduates from high school. In the meantime, Leslie needs to concentrate on strategies to help her live independently and do college level work. Leslie is less sure of her goals but basically agrees that she should be working towards these goals.

## Step 2  Discuss present levels of academic and functional performance.
*(What do we know about this child, and how does that relate in the context of content standards, or for preschool children, in the context of appropriate activities and how the disability affects the student's involvement in the general education curriculum.)*

Leslie is currently working at grade level in all academic content areas. Due to an automobile accident, Leslie's spine suffered damage resulting in loss of all neuro-motor function in her legs and limits neuro-motor function in her upper torso, arms, and hands. The limited use of her hands impacts her manipulation of objects and writing utensils. A voice-activated computer allows her to complete all written assignments at the 85% accuracy level. Extended time and adaptive equipment allows Leslie to complete manipulative (as needed) tasks at or above the 85% success level.

# INDIVIDUALIZED EDUCATION PROGRAM (IEP)

## Annual Goals and Short-Term Objectives

**Step 3: Identify needs that require specially designed instruction**

Leslie needs to continue to use her voice - activated computer to effectively access the general curriculum in all content areas.

**Step 4: Identify measurable annual goals, including academic and functional goals**

Goal # _____ Content area addressed:

Leslie will use her voice - activated computer for written assignments in all classes and will complete those assignments at 85% or higher success rate.

Benchmarks or short-term objectives

1. Leslie will check accuracy of vocal input meaning she will proof read and correct her work in a manner expected of written work.
2. Leslie will work in learning about her software packages.

**Student Progress**

(Include a description of how the child's progress toward meeting the annual goals will be measured and when periodic reports on the progress the child is making toward meeting the annual goals will be provided.)

Leslie's progress will be monitored by checking her "written" work and through observation of her computer use via a weekly checklist. Her parents will receive progress reports at the interim and end of each grading period.

**Step 5: Identify services**

Related services - consultation with _____

Service: speech therap. Initiation date: 4/21 Expected duration: 1 sch. yr. Frequency: (how often) upon teacher request

(Identify all services needed for the child to attain the annual goal and progress in the general education curriculum. Services may include specially designed instructional, related services, supplementary aids, or, on behalf of the child, a statement of program modifications, testing accommodations, or supports for school personnel)

Leslie needs a voice- activated computer (student-owned).

**Step 6: Determine least restrictive environment**

Determine where services will be provided

(An explanation of the extent, if any, to which the child will not participate with nondisabled children in the regular class.)

100 % of time in general education classroom.

# INDIVIDUALIZED EDUCATION PROGRAM (IEP)

## Annual Goals and Short-Term Objectives

**Step 3:** Identify needs that require specially designed instruction

Leslie needs adapted materials in general education classes where manipulating materials such as shapes, glassware, or substances is required.

**Step 4:** Identify measurable annual goals, including academic and functional goals

Goal # _____ Content area addressed:

Leslie will require materials that are thicker, larger, and/or constrained during hands-on activities where grasping materials, glassware, or substances is necessary. Examples include laboratories, picking up and handling paper materials.

**Benchmarks or short-term objectives**

Leslie will work slowly and carefully when manipulating objects. Leslie will also practice patience in situations which are frustrating to her.

**Student Progress**
(Include a description of how the child's progress toward meeting the annual goals will be measured and when periodic reports on the progress the child is making toward meeting the annual goals will be provided.)

Leslie's progress will be measured through observation and checklist during hands-on activities.
The parents will receive a progress report at interim and end of each grading period.

**Step 5: Identify services**

Related Services – consultation with OTH

Service: OTH _____ Initiation date: 4/2/7 _____ Expected duration: 15ch yr. _____ Frequency: (how often) as needed

(Identify all services needed for the child to attain the annual goal and progress in the general education curriculum. Services may include specially designed instruction, related services, supplementary aids, or, on behalf of the child, a statement of program modifications, testing accommodations, or supports for school personnel)

Leslie will need adaptive materials that are thick enough and large enough for her to pick up. Containers such as beakers should be plastic and when necessary attached in a flat surface. Leslie should have an area during laboratories and activities where spills are a possibility as well as general safety equipment such as goggles.

**Step 6: Determine least restrictive environment**

Determine where services will be provided
(An explanation of the extent, if any, to which the child will not participate with nondisabled children in the regular class.)

100% of time in general education class

# INDIVIDUALIZED EDUCATION PROGRAM (IEP)

## Annual Goals and Short-Term Objectives

**Step 3: Identify needs that require specially designed instruction**

In classes requiring art work, posters, or presentations, Leslie will use the drawing and presentation programs on the computer. This also eliminates any use of scissors which is very difficult for Leslie.

**Step 4: Identify measurable annual goals, including academic and functional goals**

**Goal #** **Content area addressed:**

Leslie will use computer programs such as Paint, Kid Pix, and PowerPoint to create art work, posters, and presentations.

**Benchmarks or short-term objectives**

Leslie will become more adept at using her computer programs.

**Student Progress**
*(Include a description of how the child's progress toward meeting the annual goals will be measured and when periodic reports on the progress the child is making toward meeting the annual goals will be provided.)*

Leslie's progress will be monitored by checking her assignments requiring art or presentations. The parents will receive progress reports at the interim and end of each grading period.

**Related Services** — Consultation math

**Step 5: Identify services**

Service: __OTH__ Initiation date: __4/21__ Expected duration: __1 Sch. Yr.__ Frequency: (how often) __as needed__

*(Identify all services needed for the child to attain the annual goal and progress in the general education curriculum. Services may include specially designed instruction, related services, supplementary aids, or, on behalf of the child, a statement of program modifications, testing accommodations, or supports for school personnel)*

Leslie requires a computer with appropriate drawing and presentation programs (student owned).

**Step 6: Determine least restrictive environment**

**Determine where services will be provided**
*(An explanation of the extent, if any, to which the child will not participate with nondisabled children in the regular class.)*

100% of time in general education classroom.

# INDIVIDUALIZED EDUCATION PROGRAM (IEP)

## Annual Goals and Short-Term Objectives

**Step 3: Identify needs that require specially designed instruction**

Leslie will need extended time for all assignments, written and hands-on. The extended time is necessary to direct the computer programs by voice. A space where Leslie can talk freely is also required.

**Step 4: Identify measurable annual goals, including academic and functional goals**

Goal # _____    Content area addressed: _____

Leslie will require extended time to complete written and hands-on activities in all classes. Leslie will complete all assignments when given the extended time and a space where she will not be disturbed.

**Benchmarks or short-term objectives**

Leslie will take her time and accurately do assignments at the 85% level or higher. Leslie will also practice perseverance in finishing assignments that require drawing using her computer or manipulating materials.

**Student Progress**
(Include a description of how the child's progress toward meeting the annual goals will be measured and when periodic reports on the progress the child is making toward meeting the annual goals will be provided.)

Student progress will be monitored by projects and activities completed. The parents will receive progress reports at the interim and end of each grading period.

---

**Step 5: Identify services**

Related service - consultation with _____
Service: measurative space  Initiation date: 4/21  Expected duration: term yr.  Frequency: (how often) as needed
(Identify all services needed for the child to attain the annual goal and progress in the general education curriculum.  Services may include specially designed instruction, related services, supplementary aids, or, on behalf of the child, a statement of program modifications, testing accommodations, or supports    for school personnel)

Leslie needs the accommodations of a voice-activated computer with appropriate programs, extended time, and space where she can talk comfortably to make computer assignments.

---

**Step 6: Determine least restrictive environment**

**Determine where services will be provided**
(An explanation of the extent, if any, to which the child will not participate with nondisabled children in the regular class.)

100% of time in general education class

# INDIVIDUALIZED EDUCATION PROGRAM (IEP)

## Special Factors

Based on discussions of the information provided regarding relevant special factors and other considerations as noted below, the following is applicable and incorporated into the IEP.

| | Incorporated into IEP (Check box) |
|---|---|
| **Behavior:** In the case of a student whose behavior impedes his or her learning or that of others. | ☐ |
| **Limited English proficiency (LEP)** | ☐ |
| **Children/students with visual impairments** (See IEP page ___) | ☐ |
| **Communication** | ☐ |
| **Deaf or hard of hearing** | ☐ |
| **Assistive technology services and devices** | ☐ |

## Other Considerations

| | |
|---|---|
| Physical education *Jessie participates in community activities in place of school requirement.* | ☑ |
| Extended school year services | ☐ |
| Beginning at age 14...transition service needs which focus on the student's courses of study [See IEP page ___] | ☐ |
| Transition services statement, no later than age 16 [See IEP page ___] | ☐ |
| Testing and assessment programs, including proficiency tests [See IEP page ___] | ☐ |
| Transfer of rights beginning at least one year before the student reaches the age of majority under state law (Ohio law is age 18) | ☐ |

Relevant Information/Suggestions (e.g., medical information, other information):

# INDIVIDUALIZED EDUCATION PROGRAM (IEP)

## Statewide and Districtwide Testing

Student Name: _Leslie Carr_

Student Grade (when scheduled to take this test): _6th_  Student ID: _____

School Year: _____  IEP Meeting Date: _4/31_

### STATEWIDE TESTING

| Areas of Assessment | Grade Level of Test to be Administered | Will Take Test without IEP Accommodations | Will Take Test with IEP Accommodations | Will Participate in Alternate Assessment |
|---|---|---|---|---|
| Reading | 6th Achiev. | | ✓ | |
| Writing | | | | |
| Math | 6th Achiev. | | ✓ | |
| Science | | | | |
| Citizenship | | | | |
| Technology | | | | |
| ITAC | | | | |

### DISTRICTWIDE TESTING

| Grade Level of Test to be Administered | Will Take Test without Accommodations | Will Take Test with Accommodations | Will Participate in Alternate Assessment |
|---|---|---|---|
| | ✓ | | |
| | ✓ | | |
| | | | |
| | | | |
| | | | |
| | | | |
| | | | |

A statement of why the child cannot participate in the regular assessment and will be taking alternate assessment:

_____

Excused from the consequences associated with not passing the test (Graduation Test) in the following area(s) of assessment: _____

Met participation requirements  Yes  No  Date _____
(Graduation Tests)

| Area of Assessment | List Accommodations to Assessment |
|---|---|
| Reading | sep. testing room |
| Writing | computer-assisted tech, extended time, |
| Math | CAT, extended time, sep test room |
| Science | |
| Citizenship | |

| Area of Assessment | List Accommodations |
|---|---|
| Other (Specify) | |
| Other (Specify) | |
| Other (Specify) | |
| Other (Specify) | |
| Other (Specify) | |

# Midland High School

# Transcript

**Student:**  Leslie Marie Carr

**Social Security Number:**

**Total Credits to date:**

**GPA:**

| Courses (by Subject Area) | Grade 9 | Grade 10 | Grade 11 | Grade 12 |
|---|---|---|---|---|
| Freshman English | 90 | | | |
| Sophomore English | | 89 | | |
| American Literature | | | 92 | |
| British Literature | | | | O |
| Algebra I | 95 | | | |
| Algebra II | | 96 | | |
| Geometry | | | 95 | |
| Pre-Calculus | | | | O |
| Physical Science | 97 | | | |
| Biology | | 92 | | |
| Chemistry | | | 98 | |
| Physics | | | | O |
| American History | 88 | | | |
| Government and Politics | | 90 | | |
| World History | | | 88 | |
| Economics | | | | O |
| Spanish I | | 88 | | |
| Spanish II | | | 86 | |
| Spanish III | | | | O |
| Health/Physical Education | NA | NA | | |
| Computers/Keyboarding | 94 | | | |
| Art | 95 | 98 | 96 | O |

*Note. O indicates that course is being taken during the present academic year.*

Transcript Grading Scale

| Letter Grade | Numerical Grade | GPA (4.0 Scale) |
|---|---|---|
| A | 90-100 | 4.0 |
| B | 80 - 89 | 3.0 |
| C | 70 - 79 | 2.0 |
| D | 60 - 69 | 1.0 |
| F | 0 - 59 | 0.0 |

# Standardized Testing Scores

**PSAT (Pre-Scholastic Aptitude Test) Scores**

| Date Taken: | Math | Verbal |
|---|---|---|
| October | 60 | 55 |
|  |  |  |

**SAT (Scholastic Aptitude Test) Scores**

| Test Date: | Math | Verbal |
|---|---|---|
| February | 530 | 500 |
|  |  |  |
|  |  |  |

**SAT II Subject Tests**

| Test Date | Subject | Score |
|---|---|---|
|  | Math II C | 570 |
| May | Writing | 500 |
|  | Chemistry | 530 |

**Birth** | (Last) Carr | (First) Leslie | (Middle) Marie | Sex F ( ✓ M )
**of Birth** Feb (Month) 6 (Day) ____ (Year) | Document of Birth __Certificate__ (Certificate, Passport, etc.)
**City of Birth** Midland (City) ____ (State) | Entered Aug 25 From Home Schooling (Kindergarten)

From ____

| | |
|---|---|
| S.S. No. | No. Brothers: Older ____ Younger ____ |
| | No. Sisters: Older ____ Younger ____ |
| | Father Deceased ( ) Mother Deceased ( ) |
| Withdrew | From ____ To ____ |
| | From ____ To ____ |

**Father** (Last) Carr (First) John (Middle) Allen
Address 118 West Cherry Hill Drive, Midland (in pencil)
Occupation VP Midland Chrysler (in pencil)

**Mother** (Last) Carr (First) Carolyn (Maiden) Davis
Address same (in pencil)
Occupation Homemaker

**Att. Emerg. Guardian** (Last) Shumaker (First) Jennifer (Middle) Davis (in pencil)
Address 1121 Riverhill Dr., Oakville
Occupation Chiropractor

**Stepparent(s)** (Last) ____ (First) ____ (Middle) (in pencil)
Address ____

**Stepparent(s)** (Last) ____ (First) ____ (Middle) (in pencil)
Address ____

## Annual Summary of Grades    Kindergarten - Eighth

| Grade | School Year | Teacher | Days Present | Days Absent | Times Tardy | Reading | Writing | Spelling | English | Math | Social Studies | Science | Health | Phys Ed | Art | Music | Life Skills | Tech-nology | Gifted | General Music | Inst. Music |
|---|---|---|---|---|---|---|---|---|---|---|---|---|---|---|---|---|---|---|---|---|---|
| 1 | 06-07 | Simpson | 170 | 10 | 9 | S | S | S | S | S | S | S | S | 1 | S | S | S | S | | | |
| 2 | 07-08 | Jones | 168 | 12 | 7 | S | S | S | S | S | S | S | S | 1 | S | S | S | A | | | |
| 3 | 08-09 | Moss | 171 | 9 | 7 | B+ | B | B | B | A | A | A | B | 1 | A | B- | B | A | | | |
| 4 | 09-10 | Calendar | 170 | 10 | 6 | B | B | B | B | A | A | A | B | 1 | B+ | B- | B | A | | | |
| 5 | 10-11 | Noel | 172 | 8 | 9 | D+ | B | B | B | A | A | B | B | 1 | A | B- | A | | | | |
| 6 | 11-12 | Griffith | 165 | 15 | 10 | C+ | D- | D+ | C- | C- | D | C- | B | 1 | C | C- | C- | B | | | |
| 7 | 12-13 | Cannes | 166 | 14 | 9 | B | B | B | C+ | B | C+ | A | B | | A | C+ | B | A | | | |
| 8 | 13-14 | Campton | 175 | 5 | 5 | B | B | B | B | B | C+ | A | B | | A | B | A | A | | | |

### Assignment for next year

- second grade
- third grade
- fourth grade
- fifth grade
- sixth grade
- seventh grade
- eighth grade
- ninth grade

# CUMULATIVE RECORD

|  | | |
|---|---|---|
| Name | Carr (Last) | Leslie (First) Marie (Middle) |
| Date of Birth | Feb. 6 | Sex F (✓) M ( ) |
| Place of Birth | Midland (City) | Document of Birth: Certificate |
| Date Entered | Aug. 26 | From: Home Schooling (Kindergarten) |

| | | |
|---|---|---|
| Father | Carr (Last) John (First) Allen (Middle) | Occupation V.P. Midland Chrysler (in pencil) |
| Address | 118 West Cherry Hill Drive, Midland (in pencil) | |
| Mother | Carr (Last) Carolyn (First) Davis (Maiden) | Occupation Homemaker (in pencil) |
| Address | Same | |
| Guardian | Mr. & Mrs. Shumaker (Last) Jennifer (First) Davis (Middle) | Occupation Chiropractor (in pencil) |
| Address | 1121 River Hill Dr., Oakville | |
| Stepparent(s) | (Last) (First) (Middle) | |
| Address | | |
| Stepparent(s) | (Last) (First) (Middle) | |
| Address | | |

S.S. No. _____

No. Brothers: Older ____ Younger ____
No. Sisters: Older ____ Younger ____

Father Deceased ( )
Mother Deceased ( )

Date Withdrew _____

From _____ To _____
From _____ To _____

## Annual Summary of Grades — Kindergarten - Eighth

| School | Grade | School Year | Teacher | Days Present | Days Absent | Times Tardy | Reading | Writing | Spelling | English | Math | Social Studies | Science | Health | Phys. Ed | Art | Music | Life Skills | Tech-nology | Gifted | General Music | Inst. Music |
|---|---|---|---|---|---|---|---|---|---|---|---|---|---|---|---|---|---|---|---|---|---|---|
| CVE | 1 | 06-07 | Simpson | 170 | 10 | 9 | S | S | S | S | S | S | S | S | ✓ | S | S | S | S | | | |
| CVE | 2 | 07-08 | Jones | 168 | 12 | 7 | S | S | S | S | S | S | S | S | ✓ | S | S | S | S | | | |
| CVE | 3 | 08-09 | Moss | 171 | 9 | 7 | B+ | B | B | B | A | A | S | A | ✓ | B+ | A | B- | A | | | |
| CVE | 4 | 09-10 | Callendar | 170 | 10 | 6 | B | B | B | B | A | A | A | B | ✓ | B+ | B- | B | A | | | |
| CVE | 5 | 10-11 | Noel | 172 | 8 | 9 | B | B | B | B | A | B | B | B | ✓ | A | B | B- | A | | | |
| MMS | 6 | 11-12 | Griffith | 165 | 15 | 10 | D+ | B | D- | D+ | C- | C | C | B | ✓ | C | C | C | C-B | | | |
| MMS | 7 | 12-13 | Cannes | 166 | 14 | 9 | C+ | B | B | C+ | B | C+ | A | B | | A | C+ | B | A | | | |
| MMS | 8 | 13-14 | Compton | 175 | 5 | 5 | B | B | B | B | B | A | A | B | | A | B | B | A | | | |

## Assignment for next year

- second grade
- third grade
- fourth grade
- fifth grade
- sixth grade
- seventh grade
- eighth grade
- ninth grade

Grades 9 - 12

**Name** Carr (Last) Leslie (First) Marie (Middle)

**Birthdate** Feb. 6  **Birthplace** Midland

**Address** 118 West Cherry Hill Drive, Midland

**Date Entered** 8/25   **Date Withdrew** —

**Transferred To** —

**Home Phone** 555-4565  **Work Phone** 555-4455

**S. S. No** (in pencil)

**Parent or Guardian**

ADDITIONAL INFORMATION

P.E. - Swimming, Horseback riding, Exempt from school P.E. program

### NINTH — School MHS — Grade 9 H.R. 106

| Subjects | marks 1 sem. | 2 sem. | yr. | units credit |
|---|---|---|---|---|
| Eng. | B | B+ | B | |
| S.S. | B | B+ | B+ | |
| Alg I | A | A | A | |
| Au. | A | A | A | |
| Span I | A+ | B | B | |
| Art | A | A | A | |

days pres. 175  days absc. 5  credits this yr. 6  credits total 6  class rank

### TENTH — School MHS — Grade 11 H.R. 101

| Subjects | marks 1 sem. | 2 sem. | yr. | units credit |
|---|---|---|---|---|
| Eng | B+ | B+ | B+ | |
| S.S. | A | A | A- | |
| R.Sci | A | A | A | |
| Chem | A | A | A | |
| Span III | A | A | A | |
| Art | A | A | A | |
| Bio II | A | A | A | |

days pres. 196  days absc. 4  credits this yr. 7  credits total 20  class rank

### ELEVENTH — School MHS — Grade 10 H.R. 110

| Subjects | marks 1 sem. | 2 sem. | yr. | units credit |
|---|---|---|---|---|
| Eng | B+ | B+ | B+ | |
| S.S. | A | A | A | |
| Alg I | A | A | A | |
| Bio | A | A | A | |
| Span II | A | A | A* | |
| Art | A | A | A | |
| Comp T. | A | A | A | |

days pres. 174  days absc. 6  credits this yr. 7  credits total 13  class rank

### TWELFTH — School MHS — Grade 12 H.R. 105

| Subjects | marks 1 sem. | 2 sem. | yr. | units credit |
|---|---|---|---|---|
| Eng | A | A | A | |
| S.S. | A | A | A | |
| Trig | A | A | A | |
| Phys | A | A | A | |
| P.L.I | A | A | A | |
| Comp D. | A | A | A | |

days pres. 196  days absc. 6  credits this yr. 6  credits total 26  class rank

# Chapter 7

## KIM YU-SHIN

### *Reaching Reluctant English Language Learners*

## EIGHTH GRADE

### Midland Middle School

Kim Yu-shin and his sister Jin-ho, accompanied by their parents and grandmother, arrived at Midland Middle School on the first day of school. Kim Shin was appointed manager of the Cowon Electronics Company in mid-July and has been overseeing the building of the new plant. His children, his wife, Lee Kyung-soon, and his mother, Park Hyun, arrived in Midland 2 weeks ago. The Kim family is the first of many families expected to move to Midland as the plant goes into production.

The entire family has come to enter Yu-shin in school. Mrs. Piper, the school's secretary, notices the family enter the school cautiously, then move quietly to stand in front of her desk, Mr. Kim in the lead. The family stands very straight and tall, with their hands at their sides. Lee Kyung-soon and Park Hyun stand slightly behind Mr. Kim with the children.

In formal and somewhat stilted English, Mr. Kim tells Mrs. Piper that he would like to enroll his children in school. Mrs. Piper, not quite knowing what to do, asks them to wait while she gets the principal. The principal, Mr. Geiser, invites them into his office and after some discussion determines that Jin-ho should be in fifth grade at Clover Valley Elementary School and Yu-shin should be in the eighth grade at Midland Middle School. Mr. Kim is not happy about this, as he expects Yu-shin to look after Jin-ho, and now Jin-ho will be across town at Clover Valley.

Mr. Kim tells the principal that Yu-shin and Jin-ho will study hard and do well. He says that both children will be expected to attend universities in Korea or the United States and that the university will make the children very successful. He explains that the children have desks and study materials at home and that they will be good students. He asks if they will be able to continue their violin lessons, which in Korea had been an important part of their education. Upon further questioning, Mr. Kim explains that the children's permanent records are in Korean and that he will have them translated into English as soon as possible.

Mr. Geiser takes Yu-shin and his family to Mr. Helm's eighth-grade homeroom, introduces the family to Mr. Helms, and tells the other students that Yu-shin will be a member of their class. After some awkward moments and bows all around, Mr. Geiser leaves Yu-shin with Mr. Helms and takes the rest of the family back to the office, where he calls Mrs. Sloan at Clover Valley to let her know to expect the Kims and to give them directions to the school.

After several weeks, Mr. Helms and the rest of Yu-shin's teachers share their experiences. They agree that he is quiet and very respectful, but they admit that it makes them uncomfortable when he bows. They note that he looks at the ground when they talk to him and wonder if he is paying attention to what they say. They are not sure if he is picking up much of the course content material because he rarely speaks, even to the other children. Mr. Helms remarks that he was more than surprised when the Kims showed up for parent-teacher conferences with a bouquet of flowers. A few teachers admit that they are annoyed with Yu-shin. They view his aloofness as arrogance. Some have given up trying to talk with him.

Ms. Hess, his English teacher, explains that she has tried repeatedly to include Yu-shin in the class, only to be rebuffed. She says she was excited about a technique she had read about—giving a student a card that was red on one side and green on the other and asking the child to display the red side when he or she was confused. She told Yu-shin that she would come to his desk to answer his questions when the red side was turned up. After repeated reminders to use the card, Yu-shin continues to leave it in his backpack or slide it under his books. When she insists that he keep it on his desk, he leaves it on green, even when she knows that he is completely lost.

Ms. Hess has also tried pairing him up with other students, but Yu-shin continues to work in his notebook, not acknowledging his study buddy. She thought that pairing him with Sarah Brown was a great idea, but after 15 minutes Sarah stormed up to Ms. Hess's desk, saying that Yu-shin was ignoring her. Thinking maybe this was a gender issue, Ms. Helms tried pairing him with Howard Bailey, but there was no change in Yu-shin's willingness to work with a partner.

Mr. Brandt, the social studies teacher, thinks that Ms. Hess is too worried about Yu-shin. He says that he barely notices Yu-shin, what with having to keep Malcolm Singer and his buddies in line.

Only his science teacher, Mr. Sharp, thinks that Yu-shin is doing just fine. He reports that Yu-shin is attentive in lectures and excellent in completing experiments.

Now, halfway through the year, Yu-shin is doing well in science and math. Much of the science is hands on, and he had excellent instruction in Korea. The math is basically a review for him, and the familiar numbers and equations are comforting. However, he struggles with social studies. He has no background in American history, and the reading demands are far beyond his limited ability to translate English.

In addition, he is appalled by the behavior of his classmates in social studies class. He cannot understand why the Black boy and his friends are continuously laughing and punching each other while the teacher is talking. The noise gets so bad at times that Yu-shin shuts his eyes and remembers his orderly Korean classrooms. He dreams of a time when he can return to Korea and forget that this nightmare in America took place. He contemplates finishing an engineering degree at an American university, then returning to his native community to become a successful scientist who will bring honor to his homeland.

Language arts too is a struggle. He hates to admit this to himself, but he is angry with Ms. Hess. Because his language skills are so poor, most of what she says is lost to him. He keeps up only by translating the written material every night. It is an exhausting but necessary step in trying to get a good grade without embracing the language. His 1 year of studying English in Korea did not prepare him for the extensive readings in English that this class requires. He finds the English language difficult to learn and unpleasant to listen to. Frequently he finds himself shutting out the noise to concentrate on the written word.

Ms. Hess will not leave him alone. He does not understand why she is constantly calling attention to him and why she pairs him with students he does not care to know. He is also humiliated by the red and green card that she has given him. He cannot understand why she would be so cruel as to point out to the whole class that he cannot understand something. He lives in fear that his family will find out that he is disobeying the teacher, but to publicly admit ignorance would disgrace them as well. The stress of being disobedient to the teacher or publicly humiliated keeps him awake at night. Doing poorly in any of his classes causes him great distress because he does not want to bring shame to his family.

Yu-shin finds that studying English back home in his Korean school and using it in the United States are two very different things. He reads slowly and speaks haltingly. Understanding spoken English is very difficult, and he is hampered by the use of unfamiliar words, the ever-present slang, and the fast pace at which everyone seems to speak.

He does not socialize much with the other children because of his limited language ability and his focus on family rather than friends. He doesn't much care for the American classmates he has met. They are loud and call attention to themselves. So many appear to make light of life. They appear to be children rather than young adults. Yu-shin takes his role as eldest son very seriously. When asked to join in after-school activities, he replies that his family obligations require that he be at home.

Yu-shin brings his lunch from home because he finds the school food very odd. The response from his classmates ranges from sincere curiosity to rude, derogatory remarks about what looks and smells strange to them. Yu-shin stoically ignores both the polite and the rude comments.

Each afternoon, Yu-shin walks across town to the elementary school to pick up Jin-ho, and they wait outside for someone to pick them up. Yu-shin is very protective of Jin-ho and takes his role as older brother seriously. If he finds Jin-ho out on the playground running and shouting, he reprimands her in Korean for unseemly behavior, especially if teachers are present. Neither Jin-ho nor Yu-shin remains after school for enrichment programs or sports. Yu-shin says he cannot because his mother needs him to help with shopping and other errands that require someone who speaks some English. Yu-shin says that Jin-ho is needed at home to spend time with their grandmother, who enjoys several soap operas and relies on Jin-ho's very sketchy but imaginative Korean translations. Both children have private music lessons once a week in the evening.

The entire family attends Midland Methodist Church every Sunday for both church service and Sunday school. Their social life outside the family centers on their developing relationship with their church family. The ties in the church remind them of the extended community support they enjoyed in Korea.

## TWELFTH GRADE

### Midland High School

Yu-shin, now a senior, still holds tightly to his Korean heritage and values. As the oldest child and son, he is expected to be a good student and maintain the family's good name while preparing for a future in which he can care for his parents and his grandmother and work for the benefit of his family. He has not adopted the language, dress, mannerisms, values, or interests of his classmates at Midland High School.

Yu-shin is at the top of his class in math and science. His written work is impeccable, but his teachers notice that it takes many drafts and countless hours for him to complete each assignment. Most are quite happy to answer his questions and correct his drafts so that the final version can be as close to perfect as possible. Using these same techniques, he has managed to get good grades even in English and social studies. He still translates much of his reading into Korean, and his room is piled high with the notebooks he has compiled since arriving in Midland 4 years ago.

His spoken English is not as far advanced as his parents and teachers would like. As more Korean families move to the area, Clover Valley Elementary School has begun to look into beginning a program for English Language Learners (ELLs). Over the past few years, some teachers at the high school have attempted to help Yu-shin with his language skills, but he is a reluctant learner. A few have taken time to work with him one on one, but the results have been minimal. He still has trouble with grammar and syntax and has not learned to speak as fluently as his younger sister. His sister has become more savvy about American culture as well, and their parents are beginning to rely on her knowledge and skills more and more.

In fact, the contrast between the brother and sister could hardly be more evident. While Yu-shin clings to his native culture, Jin-ho has become the embodiment of American culture. He prefers the company of his family and the Korean students who have recently moved to Midland. She prefers her American friends, both girls and boys. He still brings his lunch from home. She eats hamburgers and pizza in the cafeteria. He studies at home each afternoon after school. She plays on the ninth-grade girls' basketball team and has been elected cheerleader for the boys' team. The Kims praise Yu-shin for being a dutiful son. The teachers at Midland High praise Jin-ho for being a lively and enthusiastic student and athlete.

Mr. Dalton, one of the high school guidance counselors, has twice called in the brother and sister when their disagreements reached the level of shouting in the hallway. After reading as much as he could find on Korean culture and patiently probing Yu-shin for information, he determined that the young man was feeling estranged from his sister and, most of all, guilty for failing to care for, train, and discipline her. She is an embarrassment to him, and he and the family have lost face because of her behavior. Yu-shin tells Mr. Dalton that his parents are rightfully disappointed in him. He must not have been the good role model Jin-ho needed. He must not have fulfilled his duties as her elder brother.

Mr. Dalton encourages Yu-shin to widen his circle outside the family by joining the boys, mostly Koreans, who play on the Cowon soccer team. Many of the boys are very good, but some are beginners, and Yu-shin finds that he is pretty good—and that he enjoys the camaraderie of the other players. He has found that while many of the boys on the team still retain traditional Korean values, a small group on the Cowon soccer team have embraced the Asian punk scene. These boys have become popular with American students and hang out with the "skater" crowd. Yu-shin is worried that they may influence American perception of Koreans in a negative way.

As the year continues, Yu-shin becomes more and more worried about his future. He knows that he wants to be an engineer and that he will have to leave Midland for a university that offers a good engineering program. But he does not know how to find a university or what to do to be accepted into one. He worries that his family will stay in Midland when he returns to Korea after college. If he does go away to college, how will his family adjust to his being gone? How will he adjust to being away? Will he be as different at college as he has been in Midland? Will he be different when he returns to Korea?

Yu-shin's Cumulative Folder

# CUMULATIVE RECORD

Name: **KIM** (Last)  **YU-SHIN** (First)  _____ (Middle)

Date of Birth: **1** (Month)  **30** (Day)  _____ (Year)  Sex F ( )  M (✓)

Place of Birth: **NonSun, S. Korea** (City) _____ (State)  Document of Birth (Certificate, (Passport), etc.)

Date Entered: **10-1**  From _____

_____ From _____

S.S. No. _____
Father Deceased ( )  No. Brothers: Older _____  Younger _____
Mother Deceased ( )  No. Sisters: Older _____  Younger **1**

Date Withdrew _____  To _____

_____  To _____

---

Father: **KIM** (Last)  **SHIN** (First)  Occupation **Manager** _____ (Middle)
Address: **BIRCH RUN RD.** (in pencil)

Mother: **LEE** (Last)  **KYUNG-SOON** (First) (Maiden)  Occupation **At home** _____ (Middle) (in pencil)
Address _____ (in pencil)

Guardian _____ (Last) _____ (First)  Occupation _____ (Middle)
Address _____ (in pencil)

Stepparent(s) _____ (Last) _____ (First) _____ (Middle)
Address _____ (in pencil)

Stepparent(s) _____ (Last) _____ (First) _____ (Middle)
Address _____

---

Assignment for next year: **9th**

## Annual Summary of Grades    Kindergarten - Eighth

| School | Grade | School Year | Teacher | Days Present | Days Absent | Times Tardy | Reading | Writing | Spelling | English | Math | Social Studies | Science | Health | Phys.Ed | Art | Music | Life Skills | Tech-nology | Gifted | General Music | Inst. Music |
|---|---|---|---|---|---|---|---|---|---|---|---|---|---|---|---|---|---|---|---|---|---|---|
| YMS | 8 | | S. HESS | 150 | 2 | 0 | A | B | B | B | A | A | A | S | S | A | A | | | | | |

# Student Cumulative Record

| Name | | |
|---|---|---|
| Kim (Last) | Yu-Shin (First) | (Middle) |

| Birthdate | Birthplace |
|---|---|
| 1-30 | Nan Sam Korea |

**Address:** Birch Run Rd

| Date Entered | | |
|---|---|---|
| Date Withdrew | | |
| Transferred To | | |

| Home Phone | Work Phone |
|---|---|
| | 555-264... |

**Parent or Guardian:** KIM SHIN

**S.S. No.** (in pencil)

**ADDITIONAL INFORMATION**

---

## NINTH — School Year Grade 9 H.R. 23

| Subjects | marks 1 sem. | marks 2 sem. | yr. | units credit |
|---|---|---|---|---|
| L.A | B | B | B | 1 |
| Alg | A | A | A | 1 |
| S.S. | A | A | - | 1 |
| Bio | A | A | A | 1 |
| Art | A | A | A | 1 |
| Health | A | A | | ½ |
| Phy ed | A | A | | ½ |

credits this yr. / credits total / class rank

---

## TENTH — School Year Grade 11 H.R. 14

| Subjects | marks 1 sem. | marks 2 sem. | yr. | units credit |
|---|---|---|---|---|
| L.A | B | B | B | 1 |
| Alg II | A | A | A | 1 |
| Chem | A | A | A | 1 |
| World Hist | A | A | A | 1 |
| Phy ed | A | A | | ¼ |
| Health | A | A | | ¼ |
| French | A | A | A | 1 |

credits this yr. / credits total / class rank

---

## ELEVENTH — School Year Grade 10 H.R. 18

| Subjects | marks 1 sem. | marks 2 sem. | yr. | units credit |
|---|---|---|---|---|
| L.A | B | B | B | 1 |
| geom | A | A | A | 1 |
| Chem II | A | A | A | 1 |
| Anlaysis | A | A | A | 1 |
| Art III | A | A | A | 1 |
| Computer | A | A | A | ½ |
| Forul LA | A | A | A | 1 |

credits this yr. / credits total / class rank

---

## TWELFTH — School Year Grade H.R.

| Subjects | marks 1 sem. | marks 2 sem. | yr. | units credit |
|---|---|---|---|---|
| | | | | |

credits this yr. / credits total / class rank

---

## OTHER — School Year Grade H.R.

| Subjects | marks 1 sem. | marks 2 sem. | yr. | units credit |
|---|---|---|---|---|
| | | | | |

This record is part of the student's permanent record (cumulative folder), as defined in Section 49063 of the Education Code and shall transfer with that record. Local health departments shall have access to this record in schools, child care facilities, and family day care homes.

**This record must be completed by school and child care personnel from an immunization record provided by parent or guardian. See reverse side for instructions.**

Student Name **Kim Yu-shin**

Sex: M ☑ F ☐   Birthdate **01/30**   Place of Birth **NanSan S.Korea**

Name of Parent or Guardian **Kim Shin**   Address **Birch Run Road**

Telephone **555-3642**   City **Midland**   ZIP _____

Daytime   Nighttime

Race/Ethnicity:
☐ White, not Hispanic
☐ Hispanic
☐ Black
☑ Other: **Asian**

| VACCINE | DATE EACH DOSE WAS GIVEN ||||||
|---|---|---|---|---|---|---|
| | 1st | 2nd | 3rd | 4th | 5th | Booster |
| POLIO (OPV or IPV) | 09/14 | | | | | |
| DTP/DTaP/DT/Td (Diphtheria, tetanus and [acellular] pertussis OR tetanus and diphtheria only) | 11/12 | | | | | |
| MMR (Measles, mumps, and rubella) | | | | | | |
| HIB (Required only for child care and preschool) | | | | | | |
| HEPATITIS B | | | | | | |
| VARICELLA (Chickenpox) | 09/14 | | | | | |
| HEPATITIS A (Not required) | | | | | | |

| TB SKIN TESTS | Type* | Date given | Date read | mm Indur | Impression | CHEST X-RAY (Necessary if skin test positive) |
|---|---|---|---|---|---|---|
| | ☐ PPD-Mantoux ☐ Other | 09/14 | | | ☐ Pos ☐ Neg | Film date: _____   Impression: ☐ normal ☐ abnormal |
| | ☐ PPD-Mantoux ☐ Other | | | | ☐ Pos ☐ Neg | Person is free of communicable tuberculosis: ☐ yes ☐ no |

*If required for school entry, must be Mantoux unless exception granted by local health department.

Name  Kim Y-shin

**Transcripts for Elementary School**(¿µ¹®¼°ÀûÁõ¸í¼-ÃÊµîÇÐ±³)¾ç½ÄÀÔ´Ù.

NOT RECEIVED

**Official Academic Transcripts³É¼¨Ö¤Ã÷ÊéÕý±¾)/(¡õ Junior-high**

| | |
|---|---|
| µµ½ÃÁö¸® (Urban Geography) 3ÇÐÁ¡ | 100 |
| ÄÚ½° ¿î¿µ (English) | 92 |
| ¼öÇÐ(Mathematics) | 100 |
| ±×¸®°í Ã¼À°(Physical Education) | 100 |
| ÀÎ¹® °úÇÐ È¤À° »çÈ¸ °úÇÐ (Humanities or Social Science) | 98 |
| ¸¹è¿ó´Ù.(Japanese) | 100 |
| ½È¾îÇÕ´Ù (Science) | 100 |
| ¹Ì¼ú (Arts) | 100 |
| À½¾Ç (Music) | 100 |
| ±¹¾ (Korean Literature) | 100 |

# Part II

# ACTIVITIES

In Part II, you will find many activities that will help prepare you to build on the student diversity that you will inevitably find in your future classrooms and schools. You will empathize with Ms. Morgan as she meets her students on the first day of school. You will learn strategies for getting to know your students as the complex, different, and interesting people that they are. You will practice designing lesson plans that meet the instructional needs of *all* your students. You will learn how to communicate with your students' families—who will, of course, be as diverse as they are. And you will learn that there is no such thing as "the class," but rather an extraordinarily rich and varied collection of individuals who with skill and perseverance can be woven into a powerful and empowering learning community.

# Chapter 8

## GETTING TO KNOW YOUR LEARNERS

In this chapter, you will revisit the profiles and cumulative folders of Casey, Sarah, Malcolm, Leslie, Raul, and Yu-shin in Part I.

In Activity 1, you will work as a group to learn about your student and to discuss what questions or concerns you might have about teaching this child in your classroom.

In Activity 2, you will study the information given in a child's story and use your research skills to find the answers to any words or concepts that you don't yet understand.

In Activity 3, you will use a variety of resources to prepare a report on a particular disability.

In Activity 4, you will respond to two scenarios that will give you practice in getting to know your students.

In Activity 5, you will develop a plan for the educational needs of a student.

## ACTIVITY 1: MEETING THE STUDENTS

### Directions

Divide into groups according to your licensure area. Choose a child who is profiled in Part I. Have one person in your group read aloud the student's profile to the group. Read only as far as your intended level of licensure. For example, if you are intending to teach in the middle grades, read only the first two sections of the biography. Follow these directions to complete this exercise:

1. Talk about your perceptions and reactions to the child coming into your classroom.

2. Discuss any questions or concerns that you might have about teaching this child.

3. As a group, look through the student's cumulative folder and discuss the contents. Again, read only as far as your intended area of licensure.

4. Discuss what the documents might add to your understanding of this child.

5. As a group, complete the activities in Exercise A.

6. As a group, complete the activities in Exercise B.

7. Use the rubric to assess your group.

## Exercise A

### As a Group

1. List descriptors that are used to identify this child's background, personality, behavior, and learning style.

2. In a paragraph, describe this child in **unbiased terms**.

## Exercise B

### As a Group

1. List all sources that you could use to find out more information about this child. List at least five different people or sources.

2. Describe some strategies you could use to get to know this child on a more personal level. Describe how you would begin to find out how to reach this child academically.

**Box 8.1**      Rubric for Activity 1

| Unacceptable | Acceptable | Exemplary |
|---|---|---|
| Lack of group participation | Some group participation evident | Equal participation |
| Few descriptors | Missed descriptors | Complete descriptors |
| Biased description | Some bias terms | Bias-free description |
| Incomplete sources | General sources | Dynamic sources |
| No strategies listed | Some general strategies | Specific and useful strategies |

# ACTIVITY 2: FOCUSING ON SPECIAL NEEDS

## Directions

With a partner in the same licensure area and same discipline area, choose a child who is profiled in Part I. Read through the profile and the child's cumulative folder. As in Activity 1, read only as far as the level of your intended license area. Then complete the following exercises. You may use any source in any location to complete this activity.

1. List and find the definitions for all words in the case study and cumulative folder that are unfamiliar.

2. Answer the following questions about the cumulative folder and cite the source of your answer.

**Box 8.2**

| Question | Source |
|---|---|
| What is the child's IQ? | |
| What is the average range for IQ? | |
| What is a stanine score? | |
| What is a high percentile? | |
|   Low percentile? | |
| What does "on grade level" mean? | |
| What are grade-level descriptors for this child? | |
| List the tests used in this folder. | |
|   What do they measure? | |

3. Answer the following questions about the IEP (individualized education program) (if included in the child's folder):

   • What is an IEP? Who has one?

   • What is the least restrictive environment?

   • Who is on the IEP team?

   • What are the goals for this child?

   • How will a teacher know when the child has met these goals?

   • When is the next evaluation?

   • Does this child receive extended or year-round services?

   • What are the child's present levels of performance?

   • What is the identified disability or special need of this child?

   • What do you know about this disability? How do you know about it?

**Box 8.3**     Rubric for Activity 2

| Unacceptable | Acceptable | Exemplary |
|---|---|---|
| Some questions are not answered and few are supported with a source | All questions are answered but not all are supported with a source | All questions are answered correctly and supported with a source |

## ACTIVITY 3: EXPANDING YOUR RESOURCES

### Directions

Choose a child from Part I who has the exceptionality you wish to investigate. Then compile the following information in separate sections, listing the references in APA style.

1. Using at least two popular or news periodicals, describe what the general public might know about this exceptionality.

2. Using at least two parenting magazines or Web sites, describe what advice is given to parents about children with this exceptionality.

3. Using at least two popular teacher magazines or Web sites, describe what educators have to say about this exceptionality in the classroom.

4. Using at least three professional journals, describe the latest research on this exceptionality.

5. Compare and contrast the information you have discovered.

6. Write an analysis of how this information informs you as an educator to work with this child, talk to parents, and plan strategies for this child.

**Box 8.4**      Rubric for Activity 3

| Unacceptable | Acceptable | Exemplary |
|---|---|---|
| Lack of good summarization of information or inappropriate sources of information used | Summary of information given in appropriate sources | Correct use of and description of information in appropriate sources. |
| No attempt to use the information to address the needs of the child | Some comparing and contrasting of the information in the types of sources | Summary of articles that compares and contrasts the content of the types of sources |
| No use of APA | Use of information in addressing the needs of this child | Use of information to analyze how to address the needs of this child |
| Several grammatical errors | Few mistakes in APA and grammar | Correct use of APA references<br>Few grammatical errors |

# ACTIVITY 4: KNOWING YOUR STUDENTS

## Exercise A

Fill in the blank with the name of one of the children in the profiles in Part I.

You have been asked to coach [name of sport] for the community recreation board. At sign-up, you notice that you have _____ on your team. Consider these needs: full inclusion for success, acceptance by peers, participation by parents, handling peer and parent resistance, and making this a rewarding experience for all. How will you accommodate the special needs of this child to achieve these goals—and maybe even win a game or two?

## Exercise B

Read the profile of Raul in Chapter 5 or Yu-shin in Chapter 7. As the teacher, you wish to introduce one of these children to the rest of your class. Research the home country of this student, giving particular attention to cultural norms. Be sure to encourage the other children to welcome the new student. Write your introduction or present it orally to your group or to the class.

# ACTIVITY 5: DEVELOPING AN EDUCATIONAL PLAN

## Exercise A

### Directions

In order to best serve our students, we need to understand their nature and needs. In this activity, you will describe the nature and needs of a learner in one of the profiles, describe what services have been provided for the student, and develop a "next steps" plan for the student.

Select a student from one of the profiles. For that student, complete the following analysis by reading the profile from Part I and relevant school and community information from Chapter 1. You will not be able to find all the information for each student. Use objective words to describe your student. Then develop a response based on the questions and guidelines provided below.

Part I: Analysis—Find as much of the following information as you can.

1. The child: Demographics: gender, age, grade

   - Current family information
   - Relevant family history (include patterns of moving)
   - Description of initial identification process and results for the disability or giftedness designation (when, what label, what initial services, etc.)
   - Current identification with respect to disability or giftedness designation
   - Current academic achievement levels or specific skills (from IEP and/or teacher evidence)

· Current **adaptive behavior** strengths and challenges
· Current **social behavior** strengths and challenges
· Current functioning within at least one of the developmental theories
· (e.g., Piaget, Vygotsky, Erikson, Kohlberg)

2. The service: (Be sure to review the child's IEP or other specialized plans)

· Include relevant school demographics
· What access to the general curriculum does the child have?
· What other services are provided?
· Who provides the services? For how long?
· What adaptations (accommodations and modifications) are made for the student?
· What evidence have you seen or do you have?
· What do the general education teacher, special education teacher, child, and/or parent believe is working? What evidence is there to support this conclusion?
· What, if anything, does one or more of the above individuals believe to be ineffective? What evidence is there to support this conclusion?
· What would one or more of the above individuals recommend to add to or change the services?

Part II: The Response

1. The plan: Based on what you have learned from your exploration of this child, what would you recommend for the general education and/or special education teacher to do and/or provide the rest of the year? You may include service providers other than teachers.

Format: The analysis section can be written in bullet format. The response section should be written in narrative form.

# Exercise B

## Directions

Select a child with special needs as determined by your instructor, for example, from a field experience, tutoring assignment, or another set of cases. Complete the analysis as you did for Exercise A. Complete the plan as you did for Exercise A. Then answer the following questions:

1. How is what you saw and heard consistent and inconsistent with what you have learned to date in this and other courses in your teacher education program?

2. How have your knowledge, values, and perceptions about students' special needs changed as a result of your work on this case study?

3. If there are no changes in your knowledge, values, and perceptions, what reinforced what you already knew?

Format: The analysis section can be written in bullet format. The response section should be written in narrative form.

**Box 8.5**        Rubric for Activity 5

| Criteria | Exemplary | Excellent | Satisfactory | Unsatisfactory |
|---|---|---|---|---|
| Accuracy 5 points | XXXXXX | Product contains no inaccuracies with respect to terminology or relationships among terms | One minor inaccuracy in use of terminology that did not affect overall portrayal of student | More than one inaccuracy or misinterpretation |
| Analysis Evidence 10 points 5-child 5-service | 7 of 8 descriptors of child; 7 of 8 descriptors of service (at excellent level) Current functioning within at least one of the developmental theories (e.g., Piaget, Vygotsky, Erikson, Kohlberg) | 6 of 8 meaningful, detailed, objective descriptors of child; 6 of 8 meaningful, detailed, objective descriptors of service | 6 of 8 objective descriptors of child; 6 of 8 objective descriptors of service | Less than 6 objective descriptors of child or less than 6 objective descriptors of service OR descriptors are not objective |
| Response 8 points 4-plan 4-answers | In-depth plan and answers to questions tightly linked to evidence in analysis section | Clear plan and answers to all questions clearly linked to evidence in analysis section | Basic plan and answers to all questions consistent with evidence in analysis section | Either plan or answers to questions incomplete or inconsistent with evidence in analysis section |
| Format 2 points | Creative use of guidelines, professionally completed | Followed guidelines, professionally completed | Generally followed guidelines, professional grammar | Did not follow guidelines; grammar and/or proofing errors |

Total points:

4 – Exemplary:        25 points
3 – Excellent:        23–24 points
2 – Satisfactory:     20–22 points
1 – Unsatisfactory:   Less than 20 points

# Chapter 9

## DESIGNING ENVIRONMENTS THAT SUPPORT YOUR LEARNERS

One of the biggest surprises for teacher candidates in field experiences and clinical practices is the variety of needs—academic, social, emotional, and physical—that children bring to the real-life classroom. Facing a group of like-minded peers in a peer teaching exercise is nothing like facing a roomful of children in a real classroom. The prospective teacher learns very quickly that he or she does not "just teach" but must develop a classroom environment in which all students are supported in ways that promote their growth as whole persons. In this chapter, you will examine the influence of background and ability in designing classroom and school environments that support *all* students.

In Activity 1, you will be introduced to Ms. Morgan, a new eighth-grade science teacher, as she meets her students on the first day of school.

In Activity 2, you will discover what it is like to be on the misunderstood side of a cultural experience.

In Activity 3, you will discover strategies for designing and implementing a schoolwide behavior plan that will meet the needs of your highly diverse learners.

In Activity 4, you will respond to several scenarios that will give you practice in responding to your students in ways that increase their motivation and engagement in learning.

You may find it helpful to review the profiles in Part I before you begin these activities.

## ACTIVITY 1: UNDERSTANDING THE CULTURAL, SOCIAL, AND EMOTIONAL NEEDS OF YOUR STUDENTS—THE FIRST DAY OF SCHOOL

It is August 29, and Ms. Heather Morgan, a new teacher, stands in front of her first period eighth-grade science class at Midland Middle School. In her class of 27 students, she has Malcolm, who is busy scraping the wood off the side of his chair; Sarah, who has her face buried in the latest best seller; Raul, in the front row ready to go; Leslie, protesting loudly that she cannot wheel up to the lab tables; and an assortment of other students in varying degrees of attentiveness. The administration has not prepared her to accommodate a student in a wheelchair, and Leslie sits below table level, audibly upset. A quiet dark-haired boy who says his name is Yu-shin, but whose name is not on the roster, sits staring blankly from the side of the room. In attempting to make pleasantries with him, Ms. Morgan discovers that he understands very little English.

Ms. Morgan had enthusiastically accepted the position at Midland because she had grown up in the area and felt comfortable with the community, but the community has changed. She expected to deal with lower-income students, and she knew that she might have a student from the new section of town where several Mexican families reside, but she is surprised to find that Yu-shin is here, and she wonders where he is from and how he ended up in Midland. Malcolm is another surprise. He doesn't seem to be paying any attention to what is happening around him. As Ms. Morgan begins to call roll, Malcolm dashes out the door. Leslie has wheeled around to the front of her desk and is asking for her own desk. Casey wanders in and slides back to prop his feet on the wall. As she moves to ask him politely to take his feet down, she hears a crash from the hall. Sarah complains that science is starting off to a boring start, and Yu-shin puts his hands over his face.

Ms. Morgan is committed to the idea that through hard work, she and her students will be successful. After all, it has previously worked for her. Her own family owned their own farm, her parents did not attend college, and through her and her family's effort, she has attained a college education. Her life lessons have shown that anyone can make it if they try hard enough. Suddenly, she fears that her students do not share her work ethic.

As she struggles through the first 30 minutes of her day, she abandons her detailed lesson on phosphorescence to explain the basic vocabulary of "light." By the end of the period, she has serious doubts if her well-designed lesson plans for the unit will work at all. Casey wasn't able or willing to read a paragraph, Malcolm refused to open his book when he returned to class after a short absence, Yu-shin spent the whole period looking down at his desk, and only Leslie, content to use Ms. Morgan's desk, participated. Most disturbing to Ms. Morgan, though, is that the students didn't seem to care. Even Sarah, who seemed to be able to answer questions asked of her, did not volunteer any information. The majority of her class remained inattentive and distracted all day. Without support, a deep commitment to understanding the varied needs of her students, and the ability to make the content relevant and understandable to them, she may end up in the 50% of new teachers who quit the field within the first 3 years (Hirsch, 2002). Worse yet, her students will have spent another year with a teacher who, through not understanding the social as well as academic needs of her students, has discouraged them from discovering the value and beauty of science. Knowing that she has tried very hard and not been successful, Ms. Morgan may leave the field believing that her students, their parents, and the school were just too "bad." It was they who "didn't try hard enough." If this belief is revealed through her behavior during her last year of teaching, students may see themselves as failures also. The gap between them and education grows wider for each of them every time this occurs.

Many new teachers find themselves in Ms. Morgan's position. While Midland is still a community that is dominated by its European American citizens, students not exclusively of European descent now make up 40% of all students nationwide (Institute of Educational Sciences, 2004). One in five lives in poverty (U.S. Dept. of Education. National Center for

Educational Statistics, 1999), and over 6.2 million students were served by IDEA in 2002 (Digest of Educational Statistics, 2002). Teachers, though, are still primarily White (90%) and middle class (U.S. Dept. of Education, National Center of Educational Statistics, 1999).

According to Sleeter and Grant (1999), "There has always been a gap between teachers and students, resulting from age and role and often compounded by the differences in cultural background. This gap has recently been expanded, as an increasing number of students come from homes with alternative life styles and family arrangements. Some teachers bridge this gap and grasp the differences in student culture and life style fairly well; others do not, interpreting student behavior as part of the natural order of things that teachers need to control and discourage from being reproduced" (p. 29). The implication of any disparity becomes increasingly obvious if the powerful influence of student background and expectations on daily classroom life is considered (Fuller, 1992). These differences guide the way students and teachers behave, respond, and perform in school. Differences between student cultures and teacher culture will create dissonance unless the teacher can integrate the students' backgrounds into the curriculum and create a supportive environment for learning (Gollnick & Chinn, 2002). Because teachers gain the bulk of their knowledge through continuous reflection on everyday problems (Schon, 1987), as teachers reflect on the individual styles of students, they can build bridges between the dominant school culture and the various diverse cultures and learning styles of their students (Brown & Kysilka, 2002). But to be effective, teachers must first be aware that these differences exist. They must also believe that these differences do not mean that students are morally or intellectually deficient.

The position statement on Developmentally Appropriate Practice in Early Childhood Programs Serving Young Children From Birth Through Age 8 (NAEYC, 1996) describes three types of information and knowledge that are important to early childhood professionals, but these three can apply to teachers of students of all ages.

1. Knowledge about child development, age-related human characteristics that permit general predictions within an age ranges about what activities, materials, interactions, or experiences will be . . . interesting, achievable, and challenging to all children.

2. Knowledge about strengths, interests, and needs of each individual child in a group to be able to adapt for and be responsive to inevitable individual variation.

3. Knowledge of the social and cultural contexts in which children live to ensure that learning experiences are meaningful, relevant, and respectful for the participating children and their families. (pp. 4–5)

Because the realities of our school population are changing, many of the issues that were once the domain of the home and family and other community institutions are expected to be addressed by the teacher and the school. Without consideration of the cultural, family backgrounds, and social needs of students, the success in addressing these issues is at risk. Feeding hungry students at school addresses a poverty issue, but lack of consideration of dietary restrictions, religious fasting, or older students' embarrassment at admitting poverty can render the program ineffective.

In addition, some public and school personnel perceptions that academic failure can be primarily attributed to certain characteristics of the child or the child's family excuses the school and teacher from making beneficial changes in the structure of school and curriculum for historically marginalized students. By assuming that the much reported success of Asian students can be solely attributed to the hard work and a natural inclination toward math and science or that the lack of success of poor and African American students is due to a lack of ability or motivation allows teachers to continue having low expectations and using negative differential treatment toward some students.

As much research has shown, low expectations in and of themselves create disenfranchised students who develop low expectations for themselves. In fact, low self-esteem, a disconnect between home and school culture, and a lack of hope for the future are some of the dominant social characteristics that may lead a child to academic failure (Neito, 2004). This can be seen in the profile of Malcolm Singer. Schools themselves sometimes foster these social characteristics by choosing structural methods that separate children who are different from the dominant cultural norms. Inflexible scheduling and schedules based on historic rather than family needs, calendars that reflect only Christian holidays, tracking or ability grouping students, high-stakes testing, Eurocentric curriculum, separation of students with special needs from the general population, and lack of inclusion of children in decision making about curricular or extracurricular activities all contribute to the separateness felt by many students from their school. The profile of Raul illustrates the power of these systemic barriers.

Schools and teachers can help bridge this gap and better meet the social needs of students by valuing all students through the structure, curriculum, and treatment of all students. First, teachers and administrators must be convinced that they are responsible for all students' learning and well-being. Understanding the complexities that differences create in a perception of a situation is vital to feeling unthreatened by a student's challenge to authority or curriculum. All staff of a school must be willing to get to know all students with whom they will come in contact. Ways to find out about student background include the use of interest inventories, sociograms, discussions after readings, response questions, parent-teacher meetings, talking to previous teachers, class meetings, reading official documents about students, and observing group interaction. Listening to students with an open mind can give great insight to teachers into how their students perceive and process knowledge and if any ways of learning are more comfortable for them.

Getting rid of preconceived assumptions that have been reinforced through the media and ethnocentric beliefs is difficult. Teachers need to know that simply understanding why a child is disconnected because of unfamiliarity or lack of relevance of a lesson can make a big difference in the way they may approach that child. A 1-day professional development session on multicultural education cannot remedy a situation in which a teacher is at a complete loss as to how to reach a non-English-speaking child such as Kim Yu-shin and Raul Ramirez, who immigrate at different times in their lives but still need both emotional and academic support to survive in their new environment. It is vital that school systems support teachers and other staff members with programs designed to model and reinforce inclusive environments in their own classrooms and schools. Schools must have on staff a person who can connect teachers with a variety of strategies and support agencies to meet varied needs of students. A permanent staff member could also be in a classroom to offer feedback and share in the responsibilities of involving families. Intervention specialists need to team teach in the regular classroom to provide academic and social support for all students. Casey's frustration could have been lowered by continuous support in his inclusion classes.

In addition, it is important to create a culture of belonging, a community of learners in a school where each child feels welcomed and the focus remains on the strengths, not the weaknesses, of each individual. This would mean ensuring that all students have the opportunity to participate in and be involved in both decision making and implementation of significant school activities. Having some control over the environment allows students to feel empowered and capable. This raises self-esteem and confidence. In the case of Sarah Brown, having self-selection might have encouraged her to continue to excel in school rather than waste her time and be satisfied with less than her best performance. Images and symbols displayed in the classroom should reflect the membership and contribution of all students. Perhaps in Raul Ramirez's case, understanding the different expectations of his community and displaying Latino contributions to American and world history might have lessened his feelings of not belonging anywhere.

All members of the school community need to be sensitized to the importance of using equitable language in describing other members of the school (Hixson & Tinzmann, 1990). Teachers need to provide opportunities for students to discover what is meaningful to them and what they do well. The need to belong is one of Maslow's basic human needs. Teachers need to prioritize their classrooms to be an inclusive environment where all students can have the opportunity to feel as if they belong. Having met this more basic need, students can then feel more confident in reaching the higher needs of self-esteem and self-actualization in terms of academic success.

Creating a classroom of belonging means that it must be a place where competition is minimized and cooperation is emphasized. Competition should be kept to low-risk situations in which losing is not seen by students as defeat or humiliation. A nonthreatening environment will encourage risk taking both academically and socially. In some cases, students have specific social needs that reflect a lack of exposure in the home to good strategies for coping with everyday frustrations. Both Casey and Raul lack appropriate social knowledge that would help them to be accepted by their peers. At times, students also lack the anger management skills to positively express frustration, such as demonstrated by Malcolm. In these cases, teachers need to be in tune to what the students bring with them. Teaching social and anger management skills through direct instruction, goal setting, using social stories, and modeling may help individual students (Frye, 2005). Other strategies may be learned by the teacher to help individual students with depression, conduct disorders, or learned helplessness. Again, teachers need the support of the school community to become teachers who can support the social needs of students.

Meeting the social needs of students then can be ensured if all teachers do the following:

- Set high expectations for all students
- Make the classroom a positive environment where students can feel good about themselves
- Create opportunities for self-selection in curriculum and decisions affecting classroom climate
- Understand that students' cultural and family backgrounds greatly impact their attitudes and behaviors in the classroom, as does the cultural and family background of the teachers
- Recognize that the dissonance created by the differences in backgrounds does not indicate a deficit in the students
- Recognize that bridging the gap between school and home for students can increase student motivation and performance

- Recognize that it is their job to understand that all students have emotional and social needs that must be met to create an environment that supports all learners
- Recognize that it is their job to ensure that all learning experiences are relevant, meaningful, and respectful
- Work as advocates to make the school structure inviting and comfortable for all students
- Work to create a classroom and school environment that is inclusive, nonthreatening, and a culture of belonging
- Put support systems into place for both teachers and students
- Understand that it is their job to learn ways to specifically help individual students with individual needs

Designing an environment that supports all learners is a career-long task. If a teacher has this goal in mind, with each new experience, he or she will increase the possibility of encouraging students to become self-reliant individuals who are capable of setting and reaching their own goals.

Consider the following:

1. What are some disconnects between schools and students?

2. What are some ways that you would use to find out about your students' family and cultural backgrounds?

3. Describe some simple ways that you could create a classroom of "cultural belonging."

4. How would you feel on the first day of class if you encountered the problems that Ms. Morgan encountered?

5. How was your school different from or the same as your cultural and family background? List ways in which this fostered success or stress for you.

## ACTIVITY 2: EXPERIENCING CULTURAL DIFFERENCES

All teachers must become aware of the influences of culture, gender, religion, socioeconomic status, sexual orientation, language, and disabilities on their students in order to be inclusive teachers who can create an environment and lessons that will meet the needs of all learners. Not being aware of the influences that guide the perception and behavior of students can lead to teachers creating an unnecessary disengagement for students between the student and the school, the teacher, and the curriculum.

Consider this:

### The Parent-Teacher Conference

Imagine you are a parent from Midland, a community that like some Western cultures values independence, who has moved to the Far East into a fictitious culture that values dependency and reliance on immediate and extended family, like some Eastern cultures. As a parent, you notice that your child is not faring well in her new school. You prepare for the first parent-teacher conference by drawing up a list of questions designed to find out why your child is not doing well in subjects in which she previously excelled, such as creative writing. You plan to be actively involved in her education, and you are willing to help at home.

At the meeting, you find the teacher polite, but distant. A young man who is majoring in languages at the local university will interpret for you, but you are unsure of his ability to accurately convey your message. His English seems sketchy. When you bring out the last composition that your daughter wrote and ask why it received such a low grade, the teacher looks puzzled. After some back and forth dialogue between the teacher and interpreter, the interpreter relays the following information. The teacher is perplexed that you are questioning her grading at all. Again, some dialogue is exchanged, then she seems embarrassed as she painfully describes through the young man that your daughter wrote the composition about herself. She explains that it is not her intent to have her students "self-cherish" in their schoolwork. The aim of all education is to transcend self-worship and become part of the whole. To do this, students must not dwell on themselves. She looks embarrassed to have to spell this out to you.

As the conversation continues, you mention that you have provided everything, including a computer and book resources in your daughter's bedroom that she has had since she was 4, to help her advance her education. Again, the teacher looks embarrassed. The young man lets you know that she politely suggests that maybe part of your daughter's problems in school could be due to the early and unnatural separation of her from her parents or the family bed. She says she is subtly trying to curb your daughter of emoting. She tells you that your daughter's unhealthy need to express her feelings makes the other children uncomfortable.

As you leave the school very perplexed by the conference, hoping that the interpreter was mistaken, the teacher closes with the friendly send-off that she hopes for your daughter to be surrounded by blessed family members her whole life.

In this scenario, the teacher did not try to understand your family, your culture, or your background to better address the needs of your child. You feel frustrated that perhaps the interpreter was unable to convey your concerns. If the situation continues, it most likely will result in your daughter's confusion and possible feelings of alienation from school and schoolmates. As long as the teacher sees the cultural differences as cultural deficiencies, she will continue to grade accordingly. How much failure will it take to make your daughter see herself as a failure? How many times might this have happened to new immigrants to our own culture?

Questions to consider:

1. What assumptions does the parent make about school?

2. What assumptions does the teacher make about family?

3. What are the major contradictions in the perceptions of the parent and the teacher about the following:

   • Expectations and goals for students

   • The role of a teacher

   • The role of the family

- How "good" people behave
- How the daughter can be successful

4. How could the teacher have made the parent more comfortable?

5. What conclusions can you draw about communicating with parents from another culture when you become a teacher?

## ACTIVITY 3: CREATING A POSITIVE LEARNING ENVIRONMENT FOR ALL STUDENTS

Background: Many schools are moving toward systems of schoolwide positive behavioral support (PBS) to increase appropriate behavior, decrease inappropriate behavior, and provide more intensive behavioral interventions for students who have the greatest behavioral challenges. Midland Middle School moved in that direction when it adopted a schoolwide behavioral support plan for the building. The purposes of these exercises are to explore the concept of **schoolwide positive behavioral support**, consider why Midland Middle School faculty and administration may have thought this was the direction they needed to take, and analyze how Midland's use of a schoolwide behavioral support plan might have a positive impact on (a) the challenges detailed in the school description and (b) the needs of Casey, Sarah, Malcolm, Raul, Leslie, and Yu-shin.

 *Please note:* The term *schoolwide positive behavioral support* is very similar to *effective behavioral support* and *positive behavioral support*. As you look for descriptions, you may want to try more than one of the terms to get the best definitions and examples.

### Exercise A

1. Break into small groups as directed by your instructor. Answer these questions in whatever format your instructor chooses: oral report, written summary, or poster presentation.

2. Using Web-based professional resources or professional journals, explore the concept of *schoolwide positive behavioral support*. What is it? On what principles is it developed? Is there a research base to support it? If so, what does it reveal?

3. In the professional literature, find examples of middle schools that implemented schoolwide positive behavioral support. What impact did the system have on those buildings?

### Exercise B

1. Divide into small groups as determined by your instructor.

2. Pretend that you are the initial teaching members of the Midland Middle School positive behavioral support team that has just assembled to consider developing a schoolwide positive behavioral support plan. In your first meeting, the principal raises the following questions. How would you answer these questions? Use whatever format your instructor chooses for your product: simulated team meeting, oral report, written summary, or poster presentation.

**Box 9.1**    Rubric for Activity 3, Exercise A

| Criteria | Unacceptable | Acceptable | Exemplary |
|---|---|---|---|
| Accuracy | More than one inaccuracy or misinterpretation | One minor inaccurate statement of information or misinterpretation | Product contains no inaccuracies |
| Depth | Used one source and/or did not answer all questions | Used two appropriate sources<br><br>Clearly answered all questions | Used at least three appropriate sources<br><br>Answered all questions in depth with more than one example |
| Format | Did not follow guidelines<br><br>Multiple grammar errors | Generally followed guidelines<br><br>No grammar errors | Creative use of guidelines<br><br>No grammar errors |

- How are the principles of schoolwide positive behavioral support consistent with the principles of middle school education? (To answer this you may need to go online to explore middle-level education principles and philosophy.)
- What challenges do we now have at Midland Middle School that developing a school-wide behavioral support plan might help us address? How?
- What first steps should we take as a committee?
- Who else do we need to add to our planning and implementation team? Why?
- Should parents and/or community members be involved at this stage in the process? Why or why not?

## Exercise C

1. Divide into small groups as determined by your instructor. Decide which team member will represent each of the middle school children in the profiles.

2. Skim all six middle school profiles, with a focus on the student you will represent. Share with your group social-emotional characteristics and behaviors your student exhibits that should be considered as a schoolwide behavioral support plan is developed.

3. How might the implementation of a schoolwide positive behavioral support plan (as described in the literature or in your Exercise A plan) have a positive impact on your student's attitudes and/or behavior?

4. How might such a plan have a potentially negative impact on your student's attitudes and/or behavior?

5. Develop your product in whatever format your instructor chooses: oral report, written summary, or poster presentation.

**Box 9.2**      Rubric for Activity 3, Exercise B

| Criteria | Unacceptable | Acceptable | Exemplary |
|---|---|---|---|
| Accuracy | Multiple inconsistencies with PBS and/or middle school philosophy resulting from misconceptions of either or both concepts | Basically consistent with PBS and/or middle school philosophy<br><br>Inconsistencies that do not change the basic message | Answers fully consistent with both PBS and middle school philosophy |
| Depth | Did not answer all questions and/or did not refer to an outside resource | Answered all questions and cited one outside resource | Answered all questions in depth with several examples<br><br>Cited two professional resources |
| Format | Did not follow guidelines<br><br>Grammar and/or proofing errors | Generally followed guidelines<br><br>No grammar errors | Creative use of guidelines<br><br>No grammar errors |

**Box 9.3**      Rubric for Activity 3, Exercise C

| Criteria | Unacceptable | Acceptable | Exemplary |
|---|---|---|---|
| Accuracy | Multiple inconsistencies with PBS and your student's biography | Answers basically consistent with PBS and/or your student's biography | Answers fully consistent with the principles of PBS and your student's biography |
| Depth | Did not answer all questions and/or provide any support for impact statements | Answered all questions in depth with some support for potential positive and negative impact | Answered all questions in depth with solid support for potential positive and negative impact |
| Format | Did not follow guidelines<br><br>Grammar and/or proofing errors | Followed guidelines<br><br>No grammar errors | Creative use of guidelines<br><br>No grammar errors |

## ACTIVITY 4: SUPPORTING YOUR LEARNERS

### Exercise A

Choose a child from the profiles in Part I. On your own or with a partner, develop a plan to make this child feel socially included in your classroom. Be prepared to justify your plan with information from the biographies, the cumulative folders, and your own research and experiences.

### Exercise B

Fill in the blanks below with the name of one of the children in the profiles in Part I.

You have noticed that _____ is usually eating lunch alone. In class, when you assigned group work today, Emily refused to work with _____. Pulling Emily aside, you discover that she doesn't want to work with _____ because he or she is "too different" and doesn't work well with others. Emily says that everyone feels this way, and she is tired of trying to work with _____. Emily says that you should let everyone choose his or her own groups.

How will you handle this situation?

### Exercise C

As a teacher, you must engage your students in the subject matter you teach. How would you make the following topics relevant to Casey, Malcolm, Raul, and Yu-shin?

- The Civil War
- *A Tale of Two Cities*
- Forces and motion
- Pollution
- Solving equations with two unknowns

### Exercise D

Choose the grade level below at which you expect to teach. How would you respond to the following comments or actions of the children?

#### Grades K–3

Sarah: "I don't want to do this work. I want to play on the computer."

Malcolm: "He's looking at me funny."

Leslie: "I can't do this."

Casey: "This is dumb."

Raul: " I don't understand."

### Grades 4–8

Sarah: "She's so stupid. Why is she always asking such dumb questions!?"

Malcolm: "I'm sick. I need to go to the office."

Leslie: "I don't want to be partners with Rachel. She's not my friend."

Casey: "Can you do this problem for me?"

Raul: "Why do I have to read this stuff? It has nothing to do with real life."

### Grades 9–12

Sarah: "You don't even know how to do this. You teachers are so stupid. I don't believe this!"

Malcolm: "Can I go to my locker? I forgot my book."

Leslie: "Why do they make these lab tables so high. I can't reach this stuff."

Casey: "Where are we? I don't get it. You go too fast."

Raul: "Hey, Malcolm's looking off my paper!"

Yu-shin: Nods and smiles nervously but is unable to answer your question.

## Exercise E

Assume that all of the children in the profiles are in your classroom. Design a classroom management plan that takes into account their different backgrounds. Prepare a poster to communicate your plan to the children. Write a letter to explain your plan to their families.

## Exercise F

With a partner or small group, select one of the children in the profiles in Part I. Brainstorm ideas for motivating this student through a variety of teaching strategies and materials.

## Exercise G: For teachers or teacher candidates at the secondary level

Choose a student from the profiles in Part I. Pretend that this student has come to you for advice on what he or she could or should do after graduation. Assess the student's interest, past academic performance, and financial realities. With a partner, role-play the conversation that might take place between you and the student.

# Chapter 10

## DEVELOPING LESSONS TO MEET THE NEEDS OF YOUR LEARNERS

This chapter focuses on planning instructional activities and assessments that draw on the backgrounds and abilities of your students.

In Activity 1, you will discover how to plan culturally relevant lessons, drawing on differences in gender, socioeconomic status, race and ethnicity, and language.

In Activity 2, you will see how a teacher can plan instructional activities so that every child can learn something new every day in ways that support his or her own set of academic and behavioral knowledge and skills, as well as how to adapt your lessons to further address the special needs of your learners.

In Activity 3, you will create a thematic unit plan that includes several lessons.

Activity 4 is designed for teacher candidates in high school English or language arts.

## ACTIVITY 1: DEVELOPING LESSONS THAT ARE CULTURALLY RELEVANT TO ALL LEARNERS

Teachers who want to prepare culturally relevant curriculum and meaningful lessons must first get to know their students. Each student is unique, and being associated with one culture or ethnicity does not mean that the student will necessarily have any characteristics or background usually attributed to that culture. Therefore, teachers need to know their students individually, know their families, and know the general customs of those groups to which the students belong.

Once a teacher feels comfortable with his or her students, he or she can tailor lessons to be very specific, inclusive, and differentiated for specific students. Until that time, teachers can still be inclusive by considering several factors about student background when constructing a lesson.

The following is an example list of questions that teachers might ask themselves when considering the variety of students they will have in class. By considering these and other questions, teachers can train themselves to be more aware of not excluding some students and not assuming that every student is coming from the same background base.

Gender:

- Does my topic naturally appeal to both genders? If not, and knowing that genders tend to approach topics differently, how can I make it relevant to both genders?
- What knowledge would each gender bring to my assignment that would enhance the other gender's knowledge?
- Is my assignment or topic gender stereotypical? If so, how can I correct this?
- When appropriate, have I included materials, examples, pictures, and references to both genders?
- If one gender historically dominates the topic, have I addressed the reasons for this with my students?
- Is there an opportunity to teach about social justice and discrimination related to gender in my topic?
- Am I consciously considering asking the same amount of and quality of questions to each gender?

Economic Diversity:

- Do I consider the probability of all students being able to economically participate in my assignment?
- Do I consider using references that are not based in living in a middle-income home?
- Do I understand the cultural strengths and resourcefulness that my students in poverty may bring to this lesson?
- Can all students understand and relate to examples, pictures, and references in this lesson?
- Do my references and examples show respect for all people regardless of class or economic status?
- Is there an opportunity to teach about class and social justice in this lesson?
- Have I included a richness of examples to help students with a lack of experience understand the concepts?
- Am I planning for teaching and modeling language in a formal register?

Race and Ethnicity:

- Does my topic naturally appeal to all races and ethnicities, and if not, how can I make it relevant to all students' cultural backgrounds?
- Do I consider any conflicts in my assignment and students' cultural backgrounds, and if so, how can I address these respectfully?
- Do I select examples, pictures, and references that are inclusive of different races and ethnicities?
- Do I make global connections to my topic and assignment?
- Do I understand and incorporate the contributions of different cultures?
- Do I incorporate and encourage students to use their own cultural references and experiences in interpreting information and solving problems?
- Do my references show respect to all peoples' cultural, religious, and ethnic background?
- Do I provide opportunities for students to explore other cultures within this lesson?
- Is there an opportunity to teach about social justice and race and ethnicity in this lesson?

English Language Learners (ELLs):

- Have I considered how to reach my objectives with my students with no or limited English skills?
- Have I provided multiple strategies for reaching the objectives with all students?
- Am I considering using concrete and visual materials for my ELLs?
- Am I considering using partners or small groups for the assignment?
- How can I adapt the lesson to provide manageable steps or lengthen the time requirements for ELLs?
- Do I incorporate examples that are familiar to my ELL students' cultures?
- Can I find time to work one on one with any of my ELL students?
- Is there a way to help my ELLs be included socially in the lesson?

The importance of taking these qualities into consideration when designing lessons cannot be ignored. It may be the factor that allows a student to connect, to find relevance in a content area that he or she previously thought had nothing to do with his or life and experiences. Seeing meaning in a lesson is a strong motivating factor.

---

### SAMPLE LESSON PLAN

Ninth-Grade Language Arts

One block period: 100 minutes

#### I. Learning Goals

*State Standard*

Analyze how an author's choice of genre affects the expression of a theme or topic.

*What will your students know and be able to do at the end of this lesson?*

Students will be able to analyze and describe why Robert Frost selected poetry to examine choices in "The Road Not Taken."

#### II. Student Background Knowledge and Experience

*What prior knowledge and skills do students need in order to be successful in reaching the goals of this lesson?*

- Sufficient written expression skills to write an essay as described in assessment component of plan (see accommodations for Casey and Yu-shin)
- Ability to orally describe several differences between poetry and prose
- Sufficient listening skills to follow teacher's lecture and class discussion (see accommodations for Malcolm)
- Past experience with analysis and identification of evidence from poetry or prose

*How will you use or accommodate the diverse experiences that your students bring to class (gender, race/ethnicity, English language proficiency, economic status, exceptionalities, skill level, and learning styles)?*

- No student will be asked to supply materials.
- If I can find the poem in their first languages, I will present it to them.
- Both girls and boys can brainstorm memories, but one gender may focus on one sense more than another, and both can benefit from different perceptions.
- Students not familiar with country roads can better picture the image with this vivid description.
- They may also relate a cityscape that would present the same dilemma.
- Students' cultural references can be a source of discussion; although the situations may be different, the dilemma and speculation are similar.

## III. Teaching Materials/Resources

Students will be given a copy of the poem "The Road Not Taken" and paper and pen.

I will use a transparency of the poem on an overhead to write student comments.

Pictures of forking country roads downloaded from the Internet. Audio clip of Robert Frost reading the poem downloaded from the Internet.

## IV. Instructional Procedures

*Lesson sequence Time allotted*

*Opening:*        30 minutes

Pictures of a country road forking will be shown using images downloaded from the Internet. Through questions, students will be asked to discuss experiences in a wooded setting and to remember the smells, sounds, and feelings, as well as visuals, of a country dirt road or path. Students will have an opportunity to share how it feels to be momentarily lost or undecided in selecting a path. Students will then describe times in their own lives when they have been faced with a choice and to speculate on the path not chosen.

*Main Activities:*  45 minutes

A review of the genres of literature and discussion of the unique qualities of each and their purposes will be conducted. Students will be asked to list the unique characteristics of poetry and what type of message is best conveyed in verse. The poem will be read aloud to the class as they follow along. Students will respond to the poem as the teacher writes their responses. Students will discuss how the poem in a unique setting addresses universality. At this point, students will begin to explore how the language of a poem lends itself to symbolism more than narrative accounts do.

*Closing:*        15 minutes

A review of class comments related to feelings about the poem and how this is related to poetry as a genre will be conducted. Students will begin the first draft of an essay. Students will analyze and describe why Robert Frost selected poetry to examine choices in "The Road Not Taken."

### V. Assessment/Evaluation

The essay will be used as an assessment of the objective. Students will be evaluated on their ability to analyze and describe the choice of genre by the author, using evidence from the poem, the discussion, and the textbook.

### VI. Adaptations

Modifications (if lesson objective and/or significant content needs to be changed)

Accommodations (if other components of lesson need to be changed)

**Box 10.1**

|  | *Student Name Casey* | *Student Name Malcolm* | *Student Name Yu-shin* | *Student Name Leslie* | *Student Name Raul* |
|---|---|---|---|---|---|
| **Special Needs** | Specific learning disability in reading | Inattentive and distractible | Does not speak English well | Physical challenges | Ethnic heritage |
| **Learning Goals** (modification to indicator and/or what student will be expected to know or do) | | | | | |

*(Continued)*

(Continued)

|  | Student Name<br>Casey | Student Name<br>Malcolm | Student Name<br>Yu-shin | Student Name<br>Leslie | Student Name<br>Raul |
|---|---|---|---|---|---|
| **Teaching Methods** | Be sure to read poem orally several times so<br><br>Casey can pick up on subtleties through listening | Use predetermined silent signal with Malcolm if he goes off task | Have some questions relate to pictures so Yu-shin can be involved in discussion |  |  |
| **Teaching Materials** |  | Parallel symbolism in a cityscape | Fork in a country road picture |  | Fork in a country road in Mexico |
| **Student Activities** |  | Have Malcolm serve as one of the recorders at the board |  |  |  |
| **Student Materials** | Laptop for Casey to write essay<br><br>Encourage him to use grammar check on laptop and to use editing checklist on the wall |  | Poem in Korean language | Laptop if needed |  |
| **Assessment/ Evaluation** |  | Extra credit points built in for remaining on task throughout entire period | If poem is not available, have Yu-shim do thematic analysis based on a series of pictures illustrating choices |  |  |

## Directions:

Individually, or with a partner, develop a rubric for assessing the assignment in Part V of this lesson plan. How would you adapt the rubric to take into consideration the differences in your learners?

# ACTIVITY 2: DIFFERENTIATING INSTRUCTION TO MEET THE NEEDS OF ALL LEARNERS

"Every student has the right to learn something new every day." What does that mean? Lessons must not only be culturally relevant and meaningful, they must be appropriate for all learners' current levels of knowledge and skills. Yes, teachers must determine the impact that gender, economic diversity, race, ethnicity, religion, and English language experience might have on our learning goals, but that is not enough. They also must preassess their students to determine what academic and behavioral knowledge and skills they already possess. (Skills related to preassessment are discussed in the activities in Chapter 11.)

It is unlikely that in any one class, all students will have the same level of academic and behavioral knowledge and skills. In any one group of students, some will have already learned what you are planning to teach for the day and others will not have the necessary prerequisite knowledge and skills. How, then, do you teach your lesson? You *differentiate!*

Tomlinson and Eidson (2003) define **differentiation** as "a systematic approach to planning curriculum and instruction for academically diverse learners. It is a way of thinking about the classroom with the dual goals of honoring each student's learning needs and maximizing each student's learning capacity" (p. 3). The principles of differentiation can be summarized in the following:

- Learning experiences are based on student readiness, interest, and/or learning profile.
- Assessment of student needs is ongoing, and tasks are adjusted based on assessment data.
- All students participate in respectful work.
- The teacher is primarily a coordinator of time, space, and activities rather than primarily a provider of information.
- Students work in a variety of group configurations. Flexible grouping is evident.
- Time use is flexible in response to student needs.
- The teacher uses a variety of instructional strategies to help target instruction to student needs.
- Clearly established criteria are used to help support student success.
- Student strengths are emphasized.

Another term that is being used increasingly in inclusive settings that describes a process similar to differentiation is **universal design for learning** (UDL). The Center for Applied Special Technology (2005) defines UDL as "a blueprint for creating flexible goals, methods, materials, and assessments that accommodates learner differences."

To develop lesson plans that honor the diverse background knowledge, experiences, and needs of our students is not as complicated as one might anticipate. In the differentiation resources developed by Tomlinson (1997), the lesson plan is considered to have three components: the content (what you teach and the materials you use to teach it), the process (methods and activities you and the students use to make sense of the content), and the products (the means through which students demonstrate what they have learned). Thus, once you have determined whether or not your students have the prerequisite knowledge and skills, you can decide which part or parts of the lesson need to be adapted to meet their learning needs.

There will be times when the content, process, and products you have planned are very appropriate for the students in your classroom, with a few exceptions. For example, in the previous lesson plan (see Activity 1), all of the students in the Midland High School English class could read the poem "The Road Not Traveled" except for Casey and Yu-shin. They could all understand it, unless the teacher was not able to find the poem in Yu-shin's native language. None of them had already mastered the skills required in the essay, so the product was appropriate for all. For this lesson, the only changes that needed to be made were to make sure Casey *heard* the poem several times, rather than needing to read it himself, and to secure a copy of the poem in Yu-shin's native language. Such minor adjustments to a lesson to better match learner needs are known as accommodations. The learning goal remains the same, but there are minor changes to the teaching methods, student activities, learning materials, and/or student assessments (Wood, 2002).

Other times you will have a few students in your class for whom the learning goals are not appropriate. These students may be able to reach a part of the goal or learn the content at a more basic level. In that case, you will make modifications to that student's learning goal or goals. In other words, the student has a different or adapted learning goal and/or different content (Wood, 2002). There is not the expectation that the student will reach the same academic expectations for that particular lesson.

## Exercise A: Sample Lesson Plan

### Directions

Before class: the following sample lesson plan is designed for a Midland Middle School sixth-grade class that includes all the students in the profiles. Before reviewing the plan, read the sixth-grade profiles again.

During class

1. Break into groups of six, with each student representing one of the sixth graders in the profiles: Raul, Yu-shin, Casey, Malcolm, Sarah, and Leslie. Individually review the plan and highlight any specifics within that plan that you think would help a teacher meet the learning, social, and/or behavioral needs of the student you represent. (Do not review the adaptations section yet.) Then discuss what you have highlighted.

2. While in your group, reread the lesson plan, this time focusing on what components are differentiated. Highlight any differentiated content with one color, differentiated processes with another color, and differentiated products with a third. What are some potential advantages for differentiating in these ways? What are some of the potential challenges?

3. Now review the adaptations section. Highlight any accommodations or modifications that have been listed for the student you initially represented. In this sample, you will find overlap between the components of the lesson that are "differentiated" and those that are listed as accommodations or modifications. In reality, they do not have to be listed in both places. Be sure to follow the guidelines for lesson planning at your institution when planning lessons that are adapted to meet diverse learning needs. Changes to meet learner needs may be included in the body of the lesson plan or added as adaptations at the end of the plan.

Note: This is an 85-minute double-blocked period.

---

## I. Learning Goals

*Academic Content Standard:* History Standard: Students use materials drawn from the diversity of human experience to analyze and interpret significant events, patterns, and themes in the history of the state, the United States, and the world.

*Benchmark* (for 6th- to 8th-grade programs): Interpret relationships between events shown on multiple-tier timelines.

*Indicator:* Construct a multiple-tier timeline from a list of events and interpret the relationships between the events.

*What will your students know and be able to do at the end of this lesson?*

Day 1: Given a set of lists of events provided by the teacher, the student will select an appropriate set of events and construct an appropriate multiple-tier timeline.

Day 2: The students will interpret the relationships between these events either in writing, in a PowerPoint presentation, or orally as directed by the teacher.

## II. Student Background Knowledge and Experience

What prior knowledge and skills do students need in order to be successful in reaching the goals of this lesson?

- Understanding of sequence of events and cause and effect
- Understanding of sequence of dates
- Some knowledge about list of events chosen
- Skills to develop timeline to scale (inches to years)
- Oral and/or writing skills to discuss relationship among events
- Skills needed to work in teacher-selected pairs

How do you know if students have the knowledge and skills they need in order to be successful?

- Previous work in class on sequencing events and dates
- Previous work in class on cause and effect
- Quiz/test scores to date on various time periods

- Previous class work on simple timelines
- IEP (individualized education progarm) and/or other personal goals for oral and written language
- Observation of work in pairs for other class assignments

How will you use or accommodate the diverse experiences that your students bring to class (gender, race/ethnicity, English language proficiency, economic status, exceptionalities, skill level, learning styles)?

List of event options will vary in length (4 to 10 events), level of difficulty, and amount of information needed to interpret the relationship among the events. There will be three groups of lists: freedom movements, historical periods, and the rise and fall of civilizations. Pairs of students will be assigned a group of lists consistent with their experiences and background knowledge. Based on personal interest and experience, pairs can choose a list from within the group selected by the teacher. Any struggling readers will be paired with more fluent readers with similar interests. Laptop computers are available for any pair to use, with the expectation that Casey and Leslie will access their laptops for this assignment if their pairs choose to do written interpretations or PowerPoint presentations.

## III. Instructional Procedures

Content summary, including concepts and essential understandings

(Note: The concepts listed below should be detailed in lecture notes and attached to the lesson plan.)

- Purposes and principles of multitiered timelines
- How to think about relationships among events
- Relationship between sequence of events and cause and effect

Teaching methods for Day 1,

- Direct instruction on the purposes and principles of multitiered timelines, linking to previous work with simple timelines
- Model development of multitiered timeline, with student providing increasing input as the model is developed (use **think-aloud** approach)
- Monitor progress and provide informal feedback to pairs as they develop their timelines and prepare their interpretations

*Student grouping:* Pairs preassigned by teacher based on criteria noted above.

## IV. Resources and Materials

- Sheet with pairs and list of event options detailed
- Texts written at several reading levels to use resources for lists of events
- Graph paper, chart paper, rulers, pencils, markers, and yarn for timeline development

- Rubric for assessment of timeline and presentation of interpretation of relationship among events
- Computers with appropriate software for those who need them as assistive technology (Casey and Leslie) or the development of PowerPoint presentations

## V. Instructional Activities: Day 1

*Lesson sequence Time allotted*

Opening: 5 minutes

Discussion of timeline prepared from last unit: How did the timeline help us to better understand that period in history?

*Main activities:*

Minilecture: 10 minutes

Purposes and principles of multiple-tier timelines

Questions: 10 minutes

What are they? How might they be beneficial? How could you use them in your lives?

Demonstration: 15 minutes

Draw one for teacher's family, interpreting the relationship among events. Using think-aloud, model the process for the first tier, tell a volunteer at the overhead what to do for the second tier, and have volunteers tell the teacher what to do for the third tier. Assign pairs and selection of appropriate lists. Discuss how to use resources and rubrics.

Pairs work on timelines 40 minutes

*Each pair may take a 5-minute break.*

*Closing:* 5 minutes

What did you learn about your list of events while using resources to develop your timeline? What challenges did you face developing your timeline? For tomorrow, bring ideas about some relationships among the events to class with you to discuss with your partner. You will develop your oral, written, or PowerPoint interpretation and share it with the class.

## VI. Assessment/Evaluation

How will you know if each student has met the learning goals?

I will assess the students' timelines using the rubric shown below. The rubric has been developed to not discriminate against length or complexity of lists.

## VII. Adaptations

Modifications: If lesson objective and/or significant content needs to be changed

Accommodations: If other components of lesson need to be changed

## VIII. Reflection

If you could teach this lesson again, what would you do the same? What would you do differently? Which individual or group did particularly well? How do you account for this performance? What might you try in the future with this individual or group? Which individual or group appeared to be having problems? How do you account for this performance? What might you try in the future with this individual or group?

**Box 10.2**     Rubric for Timeline

|  | *Unacceptable* | *Acceptable* | *Excellent* |
|---|---|---|---|
| Content | Not all events included<br><br>OR events included in wrong order | All events included in correct order | All events included in correct order in ways that signal relationship among events |
| Timeline | Not multitier; not neat or easy to read | Multitier; neat and easy to read | Creative development of multitier to highlight relationships; neat and easy to read and interpret |
| Pair work | One partner did most of the work | Partners shared in the work as explained by instructor (not all pairs will have the same division of labor) | Partners actively encouraged each other during pair work and shared work appropriately |

**Box 10.3**

| Student Name | Casey | Sarah | Malcolm | Leslie | Yu-shin | Raul |
|---|---|---|---|---|---|---|
| What needs are you addressing for this student in this lesson? | Specific learning disability in reading | Advanced understanding of concepts | Attention span, background experiences | Physical challenges | Lack of reading ability in English | Ethnic heritage |
| **Learning Goals** Modification to indicator and/or what student will be expected to know or do | | | | | | |
| **Teaching Methods** | More pair assistance as needed. Make sure sample timeline uses words with which Casey is familiar. Encourage Casey and partner to explore alternative texts and online resources at their reading level | Encouragement to explore in-depth relationships among events | Will begin pair assistance with Malcolm's pair. Informal discussion with him about events if distracted | | Pair support will immediately follow support provided to Malcolm's pair | |
| **Teaching Materials** | | | | | | |
| **Student Activities** | Paired with fluent reader with similar interests | Paired with high-ability student | | | Paired with a more fluent reader with similar interests | |
| **Student Materials** | Use of laptop; may select list from any grouping | Must select list from most complex grouping | Several lists will contain events of interest to African Americans | Use of laptop | Several lists will contain events of interest to his native country | Several lists will contain events relevant to his native country |
| **Assessment/ Evaluation** | Support by partner in any writing component, include use of spell checker, thesaurus, etc. | | | | Support by partner as needed in any writing component | |

## Exercise B: Determining Accommodations

### Directions

1. Break into groups of six by grade-level interest, with each teacher candidate representing one of the students in the profiles: Raul, Yu-shin, Casey, Malcolm, Sarah, or Leslie.

2. As a group, discuss what makes an accommodation meaningful, usable, and effective? Develop a first draft of a list of criteria for effective accommodations.

3. Using an appropriate search engine, locate three lists of accommodations that would be appropriate for your learner's needs. Compare and contrast these lists as directed by your instructor. Evaluate them against the criteria you selected.

4. Discuss where the overlaps are among the accommodations. In other words, what accommodations would be appropriate for more than one of the students in the biographies? Why?

## Exercise C: Practice in Planning

### Directions

1. Break into groups of six by grade-level interest, with each teacher candidate representing zone of the students in the profiles: Raul, Yu-shin, Casey, Malcolm, Sarah, or Leslie.

2. As directed by your instructor, find and/or develop a lesson plan that includes goals and objectives, methods, activities, and some type of student assessment. This lesson should, in principle, be appropriate for the age level of student profiles your group has selected.

3. Differentiate that plan to meet the needs of your six students in the profiles. Include both differentiation in the body of the plan *and* an accommodations page that can be attached to the plan.

4. Share your plan, how you differentiated it, and what you selected as your accommodations with the rest of the class in an oral or poster presentations.

## Exercise D: Day 2 Lesson Plan

### Directions

1. Break into groups of six by grade-level interest, with each teacher candidate representing one of the students in the profiles: Raul, Yu-shin, Casey, Malcolm, Sarah, or Leslie.

2. Using the sample world history lesson above, develop a lesson plan for Day 2 as briefly mentioned in the goals and objectives section.

3. Develop a rubric for product options that are consistent with the needs and learning strengths of the students in the profiles.

4. Develop an accommodations page that shows how you will adapt the lesson to meet the needs of each of the six learners.

## Exercise E: Interview a Teacher

### Directions

1. Request an interview with a teacher in your grade or subject.

2. Ask the teacher to read one of the profiles that you have selected from Chapters 2 to 7. Make sure you have chosen a child about whom you would have some concerns if he or she were really in your class.

3. Interview the teacher to find out how he or she would accommodate this particular child in the classroom.

4. Write a summary of the interview, including your reactions to the teacher's conclusions.

5. Bring your summary to class to discuss with your colleagues what you have learned.

# ACTIVITY 3: CREATING COLLABORATIVE UNITS

## Directions

1. Select a subject area and grade that you are teaching. Pair with another teacher in the same grade selection.

   | | |
   |---|---|
   | Grade 1: LA | Art |
   | Grade 4: SS | Science |
   | Grade 4: LA | Math |
   | Grade 8: | Math/Physical Education |
   | Grade 8: SS | Music |
   | Grade 10: | Science/Language Arts |

2. You are to select a topic to create a thematic unit that you will teach collaboratively.

3. Design a week-long collaborative unit using the accepted lesson plan form.

4. In your class are all of the children described in Chapters 2 to 7. Make sure you list adaptations where needed. Describe academic, social, and cultural adaptations.

# ACTIVITY 4: DESIGNING RESPONSIVE LANGUAGE ARTS ACTIVITIES

## Exercise A: Reading List

1. Divide into trios.

2. From Chapters 2 to 7, select one student at the secondary level.

3. As a group, discuss what the reading ability level is for this student and what areas of interest this student has.

4. Construct a suggested reading list of 10 novels for this student based upon the above information.

5. For each novel, list the reading level as easy, medium, or difficult for this grade level. Describe why each was selected for this student.

6. Design a reading plan with objectives for one of the novels and construct a contract for the student that incorporates the strategies and products you will use to assess successful reaching of the objectives.

7. Share your plan and contract with the class.

## Exercise B: Writing Assignment Role Play

### Directions

1. Choose a high school student from Chapters 2 to 7. This student has refused to turn in the required rough draft of the following writing assignment:

*After reading the attached selections from a biography of a current political leader, select one incident in your own life where you have made a personal decision that has impacted your future. Describe the incident and the decision that you made. Explain why you made that decision and the reason you are satisfied or dissatisfied with that decision. Show the reader examples of how the decision impacted your future.*

With a partner, role-play the conversation between the teacher and student. The objective for the teacher is to understand why the student did not turn in the work and to get the student to write the assignment. The objective for the student is to either not do the assignment or to change the assignment. The scene will be over when the two reach a compromise that is acceptable to both.

Use information from the cases to understand the background of the student as a way of understanding reasons for not turning in the assignment. Consider all possibilities for this individual student.

2. As a class, answer the following questions:

• Analyze why the student didn't finish the assignment. Are there any other possibilities? Reflect on the compromise. Is it the best choice? Are there other suggestions?
• Reflect on the assignment. Is it the best choice for secondary students?

3. Write your response to the following: Describe some ways in which you could avoid having this child refuse to do assignments in the future.

# Chapter 11

# GATHERING DATA TO IMPROVE INSTRUCTION

Effective teachers do not teach "the class." Instead, they view the class as a unique collection of individuals with different backgrounds, interests, and abilities, and they design and implement learning activities that allow each student to develop to his or her full potential. And although we may think that good teachers have eyes in the back of their heads, even they can use a wonderfully simple technique to improve their knowledge of the children in their classes—ask the children.

In this chapter, you learn to collect data from children to learn about their interests and to analyze their knowledge and misconceptions about a variety of topics, both before and after instruction. Using these strategies will help you improve instruction for *all* children as you transfer your experiences in working with the children in this book to the children you encounter in your teaching in real classrooms and schools.

Activity 1 focuses on collecting information from children about their own interests through questioning, interest inventories, and journaling.

Activity 2 models collecting preassessment data for designing a first-grade lesson on one-dimensional shapes and a third-grade lesson in geology.

Activity 3 shows that teachers must collect data in order to see if their students are grasping the concepts behind instructional activities.

Activity 4 shows how assessment must be an ongoing process of feedback that continuously affects your lesson planning and keeps the students informed about their own progress in achieving instructional objectives.

Activity 5 explores alternatives for demonstrating that students have met national, state, or district standards through authentic assessment of their acquired knowledge and skills.

# ACTIVITY 1: LEARNING ABOUT STUDENT INTERESTS

Instruction that is based on student interest increases motivation and encourages learning. This does not mean that the curriculum is driven by student interests but rather that the teacher skillfully uses student interests to build instructional activities that simultaneously appeal to students *and* address the appropriate standards.

## Exercise A: Questioning

Engaging students in structured discussion provides a great deal of information about them and their interests. Pretend that you are an eighth-grade social studies teacher and that you have Casey, Sarah, Malcolm, Raul, and Yu-shin in your classroom. You are beginning to plan a unit on the Civil War. At the end of the unit, students must address the following:

- Causes of the Civil War
- Course of the war and its consequences
- Consequences of reconstruction

You ask the following questions:

- What do you know about the Civil War?
- If you were a time-and-space traveler and you could choose 1860 (just before the Civil War) or 1870 (just after the Civil War) and Atlanta (South) or Boston (North), which time and place would you choose? Why?

## Directions

Choose a partner and read the middle school profile of Casey, Sarah, Malcolm, Raul, or Yu-shin.

1. How do you think your student would answer the above questions?

2. What other questions could you ask to probe the interest and knowledge of your student about the Civil War?

## Exercise B: Interest Inventory

When you develop an interest inventory to probe student interests, you can provide a list of topics or allow students to generate their own lists. The list below directs students to choose topics that are well within the bounds of the required standards.

Interest Inventory: Circle the topics you might like to study as we begin our unit on the Civil War.

Army camp life

Lives of common soldiers

Lives of generals

Emergence of Abraham Lincoln as a national figure

Weapons

Army food and other supplies

Role of the horse in transportation and battle

Troop and supply movement

Communications

Lives of those left at home

Ku Klux Klan

Abolitionist Movement

Emancipation Proclamation

Slavery and human rights

Reconstruction

## Directions

With a partner from your grade level or subject area, choose a topic from the national or your state standards.

1. Develop an interest inventory for your chosen topic.

## Exercise C: Journaling

Journaling is a third way of discovering student interests. Asking students to respond to prompts provides you with a window on their interests—and also exercises their writing skills. A few days into the Civil War unit, you might ask the following questions:

- You've heard the expression "You don't really know someone until you've walked a mile in their shoes." Of the people we've talked about, whose shoes would you have liked to walk in? Whose shoes would you have *not* liked to walk in? Why?
- If you could have invented something to help your side during the Civil War, what would you have invented? What would have been its effect?

## Directions

1. With the same partner and topic from Exercise B, develop two or three journal prompts to assess your students' interests and knowledge.

# ACTIVITY 2: PREASSESSMENT OF STUDENT KNOWLEDGE

Even teachers who provide adaptations for learning preferences and disabilities through differentiated lesson planning often assume that the children in their classes are starting from the same knowledge and experience base. Assessing your children *before* you plan a lesson will dramatically improve your ability to support their learning so that they can achieve the goals you set for the end of the lesson.

## Exercise A: First-Grade Math

You are a first-grade teacher about to teach a unit on one-dimensional shapes. Among your students are Casey, Sarah, Malcolm, Leslie, and Raul. Your state curriculum guide states that students must be able to describe and create the following:

- Circles
- Rectangles
- Squares
- Triangles
- Hexagons
- Trapezoids
- Parallelograms
- Rhombuses

You design a "shape hunt" to see what your students already know about shapes. They are to hunt around the room to find one of each shape, then return to their seats to identify their shapes on the worksheet provided. Casey, Sarah, Malcolm, Leslie, and Raul complete the exercise. Their responses are described below:

Casey:     Correctly identifies circle, rectangle, square, and triangle. Has trouble following teacher's directions to "Look to your left" or "Look a little farther down."

Sarah:     Easily finds the pieces and places them correctly on the worksheet. Is at ease with oral instructions.

Malcolm:   Correctly identifies circle, rectangle, square, triangle, and hexagon. Has to be redirected to the activity when he becomes distracted with other objects in the room.

Raul:      Finds objects with help from study buddy, who uses hands to describe the shapes. Finds the English words on the word wall. Is able to place all the shapes on the proper places on the worksheet. Is not able to follow directions in English.

Leslie:    Points to and names several shapes that she is able to see from her desk.

You develop a lesson to address the following standards:

- Describe and create the plane figures as listed above
- Identify the figures in the environment
- Describe location, using comparative (before, after), directional (above, below), and positional (first, last) words

Students will play a game called Hidden Positions (Van de Walle, 2001) in which each pair of students has a manila folder and each student has a tic-tac-toe board and a collection of shapes. The manila folder hides the boards so that the players cannot see each other's boards. One student, the direction giver, places several pieces on his or her board, then gives oral directions to the direction follower, who places his or her pieces on the board, trying to match that of the direction giver. When the direction giver is done, they remove the folder to see if their boards match. The two trade roles, and the activity is repeated. The adaptations for each student, based on the preassessment, follow:

**Box 11.1**

| Student Name | Leslie | Casey | Malcolm |
|---|---|---|---|
| | Special Needs<br>Wheelchair/<br>Limited use of<br>hands | Special Needs<br>Reads below grade level | Special Needs<br>ADHD |
| Learning Goals (modification to indicator and/or what student will be expected to know or do) | | First, Casey and Malcolm will play the game using just shapes. One will call out a shape and the other will pick out the correct shape. Then they will check. They will proceed with the activity if they pick out the correct shapes consistently. | First, Casey and Malcolm will play the game using just shapes. One will call out a shape and the other will pick out the correct shape. Then they will check. They will proceed with the activity if they pick out the correct shapes consistently. |
| Teaching Methods | | Prior to activity, additional time will be spent working with the shapes. The goal is to improve Casey's understanding of the geometric words and directionality. | Prior to activity, additional time will be spent working with the shapes. The goal is to improve Malcolm's understanding of the geometric words and directionality. |
| Teaching Materials | Shapes are larger and thicker so that they are easier to grasp. Tic-tac-toe board is larger. | | |
| Student Activities | | Simpler version and regular version | Simpler version and regular version |
| Assessment/ Evaluation | Leslie will be using KidPix to draw her picture (computer art program). | Additional time for drawing (hand drawing might help with coordination) or KidPix if concentrating on shapes. Might need to reduce the number of shapes used. | Additional time for drawing or KidPix useful to encourage attention to task. Might need to reduce the number of shapes used. |

*(Continued)*

(Continued)

|  | Raul | Sarah |
|---|---|---|
|  | Special Needs ELL | Special Needs TAG |
| Learning Goals (modification to indicator and/or what student will be expected to know or do) |  | To extend, expand, or accelerate her knowledge |
| Teaching Methods | Prior to activity, additional time will be spent working with the shapes, English words, and translations. The goal is to improve Raul's understanding of the geometric words and directionality | Student paired with another TAG student. Sarah and her partner will build their shapes in three dimensions. They will use a Quadrant I (all positive) system coordinate system rather than a tic-tac-toe board. |
| Teaching Materials |  | Same as class plus Quadrant I coordinate system |
| Student Activities | Simpler version and regular version | Quadrant I coordinate activity |
| Assessment/ Evaluation | Additional time and help with English words. | Sarah will journal using the following questions:<br><br>*How did adding the third dimension change your directions for the shape tic-tac-toe activity?<br><br>* Describe the coordinate system you learned about today.<br><br>*Where might this kind of system be useful?<br><br>The answers to these questions will be added to Sarah's portfolio. |

## Directions

1. With your partner, discuss the adaptations in the lesson plan. Do they seem reasonable? What other adaptations might you choose? How will you assess each child's demonstration of the stated objectives?

## Exercise B: Third-Grade Science

Imagine that you are a third-grade teacher and that among the children in your classroom are Casey, Sarah, Malcolm, and Leslie. Your state standards in science require that the children observe and investigate that rocks are often found in layers. They must know the following:

- Rocks can form in layers.
- The oldest layers are usually but not always found on the bottom.
- The youngest layers are usually but not always found on the top.
- We can learn about the history of the earth by studying the layers of rocks.

You begin your lesson by showing several pictures of the dramatic rock layers of the Grand Canyon and ask the children to tell you about the pictures. Their comments follow:

Casey:    Rocks come from the ocean, and some rocks are spit out of volcanoes. My dad told me they did.

Sarah:    Those rocks are put down in layers, and the oldest ones are on the bottom. They are from a long time ago. There are three kinds of rocks, and they are all made differently. Do you want to know what the three kinds of rocks are?

Malcolm:  Our neighbor has a big rock in his yard and sometimes I go climb on it. [Makes climbing motions.] I can throw rocks too! [Makes throwing motions and cracking noises.]

Leslie:   Rocks are hard. Haven't they just always been like that?

As the children speak, you record their comments on the board.

## Directions

1. Suppose that you had planned to follow this opening activity by having the children make a model of layered rocks with white bread on the bottom, whole wheat in the middle, and rye bread on the top, held together with jelly between two of the layers and peanut butter and raisins between the other two (this lesson is adapted from Peanut Butter and Jelly Geology (www.nevadamining.org/education/projects/proj_936169 200.html). You ask them to identify the oldest part of their sandwich (bottom layer, white bread) and the newest part of their sandwich (top layer, rye bread). Which of the children might have difficulty with this part of the lesson? What would you do to adapt this activity to meet their specific needs? Which of the children would not learn anything new from this activity?

2. You then ask the children to model the forces that move the earth. They are supposed to bend their sandwiches to form troughs, mountains, and valleys. They are supposed to cut their sandwiches in two and move one side up or down and push the two parts together. You ask them to draw these formations on paper. Which of the children might have difficulty with this part of the lesson? What would you do to adapt this activity to meet their specific needs? How would you make sure that Sarah learned something from this lesson?

3. At the end of the activity, you return to the children's original comments. What questions would you ask them that would relate what they have learned in this lesson to what they knew before the lesson? How would you know if they had learned the content of the lesson? How would you know if they had learned something new?

# ACTIVITY 3: CONCEPT ASSESSMENT

Often teachers ask students to complete an instructional activity and then assume that students will get it by simply doing the activity. Understanding concepts is much different from completing activities, as you will see in the following scenarios.

Third-graders Malcolm, Casey, Sarah, Raul, and Leslie have just completed an observation in which water, vinegar, and iodine are added to sand, sugar, baking soda, baking powder, and cornstarch. When asked to describe what they observed, they wrote the following:

Malcolm: I know some are different colors. Some chemicals fizz and dissolve so you can't see them, and others are cloudy. Some look like glue. Some are good and some are bad.

Casey: Som stuf disaper. Som stuf mad a difrent colar. Som stuf bubled.

Sarah: I know chemicals can dissolve, turn colors, and fizz or bubble. A lot of chemicals dissolve, I know chemicals can be acid, base or neutral, some can be solution or suspension. They can be a crystal.

Leslie: Chemicals can be dangerous. You need to follow the safety rules. Do not taste, wear your goggles, and follow directions.

Raul: (Blank page)

## Directions

1. With a partner, answer these questions.
   - Did any of the children reach the goal of understanding what is meant by a physical and chemical change by doing the activity?
   - What could have been done before or during the activity to make sure that the children achieved the objective?

# ACTIVITY 4: GOAL ASSESSMENT

In addition to assessment prior to designing a unit or lesson, good teachers continuously assess their students' progress toward an instructional goal. As Wiggins and McTighe (2005) states, assessment must be a continuous process so that we do not "teach, test, and hope for the best."

You are a Biology I teacher, and most of your students are 10th graders at Midland High School. In your class are Casey, Sarah, and Malcolm. They have been studying the process of cell division in preparation for a departmental assessment as well as the state achievement test scheduled for 2 months from now. You are curious about their grasp of the topic and develop an activity designed to assess their progress. You split the class into two groups that are given pop beads, string, and bits of cloth to model the process of mitosis (replication and division of the nuclear material during cell division for cells other than sex cells) or meiosis (division of the nuclear material of cells that become sperm and eggs).

At the end of 15 minutes, you observe the following:

Casey: Casey sometimes stumbles but generally could walk through the phases in order. He does have some difficulty in characterizing the phases when they are called out of order during the game.

Sarah: Sarah leads her group in creating the steps and using the materials in a way that illustrate mitosis and meiosis. She obviously has a strong grasp of the steps and does not hesitate in moving from one phase to another. She easily transitions from one phase to another and can accurately point out incorrect models.

Malcolm: Malcolm has difficulty in remembering the different structures (for example, nuclear membrane and centrioles) and when they move, appear, and disappear. He also has difficulty remembering the order of the phases (prophase, metaphase, anaphase, and telophase).

Based on your observations, you assign the following:

Casey: Create a flipbook that shows mitosis and meiosis.

Sarah: Read an article from *National Geographic* on the medical implications of stem cell research and its accompanying ethical dilemmas. Write an editorial supporting or condemning stem cell research to be sent to a publication selected by Sarah.

Malcolm: Use an animated Web site that demonstrates the processes of mitosis and meiosis.

## Directions

1. With a partner, discuss these questions. If a test had been given on cell division at this point, who would have done well? Who would have failed? How would you use this information in planning subsequent lessons?

2. Discuss the assignments made as a result of the ongoing assessment. Were these activities reasonable? What was their purpose? What other instructional activities might you have assigned?

## ACTIVITY 5: AUTHENTIC ASSESSMENTS

When you think of assessment, you may think of paper-and-pencil tests, and there are indeed many times when your students will be assessed in this way. However, your students can show you that they have learned the knowledge and skills of the appropriate standards in many ways, including through use of "authentic assessments," or assessments that mirror what people do in everyday life. Some examples of authentic assessments are as follows:

- Poster
- Presentation
- Newspaper article
- Video or film
- Debate
- Interview
- Drawing or other artwork
- Play or readers' theatre
- Lesson plan

## Directions

1. With a partner from your grade level or subject area, choose a goal from the national or your state standards.

2. Brainstorm a list of authentic assessments that could be used to demonstrate a student's achievement of the goal.

# Chapter 12

# COMMUNICATING WITH FAMILIES

**C**ommunicating with families is an essential part of each teacher's job. Only through understanding each child within the context of his or her life outside the classroom can you help that child develop and grow to his or her fullest potential. This chapter focuses on developing your skills in communicating with families.

In Activity 1, you will conduct simulated conferences in which you take the role of teacher and address a particular problem of one of the children profiled in Chapters 2 through 7.

In Activity 2, you will take part in a simulated individualized education program (IEP) conference as a general educator, special educator, principal, parent, or guardian of one of the children profiled in Chapters 2 through 7.

In Activity 3, you will have the opportunity to develop a variety of parent communication documents.

## ACTIVITY 1: LEARNING TO LISTEN

### Exercise A

*Purpose:* To develop basic skills in active listening and use them in simulated conferencing situations. Each of the scenarios will be based on the information you have on one of the children profiled in Chapters 2 through 7: Casey, Leslie, Malcolm, Raul, Sarah, or Yu-shin.

*Before class:* Read thoroughly the town and school information (Chapter 1) and the profiles prior to coming to class. You need to be familiar with all the profiles, since you don't know which one you will have to use as you prepare for your conference.

### Directions

You and a classmate will be paired randomly from those assigned to conduct simulated conferences on a specific class date. The person picked first will be the teacher, and the person picked second will be the child's guardian or other significant person.

After the first 5 minutes, you will switch roles, continuing the conference rather than starting all over again. The "teacher" will be evaluated on his or her use of active listening skills, while the "caretaker" will be evaluated on skills at staying "in character" based on profile descriptions. Even though we *all* will have read the scenario, you have to act as though the person bringing the problem to the conference has not shared it with the other person before. Thus you have to use your time to draw out the feelings of the individual bringing the problem to the conference and the details of the problem situation. Do not try to solve the problem in your 10-minute miniconference—your task is to listen and to clearly and accurately reflect the emotions and nature of the content of the person(s) bringing the problem to the conference.

**Box 12.1**   Assessment Rubric

| Skills | Unacceptable | Acceptable | Excellent |
|---|---|---|---|
| Nonverbals (examples: eye contact, body language, positioning of furniture) | Nonverbals disinviting and/or inconsistent with verbal messages | Nonverbals neutral and consistent with verbal messages | Nonverbals inviting, appropriately positive, and consistent with verbal messages |
| Opening the conference (examples: introductions, positive opening remarks) OR Transitioning to second half (picking up on what happened in the first half and making a smooth transition) | No introduction and no opening positives OR Second half of conference inconsistent with the first half | Introduction or opening positive remarks OR Second half generally consistent with first half | Appropriate introductions and positive opening remarks OR Smooth transition and consistency |
| Paraphrasing (accurately identifying and reflecting emotions) | No attempt to reflect emotional component | Attempts to identify and reflect emotional components of message | Clear and accurate reflection of emotions |
| Paraphrasing (accurately identifying and reflecting nature of content) | Inaccurate and/or limited attempts to reflect content | Clear and accurate reflection of content; but conference seems stalled | Clear, accurate reflection of content; develops depth of understanding as conference proceeds |
| Staying in character (based on information in profiles and scenarios) | Difficulty staying in character | Stayed in character most of the time | Stayed in character through conference |
| Inappropriately attempts to solve the problem, give advice, or minimize participant's feelings or the situation | Multiple instances of problem solving, advice giving | One instance of problem solving, advice giving | Did not attempt to problem solve or give advice |

### *Active Listening Scenarios*

Please make sure you have read the scenarios well enough to role-play the parent/caretaker consistent with the personality described in the profile. Also remember to think about the personality of your student as described in the profile. Consider the special needs or diverse backgrounds of your student. The names in **bold** will be those talking in the conference, although you can imagine referring to the other conference participants.

**Box 12.2**    Active Listening Scenarios

| *Scenario A* | *Leslie: Grade 1* |
|---|---|
| **Who is attending?** | **Mother, teacher,** school nurse, Leslie's aide |
| **Problem:** | Leslie is not requesting the necessary assistance with her catheter and bladder control needs. |
| **Details:** | Leslie has had two accidents at school and refuses to ask for help. How can we get Leslie to communicate her needs? |
| *Scenario B* | *Leslie: Grade 6* |
| **Who is attending?** | **Father and teacher** |
| **Problem:** | Mr. Carr is concerned about Leslie's academic downturn and obvious depression. |
| **Details:** | Leslie has withdrawn from physical and social activities. She is shutting down in her strongest areas of interest (math, science, and art). She refuses to go to class on time, take notes, or participate in class. |
| *Scenario C* | *Leslie: Grade 10* |
| **Who is attending?** | **Mother, teacher,** Leslie, age 15 |
| **Problem:** | Leslie wants to go to college and major in forensics. However, no postsecondary planning has been started. |
| **Details:** | Leslie's parents have "agreed" to purchase an appropriately equipped van to allow her to drive and have the independence and mobility that driving provides as soon as she is old enough. However, they have been hesitant to discuss Leslie "moving out" to go to a college where she can study forensics. In the past, whenever the teacher or Leslie has brought up the topic, Mr. and Mrs. Carr have said, "We'll worry about it later." |

*(Continued)*

(Continued)

| Scenario D | Casey: Grade 6 |
|---|---|
| **Who is attending?** | **Teacher and mother** |
| **Problem:** | Irregular attendance coupled with not completing homework, not studying for tests, not taking tests seriously |
| **Details:** | The teacher has tried to have this conference three different times. The first two times neither parent showed up, and the third time, Mrs. Griffith called to say she had to work overtime. This time she arrives, but 15 minutes late! |
| Scenario E | Casey: Grade 10 |
| **Who is attending?** | **Teacher and father** |
| **Situation:** | It is nearing IEP conference time. Casey's parents were sent a letter telling them that this time Casey needs to have a "transition plan" written as part of his IEP. They have been asked to talk with Casey about what he wants to do after high school before they come to the IEP conference. |
| **Details:** | Casey's father shows up unannounced one day after school demanding to see the teacher. He indicates to the principal the he wants to know what this transition planning stuff is all about. He says he is tired of the school trying to run Casey's life and his life too! The teacher agrees to meet with Mr. Griffith. |
| Scenario F | Malcolm: Grade 6 |
| **Who is attending?** | **Teacher and mother** |
| **Problem:** | Malcolm is exhibiting several inappropriate behaviors at school (see profile) that are having a negative impact on his learning and minimizing the amount of instruction he receives. |
| **Details:** | Mrs. Males does not realize what he is doing at school. The teacher tried to reach her earlier in the school year when the behaviors started to increase, but did not succeed in contacting her. Now Malcolm is spending more time in the office than in the classroom and is gaining attention from older students who are also often in trouble. |

| Scenario G | *Malcolm: Grade 10* |
|---|---|
| **Who is attending?** | **Mother, teacher,** grandmother (Malcolm was invited but chose not to attend.) |
| **Problem:** | Malcolm has threatened to drop out of school. He has hinted that he wants to "join up" with his father, who is deeply involved in drug trafficking. |
| **Details:** | Malcolm now lives with his grandmother. Both his mother and grandmother want Malcolm to stay in school, and both are "worried sick" that he might take off and return to Philadelphia to live with his father. Both have in the past told the teacher they just do not know what else to do with Malcolm. |
| Scenario H | *Raul: Grade 6* |
| **Who is attending?** | **Teacher,** mother, father, guidance counselor (**person in triad can be mother or father**) |
| **Problem:** | Raul is not completing his work in English or social studies, and his teachers have been worried that he does not understand the material. |
| **Details:** | The teachers who are just getting to know Raul have interpreted his lack of interest as lack of understanding. Because Raul is Mexican, their first assumption is that he has a language barrier. Although he may not be as proficient with English as his native-speaking peers, it is likely that there is also a cultural barrier that Raul's teachers have not addressed. Mr. and Mrs. Ramirez are confused. They know that Raul is smart, speaks English relatively well, and has had success in these subjects before. Because of their lack of English-speaking skills and their complete trust in the wisdom of the teachers and school, they are willing to agree to anything the school suggests. |
| Scenario I | *Yu-shin, Grade 12* |
| **Who is attending?** | Yu-shin, Jin-ho, **father and guidance counselor, Mr. Dalton** |
| **Situation:** | Yu-shin and his sister, Jin-ho, have had another shouting match in the hall during the common lunch period. Since previous requests to refrain from verbal fights at school have not changed their behavior, Mr. Dalton requests a meeting with their parents. |
| **Details:** | Their latest verbal altercation occurred when Yu-shin spotted Jin-ho in the lunchroom. She had taken off the sweater she had worn to school that morning, revealing a very tight tank top that did not meet the waist of her jeans. The rest of the girls at her table are dressed in a similar fashion. |

| Scenario J | Sarah: Grade 2 |
|---|---|
| **Who is attending?** | **Mother** and teacher |
| **Problem:** | Sarah is making fun of the other children when they make mistakes in reading. |
| **Details:** | Two parents have called in to report that their children have come home in tears following Sarah's comments to them. |
| Scenario K | Sarah: Grade 12 |
| **Who is attending?** | **Mother, teacher** and guidance counselor |
| **Problem:** | Sarah has not yet applied to any of the colleges her family would like her to attend. |
| **Details:** | Sarah will need financial aid to attend college. |
| Scenario L | Yu-shin, Grade 8 |
| **Who is attending?** | Yu-shin, **father**, mother, **and Mr. Helms, his homeroom teacher** |
| **Problem:** | Yu-shin does not look at his teacher in the face whenever he is talking to him. Yu-shin tells his father that he thinks his teacher is angry at him most of the time. |
| **Details:** | Yu-shin is not used to looking elders in the face when being scolded. He is under the impression when Mr. Helms is talking to him that he is being scolded because his teacher has wide eyes and dark, bushy eyebrows. Mr. Helms's eyes remind him of his father's eyes when his father is angry with him. Mr. Helms has always required students to make eye contact, and they have done so without exception. Since he has not required the same of Yu-shin, other students are starting to say he is being unfair to them. |

## Exercise B

### Directions

1. Break into groups as directed.

2. As a group, roll a die to discover your situation:

| Die | Child | Characteristics | Grade |
|---|---|---|---|
| 1 | Malcolm | Hyperactive and distracted | Grade 3 |
| 2 | Casey | Problem getting along with others | Grade 6 |
| 3 | Sarah | Refusal to follow directions | Grade 8 |
| 4 | Raul | Language barrier | Grade 1 |
| 5 | Leslie | Not accepted by peers | Grade 5 |
| 6 | Yu-shin | Refuses to eat food provided for field trip | Grade 7 |

3. Individually, roll the die to discover your role:

| Die | Role | Attitude |
|---|---|---|
| 1 | Teacher | Frustrated |
| 2 | Parent | Angry |
| 3 | Principal | Placating |
| 4 | Child | Aloof |
| 5 | Counselor | Mediating |
| 6 | Intervention Specialist | Advocate for child |

4. Conduct the conference based on the roles you have chosen. The rest of the class will take notes as the scenario unfolds.

5. As a class, discuss the conference and give suggestions for how it could have been better.

6. Write an individual reflection on how the problem could best be handled by the teacher and/or other appropriate participants.

## ACTIVITY 2: SIMULATED IEP CONFERENCE

*Background:* IEP conferences are as challenging for parents as they are for teachers and administrators. Documenting student performance and progress in a meaningful way, preparing multiple copies of multiple documents, and taking care of all the conference logistics are all time-consuming yet critical components of both successful IEP conferencing *and* successful IEP implementation. Perhaps when you were in school, IEP conferences were only the concern of special education teachers and their students. That is no longer the case. With more and more students with IEPs spending all or most of their days assigned to general education teachers and in general education classrooms, all teachers need to be well informed about IEPs. All teachers need to be aware of how IEPs are developed, what their roles as general and special educators are, and how to maximize parent/guardian involvement in the IEP process.

*Purpose:* This activity is to stimulate your thinking about the IEP process and provide you with practice using language that promotes collaboration between parents/guardians and school faculty/administration. The final product for this activity is a simulated IEP conference. However, the process contains many steps that are detailed below. Your instructor will indicate which, if any, of the process steps need to be documented for him or her or if the simulated conference is the only product. Your instructor will determine the length of the conference. Group size also may be modified to better meet the needs of your education class.

### Directions

Before class:

1. Investigate what the purposes of an initial IEP conference are. What should be the end result of such a conference? Who needs to be there? Why? You may want to search online for federal and state mandates related to IEP development and conferences.

2. Reread the profile of Casey in second grade, paying particular attention to the following artifacts: (a) referral for evaluation in Grade 2, (b) **evaluation team report (ETR)**, and (c) initial IEP.

In and/or between classes:

1. Divide into groups as assigned by your instructor. Assign yourselves to the roles of Clover Valley Elementary School building principal (Mr. Stephens), second-grade general education teacher (Mr. Jones), special education teacher (Mrs. Rose), Mr. or Mrs. Griffith, and the observer. Change the gender of the assigned role as needed. It may be helpful to have your roles on 4 × 6 index cards hung around your neck with yarn so that you do not forget who is playing what role. Discuss with your colleagues Casey's IEP. Make sure you understand what the plan for his IEP is really saying. If no one in your class can interpret the IEP, to whom might you go?

2. Mr. Stephens, Mr. Jones, and Mrs. Rose need to plan the IEP conference. There is much published on IEP conferencing. Develop a list of "tips for effective IEP conferences" from a search of several professional resources. (You will find more than you can ever imagine.) Duplicate this list for the rest of your class if so directed by your instructor.

3. Mr. and Mrs. Griffith need to preplan the attitude and behaviors they will bring to the conference. Think about why you decide on certain attitudes and behaviors. Be ready to answer the question, What in the Casey profile prompted you to behave the way you did?

4. The observer needs to look at the IEP conference plan the professionals at Midland have developed. Prior to the simulated conference, ask them on what components of the conference they want you to focus your attention. Develop a way of providing them with feedback.

5. Practice your conference, with the observer taking notes. After the practice conference, have the observer share with you what tips you followed and which ones you ignored. Did everyone stay in character? If not, why not? Decide what you will do the same and differently for the simulated conference you prepare for the class and/or your instructor.

6. Conduct a simulated conference as directed by your instructor. The observer needs to provide the conference participants with feedback in front of the class and/or the instructor as directed.

## ACTIVITY 3: PARENT-TEACHER COMMUNICATIONS

### Exercise A

#### Directions

Select one of the students in the profiles. Then select one of the following communication tasks:

**Box 12.3**     Rubric for Activity 2

| Unacceptable | Acceptable | Excellent |
|---|---|---|
| Participants were unable to stay in character for much of the conference; observer provided limited general feedback to participants; principles of active listening were not followed. Oral and/or body language was too informal or unprofessional; comments were made to parent that may have made him/her feel put down, cut off, or not having anything to offer to Casey's education. | All participants attempted to stay in character; observer provided conference participants with general positive and negative feedback; tips for IEP conferences were given to the rest of the class and followed at least 75% of the time; genuine attempts to listen actively were made; oral and body language were generally professional; parent was not put down, cut of, or made to feel as if his/her opinion did not matter. | All participants stayed in character most of the time; observer provided conference participants with meaningful feedback; tips for IEP conferences were given to rest of class and followed by conference participants; active/reflective listening skills were consistently used; oral language was professional and as jargon-free as possible; body language was matched to oral language and professional; parents were viewed as valuable contributors to the educational process by faculty and administration. |

1. Assume the role of one of your student's teachers. As the teacher, write a personal note home to his or her parents/guardians about the positive things you have noticed about this child.

2. Assume the role of one of your student's teachers. Develop the script for what you would say if you were to make a telephone call home to the student's parents/guardians about a particular challenge that your student is having.

3. Assume the chair role for the schoolwide positive behavioral support (PBS) planning team at Midland Middle School. You need to secure several parents/guardians to serve on the PBS planning team. Describe the steps you would take to secure volunteers. Include either one document you would use *or* the script from a call or e-mail.

**Box 12.4**     Assessment Rubric

| Unacceptable | Acceptable | Exemplary |
|---|---|---|
| Document contains inaccuracies or is inappropriate. | Accurate document that is appropriate for situation. | Accurate, professional, creative document appropriate for situation. |

## Exercise B

## Directions

1. Select a grade or subject that you will be teaching.

2. Imagine that you are the teacher of the children whose profiles are in Chapters 2 through 7, as well as many other children. It is the beginning of the school year, and you need to write a letter introducing yourself to the families of your students. As you write, consider the community and the parents to whom you are writing. Make sure you include the following:

- Something about your background
- Your philosophy of education
- Your classroom policies
- What you hope to accomplish this year in your grade and/or subject area
- A description of the units or projects the students will complete this year
- Your expectations of students—academically and behaviorally
- Your suggestions for how the parents can support their children's progress
- A welcoming invitation to contact you at any time

# GLOSSARY

**Accommodation**  A change made to teaching methods, student activities, teacher or student materials, or student assessments that addresses specific learner differences. When an accommodation is made, the goals and/or objectives of the lessons remain the same.

**ACT**  A four-year college admissions test given to juniors and seniors that assesses their English, science, social studies, and mathematics skills.

**Adaptation**  Any change made in a lesson that is designed to improve the likelihood that the lesson will address specific learner differences.

**Adaptive behavior**  Behavior that enables an individual to better meet the specific requirements of his or her environment. In an academic setting, the term refers to behaviors that are needed to be successful in social settings and in carrying out daily living activities. For example, a 10-year-old child with "adaptive behavior deficits" still might have difficulties dressing himself or herself or talking to adults other than his or her parents.

**Adderall**  A prescription stimulant medication that has been recently added to those used to treat ADHD.

**Advocate**  An individual (n.) or process by which (v.) someone pleads the case for, encourages, or supports individuals or groups in their attempts to reach their goals.

**Apgar**  A noninvasive clinical test designed by Dr. Virginia Apgar in 1953 that is performed on a newborn, with a score given for each of five signs or behaviors at 1 minute and 5 minutes after birth. Apgar is an acronym for Activity (Muscle Tone), Pulse, Grimace (Reflex Irritability), Appearance (Skin Color), Respiration.

**Attention-deficit/ hyperactivity disorder (ADHD)**  A neurobiological disorder defined in the *DSM IV* that is characterized by chronic patterns of inattention and/or impulsivity and hyperactivity that last at least 6 months, are inconsistent with age-level expectations, are observed in at least two settings, and have a significant negative impact on educational performance.

**Auditory discrimination**  Being able to perceive the difference between two sounds or sound patterns. For example, a child with an auditory discrimination problem may not be able to hear the differences between a short *e* sound and a short *i* sound.

**Clonidine**  A prescription medication often used to treat high blood pressure. It also has been found effective in treating ADHD, although it is not currently approved by the FDA for this use.

**Cognitive behavior modification**  A therapeutic approach that focuses on teaching individuals to monitor their own behavior by using principles of operant conditioning as they become aware of that behavior.

**Conners Rating Scales**  Checklists with versions for both parents and teachers that allow them to rate an individual's inattentive, impulsive, and/or hyperactive behaviors; often used as one of several diagnostic tools to identify ADHD.

**Differentiation**  An approach to planning curriculum and instruction that increases the likelihood that the needs of academically diverse learners will be met. Historically, the term was used in describing the processes needed to adapt lessons to meet the needs of learners who were talented and gifted, but the term is now used to refer to the processes needed to adapt lessons to meet the needs of *all* learners.

*DSM*  *Diagnostic and Statistical Manual of Mental Disorders,* published by the American Psychiatric Association, is the handbook used most often in diagnosing mental disorders in the United States and internationally. The latest version, the *DSM IV,* was published in 1994.

**Dyslexia**  A term used to describe a pattern of behaviors exhibited by individuals of average or above-average intelligence who, though they have been provided with appropriate reading instruction, have not been able to learn to read or read fluently. Dyslexia is currently thought to be based on difficulties in mastering sound-symbol relationships due to some combination of genetic and/or neurological auditory and visual processing deficits.

**Encopresis**  A medical term for the unintentional passage of stool that has no clear cause; fecal incontinence.

**Enuresis**  A medical term for the involuntary discharge of urine; incontinence of urine.

**Evaluation team report (ETR)**  The report completed by the multifactored evaluation team that summarizes the results of a variety of assessments used to determine whether or not a child has a disability that can be identified under the Individuals With Disabilities Education Improvement Act (IDEIA) 2004.

**Fine motor**   The use of small muscles, such as those that permit movement of the fingers, to accomplish such tasks as cutting and printing.

**Goldstein Behavioral Observation Checklist**   An informal assessment in which patterns of behaviors can be documented historically, it has been used as an observation option in the diagnosis of ADHD.

**Gross motor**   The use of large muscles, such as those in the arms and legs, that permits individuals to walk, carry or catch items, and so on.

**Hydrotherapy**   The use of water as a therapeutic tool for enhancing movement, strengthening muscles, and minimizing stiffness and pain; often used as a form of rehabilitation.

**Individualized education program (IEP)**   The plan for instruction and accommodations tailored to the specific needs of each and every student, age 3 through 21, who has been identified with a disability under IDEIA 2004. The initial IEP is developed from the evaluation team report as part of an IEP team meeting that includes parents, a building administrator, and relevant teachers. It is rewritten whenever there are changes in services and/or placements or once a year, whichever occurs first. The IEP serves as the "road map" for the individual child's education.

**Intervention assistance team (IAT)**   A group of teachers (usually both general and special education teachers) and a building administrator to whom other educators bring specific challenges they are facing with individual students. The IAT works with educators to help them identify other ways in which they can work with the student, gather additional information from guardians and other relevant adults, and provide support to the teachers as they try to provide more successful instruction. According to IDEIA 2004, some type of prereferral activity, such as that completed through an IAT process, is required prior to referring a student for a multifactored evaluation for potential identification as a student with a disability.

**IQ (Intelligence quotient)**   A somewhat dated, though still commonly used, term to refer to the quantitative measurement of an individual's intellectual capacity, ability, or learning potential. Most often it refers to that individual's capacity to learn academic types of concepts and skills, although more current theories of intelligence include ways of measuring learning potential that extend beyond academic areas.

**Modification**   Changing the learning goal and/or objective and/or changing the difficulty of the content to meet the needs of learners who either do not have the prerequisite knowledge and skills for the stated learning goal and/or objective or have already mastered that goal and/or objective.

**Multifactored evaluation (MFE)**   The name of the assessment process that occurs when legal guardians have given consent for a team of educators to determine whether or not their child has a disability recognized by IDEIA 2004. The multifactored evaluation always includes multiple measures that are conducted by professionals with sufficient expertise to use the relevant assessments. The MFE must be preceded by documentation of prereferral intervention steps that were not sufficient for the student to be successful.

**Multisensory approaches**   Teaching methods that simultaneously appeal to more than one sense and that help learners with strong sensory preferences to benefit from the lesson. For example, a multisensory lesson might include lesson components that require the use of the visual, auditory, and tactual senses.

**Postsecondary options**   Opportunities that students may have to continue their education and/or training after graduating from high school. IEPs written for students with disabilities, age 16 through 21, must include some reference to postsecondary options in their transition plans if they are appropriate for those students to consider.

**PSAT**   A precollege admission test typically given to high school students during their junior year, although students identified as talented and gifted initially may take it during their junior high years. Performing well on the test may qualify students for the National Merit Scholarship Program.

**Pull-out program**   Usually a special education placement where it has been decided that a student's least restrictive environment for a particular special education service is in a setting separate from the one in which he or she would be with his or her peers who do not have disabilities. In general, this type of a program is considered more restrictive than providing services in an inclusive setting.

**Ritalin**   A prescription stimulant medication, chemically related to an amphetamine, that acts as a mild stimulant of the central nervous system and is used in the treatment of ADHD.

**Round-robin**   A reading practice in which students take turns reading orally. It can be a challenge to students who have either a difficult time paying attention or reading difficulties. It is usually not recommended practice past the earliest years of reading instruction.

**SAT**   A 4-year college admissions test given to juniors and seniors that yields a score in the subject areas of English and mathematics, as well as a combined score.

| | |
|---|---|
| **Schoolwide positive behavioral support** | A systems approach to discipline that emphasizes the prevention of problem behaviors through instruction and consistent reinforcement, data-based decision making, and more intensive behavioral intervention if preventive approaches are not sufficient. |
| **Social behavior** | Interpersonal behavior; behavior patterns exhibited in social settings. In schools, the term often refers to expected patterns of behavior at certain ages and stages that children exhibit as they interact with teachers and peers. |
| **Social skills assessment** | The use of a variety of measures (checklists, interviews, role plays) to determine what behaviors individuals can and will use in social settings. |
| **Sound-symbol relationships** | In reading, the understanding that letters (the symbols) each represent one or more sounds that, when combined, make up words. |
| **Specific learning disability (SLD)** | Also referred to as "learning disability," a disorder in one or more psychological processes used in the production or reception of language that has a significant impact on educational performance and is not due to sensory deficits, for example, hearing or vision problems; mental retardation; emotional disorders; or environmental, cultural, or economic disadvantages. Academic areas in which the specific learning disability may have a significantly negative impact are reading (word recognition and/or comprehension), mathematics (calculations and/or reasoning), written or oral expressions, or listening comprehension. |
| **Talented and gifted (TAG)** | An identification that refers to individuals with outstanding talent who perform or show the potential to perform at extremely high levels when compared to their peers in one or more of the following areas: intellectual capacity, creative and/or artistic endeavors, leadership potential, or specific academic disciplines. |
| **Think-aloud** | A teaching strategy or method where the teacher first models a process, orally describing the steps taken or components considered, then slowly transfers that process to the students until the students can silently think through the steps of the process independently. |
| **Transition plan** | The portion of a student's IEP that focuses on measurable postsecondary goals and services needed to prepare the student for those goals; must be included by the time a student is 16 years of age, if not sooner. |
| **Unbiased terms** | The systematic use of language that minimizes the likelihood that a particular group either (a) will not have had experience with the word(s) and thus be at a disadvantage or (b) will be prejudiced by the connotation of particular words. |
| **Universal design for learning (UDL)** | A plan for creating goals, methods, materials, and assessments that address learner differences. This plan is developed from information |

obtained through the preassessment of learners and builds in any needed changes prior to the time the lesson is taught.

**Visual discrimination**

Being able to perceive the difference between two visual images. For example, a child with a visual discrimination problem may see a *b* but interpret it as a *d*.

**Wechsler Intelligence Scale for Children (WISC)**

A widely used individual intelligence test, standardized for children ages 6 to 16, that yields three overall scores: a score that reports the composite of verbal subtests, a score that reports the composite of performance subtests, and a full-scale score that reports an overall score of intellectual potential. The mean score is 100 and the standard deviation is 15. Versions still in use include the WISC III and the WISC IV, with the WISC IV published in 2003.

**Woodcock-Johnson Test of Cognitive Ability**

One major component of the Woodcock-Johnson Psycho-Educational Battery. This component is designed to measure general academic and thinking skills needed to be successful in school versus achievement in specific academic areas.

# REFERENCES

Brown, S. C., & Kysilka, M. L. (2002). *Applying multicultural and global concepts to the classroom and beyond.* Boston, MA: Allyn & Bacon.

Frye, H. N. (2005). How elementary school counselors can meet the needs of students with disabilities. *Professional School Counseling, 8*(5), 442–449.

Fuller, M. (1992). Monocultural teachers and multicultural students: A demographic class. *Teaching Education, 4*(2), 87–93.

Gollnick, D., & Chinn, P. (2002). *Multicultural education in a pluralistic society.* Upper Saddle River, NJ: Merrill Prentice Hall.

Hirsch, E. (2002, January). *Program of education.* National Conference of State Legislatures (NCSL). Symposium conducted at Holmes Partnership Sixth Annual Conference, San Antonio, TX.

Hixson, J., & Tinzmann, M. B. (1990). *Who are the "at-risk" students of the 1990s?* North Central Regional Educational Laboratory. Retrieved August 12, 2005, from http://www.ncrel.org/sdrs/areas/rpl_esys/equity.htm

Institute of Educational Sciences: National Center for Educational Statistics, U.S. Department of Education. (2004). Retrieved April 7, 2006, from http://nces.ed.gov/programs/coe/2005/charts/chart04.asp

National Association for the Education of Young Children. (1996). *Developmentally appropriate practice in early childhood programs serving young children from birth through age 8.* Washington, DC: Author.

National Center for Education Statistics. (1999). *Digest of education statistics.* Washington, DC: U.S. Government Printing Office.

Neito, S. (2004). *Affirming diversity: The sociopolitical context of education.* White Plains, NY: Longman.

Schon, W. (1987). *Educating the reflective practitioner.* San Francisco: Jossey-Bass.

Sleeter, C., & Grant, C. (1999). *Making choices for multicultural education: Five approaches to race, class, and gender.* New York: Wiley.

Tomlinson, C. A. (1997). Differentiating instruction. In *ASCD Professional Inquiry Kit, Facilitator's Guide* (pp. 67–68). Alexandria, VA: ASCD.

Tomlinson, C. A., & Eidson, C. C. (2003). *Differentiation in practice: A resource guide for differentiating curriculum, grades k–5.* Alexandrea, VA: Association for Supervision and Curriculum Development.

Wiggins, G., & McTighe, J. (2005). Understanding by design: Professional development workbok (2nd ed.). Alexandria VA: ASCD.

Wood, J. W. (2002). *Adapting instruction to accommodate students in inclusion settings.* Upper Saddle River, NJ: Merrill Prentice Hall.

# ABOUT THE AUTHORS

**Joy R. Cowdery**, EdD, is Assistant Professor of Education at Muskingum College. She holds an EdD in Educational Leadership/Critical Pedagogy, an MA in Communication from West Virginia University, and a BA in English, Speech, and Drama from Marietta College. She has taught English and communication in high school. Currently she teaches diversity education and secondary language arts methods at Muskingum College and serves as an adviser for Kappa Delta Pi national education honorary. She is a Praxis III assessor for the Ohio Department of Education and serves as a member of the Ohio Department of Education accreditation teams. She belongs to and presents at numerous professional organizations. Areas of professional interest are multicultural education, social justice, and rural poverty.

**Linda Ingling**, PhD, is Associate Professor of Education and Chemistry at Muskingum College. She holds a BS in Biology from Westminster College, Pennsylvania; an MEd from the University of South Carolina; a BS in Chemistry from Clarion University, Pennsylvania: and a PhD in Chemistry from Duquesne University, Pennsylvania. Her experiences in education include teaching biology, chemistry, physics, and assorted math courses at the middle and high school level as well as chemistry at the college level. She is a member of the American Chemical Society, the Science Education Council of Ohio, and the Ohio Association of Teacher Educators. She currently teaches courses in math and science methods for grades kindergarten through 12th grade.

**Linda E. Morrow**, PhD, is Professor of Education and Special Education Program Advocate at Muskingum College. She holds a BA in Psychology from Muskingum College, an MEd in Special Education from Ohio University, and a PhD in Teacher Education, with minors in educational psychology and reading, from Ohio State University. Her experiences with children and families in southeastern Ohio include teaching high school students with specific learning disabilities, parent education, social work, and youth ministries. She is a member of the State of Ohio Advisory Panel for Exceptional Children, the Ohio Special Education Personnel Development Advisory Committee, and the Center for Improving Teacher Quality project, and served on the Ohio Department of Education's Ohio Teacher Education Licensure Advisory Commission from 1998 to 2002. She currently teaches graduate courses in special education. Her research focuses on schoolwide positive behavioral support and adolescents with reading challenges. She lives with her husband on a farm and has two grown sons and two grandchildren.

**Vicki A. Wilson**, PhD, is Professor of Education and Associate Dean of Academic Affairs in Teacher Education at Muskingum College. She holds a BA in English from the University of Dayton, an MBA in Business/Government Relations from American University, and a PhD in Educational Administration, with a minor in educational research, from the University of Southern Mississippi. Her experiences in education include teaching middle school in inner-city Tampa, Florida, coaching teachers in math and language arts in rural Mississippi, and teaching scuba diving to hearing-impaired adult students. She served as the President of the Ohio Association of Private Colleges of Teacher Education from 2003 to 2005 and on the Ohio Department of Education's Ohio Teacher Education Licensure Advisory Commission from 2001 to 2005. She currently teaches a course in educational issues for student teachers at the undergraduate level and directs research projects at the graduate level. Her scholarly interests include gifted education and educational research.